Interrelated macro-economic systems

Tilburg Studies on Economics

9

Edited by the

Tilburg Institute of Economics

of the Tilburg School of Economics, Social Sciences and Law

A study on International Trade

Interrelated macro-economic systems

P.J.L.M. Peters

Lecturer in macro-economics at the Erasmus University Rotterdam (graduate School of Management, Delft)

Foreword by

D.B.J. Schouten

Professor in General Economics and Economic History

1974
Tilburg University Press
The Netherlands

Translated by J. van den Dool-Phelps

Distributors: Academic Book Services Holland, P.O. Box 66,
Groningen, the Netherlands
ISBN 90 237 2913 7

Foreword

The study presented here by P. J. L. M. Peters demonstrates clearly the author's capacities as a master in his subject. Not only does he impress us with his didactic talents to express extremely difficult interrelations involving interregional dynamic relations in a particularly lucid way but his command of mathematics and statistics also proves to be such that he can adopt a critical standpoint towards a purely empirical view on economic life.

For that very reason he decided upon a rather theoretical study since he felt that measuring and observing without a thorough understanding of what we should in fact be measuring is a somewhat pointless and often unrealistic pursuit. The results are, consequently, particularly interesting for empiricism. He demonstrates that the testing of macroeconomic models, based on the hypothesis that foreign variables are completely independent of domestic events, results in a completely wrong understanding of the characteristics of the national economy. He has considerably enlarged our knowledge of the mutual repercussions and transference of the consequences of the improvements in one's own national structure to other nations. To this purpose he uses dynamic two-sector models which not only recall simple demand models à la Keynes but in which supply factors, in particular the development of production capacity and its degree of utilization also play an important role. A certain degree of integration of business cycle and structure analysis is thus achieved. All this is of great importance for an international or interregional coordination of economic policy.

Rationally and ethically (in the sense that other nations or regions are not put in an unfavourable position) we can only pursue our national interests through a coordinating supra-national authority which supervises all interrelations and prevents too many unilateral activities.

Once again, attention everywhere is being centred on the consequences of monopolistic concentrations of power. How much power do trade unions have with regard to the determination of wages, how much power does trade and industry have with regard to the determination of prices, who is in fact truly autonomous or which nation can really still feel sovereign now that an analysis of the sum total of the international relations shows that each part is in turn dependent on the whole.

The author provides us, to the best of his knowledge and without dogmatic bias, with a fascinating answer to the time-honoured question of 'Power or economic law?': in theory, a supra-national authority can achieve much; in practice however, in the presence of countless national authorities, it becomes an uncoordinated muddle, where nobody really plays a dominating role.

A game-theoretic elaboration of the possibilities of planning economic policy presented here, as well as a better integration of the monetary factors in the models he has used, is a study which we may expect from the author next.

D. B. J. Schouten

Preface

Anybody who has ever made a study of dynamic systems will have probably reached the conclusion that although each individual relation may be clear, the operation of the relations as a whole is hardly comprehensible. In other words, although we can understand the separate relations, it is almost impossible to understand the complete system let alone describe it in a simple manner.

This presents the economist with not unimportant problems since it is usually expected that his reasoning can be understood and checked by those who have asked for advice. It must also be possible to compare the value of his arguments with that of other arguments, which sometimes prove the contrary. In positive economic science, it is not (yet) possible to say: 'the given recommendations can be obtained by having the computer verify my model, which is constructed on the best available ideas.' Such an allegation still sounds unbelievable in our profession, because despite all the progress that has been made in econometrics, the quantitative views are not nearly definite enough.

The consequence of this methodological uncertainty is that the practice of economic science consists to a not unimportant degree of weighing the pros and cons with regard to the question of which of the many possible mechanisms predominate in a specific concrete situation. In this connection it is important to point out that the method of the current econometric model estimation implies that the specified mechanisms operate constantly, ex hypothesi, during the whole period of observation on which the estimates are based. There are, however, arguments which assert that it is plausible that at nearly all points of the system of the supply of goods first one, then another mechanism predominates.

However, this study is based on the methodological assumption that it is impossible in the (macro-) economy to obtain an idea of the functioning of the economic system by using statistical observations only, also because of the meagre possibilities for experiment.

It is quite impossible, by using this method, to pay sufficient attention to the gradually changing structures, although we acknowledge that econometric models are of use for rough estimates if the structure is not submitted to large changes.

Since it seems reasonable to assume that structural changes do occur regularly in reality, it is essential to be acquainted with theoretical mechanisms when operating in isolation, to discover their characteristics and to compare them with the empirical characteristics.

In this study we have attempted to examine and to explain in understandable economic terms a relatively large number of dynamic mechanisms, traces of which have in fact been found.

In this regard we were able to rely, to an important degree, on the work of Professor Schouten. The book *Dynamische macro-economie* (Dynamic macroeconomics) (1967) presents the first results of this work.

In a way, our study is a logical continuation of Professor Schouten's work. However, while he confined himself, at the time, to the integration of the theory of business cycle and structure in terms of pure macro-theory, we have assigned ourselves the task of giving an integrated cyclical-structural analysis of des-aggregated multi-country, or multi-region models.

The models do of course become because of this more complicated. However, the variety of problems which are included in the analysis makes up for the increased intricacy. Some examples of the new problems can be mentioned: in the first place, problems dealing with international coordination of economic policy. We hope to show that comments on this can only be made within the scope of the multi-region model and that the use of macro-theory can lead to faulty recommendations to the individual regions (or countries).

Another comment on economic policy of large regions is: apart from the inter-regional (international) coordination of economic policy, it will be possible for large regions within a community to be confronted with the consequences of their measures (whether lagged or not) by means of international contacts. This does not necessarily involve measures of resistance deliberately taken by the partner regions to avoid any possibly harmful effects caused by the active regions. These international circular effects can also appear as a result of the endogenous operation of the international system.

It should be clear that everything we have just stated about the international economic system is also applicable, to an even greater extent, to the inter-regional problems within one single country because of the considerable degree of interdependence.

Although we consider that a number of the matters we have dealt with can also be of concrete significance for Applied Science we are also quite convinced that the restrictions we had to make are such that some readers will feel disinclined to read further. To enable the reader to decide at an early stage whether or not to continue reading, we have made a list of the restrictions in question.

1. The international (inter-regional) contacts we have treated are active only on the goods market: international mobility of production factors has not been treated.

2. The possibility of equilibrium growth plays a principal role in our explanation. We shall be assuming in a large section of our book that the economy is approaching the equilibrium growth situation. We have made this assumption because we have not found the opportunity to describe verbally the dynamics of systems which find themselves far from equilibrium growth.

When almost all the important structural aspects are continually changing (productivity of capital, technical progress, saving and investment tendencies etc.) the description of the operation of the system becomes very lengthy. The mathematics of this situation also becomes extremely complicated. As far as we can now judge, we can conclude that we can only achieve something regarding the analysis of the systems not characterised by equilibrium growth, by computer simulation.

3. Partly in connection with point 2, the labour market plays a dominating role in our models. Although this would not seem to be an unrealistic assumption for the interpretation of Western economies, we have been rather partial as far as this is concerned. Important sub-systems in the economy, such as for example the monetary mechanism have not been assigned an endogenous role in our models.

We regard the integration of the monetary factors as an important, as yet unfinished task.

THE CLASSIFICATION OF THE MATERIAL

As we have already stated, the main purpose of our study is to desaggregate previously developed macroeconomic models. In this way, a certain generalisation of macro-theory is obtained.

We begin our task immediately in Chapter I. The suppositions made there are however still kept very simple; in particular the demand side of the labour market, since it is still assumed that the demand for labour is exclusively dependent on the number of available physical labour positions.

In the following chapters we depart from this simplified supposition in particular. It is then assumed that effective demand is also a determining factor for the demand for labour.

Since this supposition evokes rather more problems in the integrated multi-region models than in the simpler labour positions theory, some macroeconomic preparation was necessary. This appears in Chapters II and III. The emphasis in our study is however on Chapters IV and V in which the cyclical and structural models which are des-aggregated in regions (or countries) are dealt with in detail. The models presented in IV and V can be interpreted as multi-sector models, depending on how closely the production factors are connected with the production sector, so that we are in fact dealing with separate factor markets.

In short, our study can be regarded as a contribution towards the integration of the multi-sector growth theory on the one hand and the short-term business cycle theory on the other hand.

EMPIRICISM

Empiricism plays a subordinate part in our book. In general we have not dealt with it explicitly. The achievements of others in this field did however serve as an inspiration. In fact, most of the relations we have used, can be found in, for instance, Central Planning Bureau models, although often in a much more complicated specification.

We have departed from our general rule on several instances, notably, with regard to parts of our system with a dominating role i.e. the wage determination function (see appendix A 2.2) and the import and export relations (par. 3.2.1).

THE MATHEMATICS USED

We have used mathematics of an elementary nature. The most important aid is the linear difference equation.

Because of the simplicity of the mathematics employed, we have also avoided mathematical illustrations and evidence as much as possible. An exception is made for the reduction of a simultaneous system of m linear difference equations with scalar variables, to a vector-difference equation of the 1st degree. A brief appendix (A 1.2) is devoted to this.

Hardly any attempt has been made to publish a regional or sectoral des-aggregation of the so-called business cycle structure models. For these reasons we had little cause to include direct references (to publications).

Publications about economic growth as it developed in the fifties and sixties, have served as a background for our short-term analysis. We have, as well, consulted some empirical work which we can use to defend the actual relevance of our relations.

A list of reference material which we have consulted is added at the end of the book.

Contents

I. A model with constant profit expectations

1.0 INTRODUCTION

In this chapter we shall give a brief impression of the nature of the problems to be treated in our study. This will be based on a number of simplified assumptions.

The most important, those which determine the character of the analysis, will be described broadly in par. 1.1.

1.1 GENERAL ASSUMPTIONS

1. As far as technology is concerned, complete complementarity is assumed. Furthermore, only two homogeneous production factors work together, i.e. labour and capital.

Demand for labour is solely determined by the available production capacity; actual production has no influence on employment. This assumption in particular, seems to have far-reaching consequences (see Chapters II, IV and V).

2. With regard to spendings, we assume that the wage earners use their whole income for consumption. The non-wage incomes on the other hand are used partly for financing investment goods and partly for consumer goods.

3. The employers work with a constant (monopolistic) profit margin on wage costs. With this assumption an important correction automatism of cyclical disequilibrium disappears. The mechanism we refer to here, that which ensures that the growth rate of the capital goods stock at a time of high wage costs rises less quickly, and vice versa, will play an important part in later chapters.

1

4. The natural growth rate amounts to 0. We therefore have a stationary structure (this is not a very essential assumption which can be removed easily).

5. Where applicable, fixed rates of exchange are assumed.

1.1.1 *Contents*

In par. 1.2.1, a simple macroeconomic model is specified, based on the above mentioned assumptions. It is preceded by an exact definition of *equilibrium growth* since we shall be continually observing the variables against that background. With regard to the assumed technical complementarity, equilibrium growth can be easily defined as the situation which is characterised by full utilisation of the production factors, while the 'normal' production coefficients remain valid.

A brief definition of the (well known) macromodel will be followed by the specification of a two-regions model, in which the macroeconomic model of par. 1.2.1 is split up into a model of two regions (countries) to which all relations of the macromodel apply, but which, at the same time, have trade relations with each other according to simple import and export functions. Here we come to the core of that which we regard as our contribution: the disaggregation of dynamic macro systems. The disaggregated model, though still integrated by means of inter-regional relations, will then be dealt with extensively: its reaction after autonomous impulses will be illustrated by use of numerical examples. We will also examine how a number of traditional problems of economic policy (employment and stabilisation policy) can be solved, in our model.

It is also possible, within the framework of our models, to consider the problem of the international coordination of economic policy.

In the first place, we assume a completely uniform structure of both countries. In view of the real situation it is of course more interesting to analyse the possibilities of symbioses of lands with dissimilar structures. However interesting this may be, we have not pursued it further. The only case of asymmetry, that we have presented in an appendix to this chapter, concerns the meaning of the differences in size between countries (regions) with an otherwise similar economic structure (see Appendix A 1.1).

1.2 RELATIONS OF THE MODEL

1.2.1 Equilibrium growth (stationary situation)

The situation of equilibrium growth (with an assumed natural growth rate of 0, a stationary situation) can best be described by a confrontation of means and spendings (see table 1.2.1 below). In view of the numerical examples which appear in the sequel to this chapter, the quantitative values in the equilibrium growth phase are also indicated.

Table 1.2.1 *Confrontation of means and spendings in the situation of equilibrium growth:* ($y_{E_t} = y_{E_{t-1}}(1 + g_n)$)

(Here, g_n is the natural rate of growth)

Means		Spendings	
Income of wage earners $y_{LE} = l_E w_E$	$= 100 \times 1 = 100$	Consumption of wage earners $c_{LE} = y_{LE}$	100
Gross profit income $y_{RE} \equiv k_E r_E = (1 - \lambda_m) y_E$	$= \frac{1}{2} \times 200 = 100$	Consumption of non wage earners $c_{RE} =$	20
National income (gross)		Investments: i_E	80
		Gross national spending	
$y_E \equiv y_{LE} + y_{RE}$	200	$y_E \equiv (c_{LE} + c_{RE}) + i_E$	200

Apart from the relations already mentioned in the table we must take note of several other simple relations which apply in the stationary situation. In the first place, the balanced capital goods stock can be calculated only if the capital coefficient belonging to a normal degree of utilisation of capacity is known, thus:

$$k_E = \kappa y_E = 4 \times 200 = 800 \tag{1.2.1}$$

Since we assume a stationary situation, the depreciation rate in our example is obviously 10%.
    The following applies:

$$i_{B_E} = (\delta + g_n) k_E = (0,10 + 0) 800 = 80 \tag{1.2.2}$$

As demand function for labour we suggest the following:

$$l_v = \alpha y_E = \frac{1}{2} \times 200 = 100 = \bar{l} \tag{1.2.3}$$

1.2.1.1 *Structural relations (the closed economy)*

The 'relations' in the previous paragraph were still of a purely defining, tautological character. The operation of the system, however, is of course determined by the causal structural relations. These are only few in number in the closed economy and consist of several *consumption* functions, an *investment* function, an *accumulation* function and a *profit-earning* function.

As already stated in the introduction, we assume that a fixed (monopolistic) profit margin is imposed on wage costs. Then there is obviously a fixed relation between wage costs and profit. Thus:

$$y_R = \frac{1-\lambda_m}{\lambda_m} y_L = (1 - \lambda_m) y \tag{1.2.4}$$

Here, therefore, $(1-\lambda_m)$ is the constant profit share of production. The assumed consumption function of wage earners is quite simple; it is assumed that the total wage income is consumed immediately.

$$c_L = y_L \tag{1.2.5}$$

The consumption function of the capitalists is rather more complicated and is as follows:

$$c_R = \tilde{\gamma}_R(1 - \lambda_m)\frac{1}{\kappa} k + c_{\underline{R}} = \tilde{\gamma}_R y'_{\underline{R}} + c_{\underline{R}} \tag{1.2.6}$$

Here, $y'_R = \dfrac{(1-\lambda_m)}{\kappa} k$.

The consumption of the profit earners is, in other words, based on available production capacity, from which, given a fixed profit margin, an income can be expected that can be calculated according to the formula:

$$(1 - \lambda_m)\frac{k}{\kappa} \equiv (1 - \lambda_m) y'.$$

It is possible to relate the above to the established phenomenon of the stabilisation of the dividend payments, available for consumption purposes. Investments, as well as consumption are based on profit expectation, but a correction takes place when the actual production volume y deviates from the production capacity (flexible accelerator), thus:

$$i = \tilde{\sigma}_R(1 - \lambda_m) y' + \zeta\kappa(y - y') + \underline{i} =$$
$$= \tilde{\sigma}_R y'_R + \zeta\kappa_R(y_R - y'_R) + \underline{i} \tag{1.2.7}$$

4

Here $\kappa_R \equiv \dfrac{\kappa}{1-\lambda_m}$.

Taking account of the definitions

$$y \equiv y_L + y_R \equiv c_L + c_R + i; \tag{1.2.8}$$

we obtain

$$y_R = M\left(\tilde{\sigma}_R + \tilde{\gamma}_R - \frac{\zeta\kappa}{1-\lambda_m}\right) y_R' + M\underline{x} \tag{1.2.9}$$

Here, $\underline{x}$ is total autonomous spendings, while M is an (important) spending multiplier:

$$M \equiv \frac{1}{1-\zeta\kappa/(1-\lambda_m)}$$

In the case of equilibrium growth, there is no over- or undercapacity, in which case the following applies:

$$y_R = y_R' \tag{1.2.10}$$

We can deduce from this that:

$$y_{R_E} = \frac{M}{1-M\left(\tilde{\sigma}_R + \tilde{\gamma}_R - \dfrac{\zeta\kappa}{1-\lambda_m}\right)} \underline{x} \tag{1.2.11}$$

The conclusion is familiar:

Equilibrium growth is not produced spontaneously by the system, but a very definite amount of autonomous spending 'x' is required in order to reach the equilibrium.

The actual meaning of the constant profit margins is now obvious. When lasting discrepancies between effective demand on the one hand and production capacity on the other, do not lead to adequate adjustment of the profit margins, then the equilibrium growth is coincidental and will be realised only with, for example, a well considered spending policy. On the other hand, it is possible that every arbitrary increase of production capacity is realised by a single spending pull while maintaining the capacity equilibrium.

The relevant subject matter is too well known to be treated here once again. It concerns, in fact, a variant of Harrod's stability problem. Furthermore, it is obvious that in the model in question an equilibrium basic situation can be maintained without autonomous spendings being necessary. We need only to apply the following:

$$\tilde{\gamma}_R + \tilde{\sigma}_R = 1.$$

In the sequel to this chapter we shall analyse only this (important) casus (complete marginal spending of profit income).

As working hypothesis for the rest of this chapter, we shall assume that a balanced production capacity has been built up in the basic situation, because of an adequate spendings policy in the past. It is clear that if thereafter no further autonomous spending impulses occur, the equilibrium stationary situation, characterised by full employment and a normal utilisation of the capital goods stock, will be maintained forever.

It can also be noted that although autonomous impulses on consumption or investments do influence the short term solutions, they do not evoke any business cycle.

Furthermore, we will come across systems in the rest of this chapter in which it is precisely the cyclical fluctuations that play a major part. Finally, it is worth noting that labour market situations do not play an endogenous part in the functioning of the macromodel described above. Even lasting situations of over- and underemployment are of course possible, but do not produce any feedback impulses which could restore the equilibrium.

1.2.1.2 *Structural relations of the two-regions model*

We shall now leave the macroeconomy; a not particularly interesting topic as far as our present model is concerned. Instead, we will assume that not only one final product, but two types of goods, y_A and y_B are produced. This takes place in two geographically separated areas (lands, regions) A and B. In theory, both regions have their own structural relations.

The mutual relations between both regions can be described with the aid of some simple import and export relations. It is assumed that with normal prices (the prices of the equilibrium basic situation are assumed to be 1), a 'normal' part of the spending of region A will take place in the partner region B and vice versa. In the situation of equilibrium growth, an equilibrium of the current account of the balance of payments is of course relevant.

The relationship between actual imports and exports will deviate from the abovementioned equilibrium relationship, when actual prices deviate from the equilibrium ones. In later chapters we will deal with other specifications of the import and export relations.

6

In concrete terms, the following relation is assumed for the balance of the current account.

$$(e_A - m_A) = -e_{E_A}\eta(p_A - p_B) = -\mu_{0_A}y_{E_A}\eta(p_A - p_B) =$$
$$= -(e_B - m_B) \qquad (1.2.12)$$

In the last equation the coefficient symbolises the total sum of the import and export elasticities. With regard to price determination, we also have the simplest possible assumption; i.e. we assume that wage costs are partly calculated into prices, thus:

$$p = \psi p_L \qquad (1.2.13)$$

An endogenous wage determination function of the well known Phillips type is also assumed for each region. In Chapter II we will have more opportunity to pay attention to the wage determination relation (also to its empirical aspects). For the moment we will suffice with the algebraic version of that variant of the Phillips curve which shows that the wage *level* has a lagged relation to the employment *situation* by means of a constant elasticity, as follows:

$$\frac{p_L - p_{L_E}}{p_{L_E}} = \beta\left(\frac{l_{v-1} - \bar{l}}{\bar{l}}\right) \qquad (1.2.14)$$

or, when $p_{L_E} = 1$ (as supposed):

$$p_L = 1 + \beta\left(\frac{l_{v-1} - \bar{l}}{\bar{l}}\right) \qquad (1.2.15)$$

The employment function also plays an important part. For the present, i.e. in this chapter, we shall assume that the demand for labour is determined by the number of labour positions available which is, in turn, linearly dependent on the available production capacity.

The algebraic equation applicable here is:

$$l_v = \alpha y' \qquad (1.2.16)$$

Some simple substitutions produce the following relationship between the balance of the current account of land A on the one hand and the production capacities on the other hand:

$$(e_A - m_A) = -\mu_{0_A}y_{E_A}\eta\left[\psi_A\beta_A\left(\frac{y'_{A-1}}{y_{E_A}} - 1\right) + \right.$$
$$\left. -\psi_B\beta_B\left(\frac{y'_{B-1}}{y_{E_B}} - 1\right) + \psi_A - \psi_B. \right] \qquad (1.2.17)$$

In the case of a symmetrical structure of both lands, equation (1.2.17) changes into the following simple form:

$$(e_A - m_A) = -\mu'(y'_{A-1} - y'_{B-1}) = -(e_B - m_B) \qquad (1.2.18)$$

Here:

$$\mu' = \mu_0 \eta \psi \beta$$

This is a simple way of expressing the popular conception:

The deficit in the current account is explained by the difference between internal and foreign tension. (With a given supply of labour, a high y' indicates a high degree of cyclical stress.)

1.2.2 *Summary of the model*

In the model outlined below, the relations obtained so far have been arranged in such a way that the solution can be obtained, simply and directly, in the form of a difference equation. In order to avoid repeating practically the same relation for regions A and B, we have used the more efficient matrix notation. The variables then become vectors of the form:

$$\{c_R\} = \begin{Bmatrix} c_{R_A} \\ c_{R_B} \end{Bmatrix}, \qquad \{i\} = \begin{Bmatrix} i_A \\ i_B \end{Bmatrix}, \qquad \text{etc.}$$

We see that the mathematical structure of our two-regions model is as simple as that of the macromodel. The only complication is equation (4) in which the inter-regional relations are described.

It is possible to generalise the model to more than two regions; we only have to set up a further distribution model for the international trade currents, whereby (4) becomes more complicated, compared with the given specification. We have refrained from doing this in the present study.

In the foregoing equations, we have made allowance for quantitative differences in structure between the two regions. A detailed elaboration of the asymmetrical structures would, however, require a separate study. We have only added an appendix to this chapter dealing with the meaning of differences in size between the two regions.

1.2.2.1 *The autonomous impulses*
In the survey of the model (model 1.2.1) we have already included the autonomous impulses (c_R, i, p_L).

Because of their importance, some further explanation seems desirable.

Model 1.2.1 Summary of the basic model I

$$\{c_R\} = (\tilde{\gamma}_R)\,\{y_R'\} + \{\underline{c}_R\} \tag{1}$$

$$\{i\} = (\tilde{\sigma}_R)\,\{y_R'\} + (\zeta\kappa_R)\,\{(y_R - y_R')\} + \{\underline{i}\} \tag{2}$$

$$\{c_R\} + \{i\} \equiv \{y_R\} - \{e - m\} \tag{3}$$

$$\{e - m\} = -(\mu_0 y_E \eta) \begin{bmatrix} 1 & -1 \\ -1 & 1 \end{bmatrix} \{p\} \tag{4}$$

$$\{p\} = (\psi)\,\{p_L\} \tag{5}$$

$$\{p_L\} = \{1\} + (\beta)\left\{\frac{y_{R-1}'}{y_{R_E}'} - 1\right\} + \{\underline{p}_L\} \tag{6}$$

$$\{y_R'\} = (1 - \delta)\,\{y_{R-1}'\} + \left(\frac{1}{\kappa_R}\right)\{i_{-1}\} \tag{7}$$

To complete the picture, we include an explanation of the meaning of the matrices:

$$(\tilde{\gamma}_R) = \begin{pmatrix} \tilde{\gamma}_{R_A} & 0 \\ 0 & \tilde{\gamma}_{R_B} \end{pmatrix}; \qquad (\tilde{\sigma}_R) = \begin{pmatrix} \tilde{\sigma}_{R_A} & 0 \\ 0 & \tilde{\sigma}_{R_B} \end{pmatrix};$$

$$(\zeta\kappa_R) = \begin{pmatrix} \zeta_A \kappa_{R_A} & 0 \\ 0 & \zeta_B \kappa_{R_B} \end{pmatrix}$$

$$(\mu_0 y_E \eta) = \begin{pmatrix} \mu_{0_A} y_{E_A} \eta_A & 0 \\ 0 & \mu_{0_B} y_{E_B} \eta_B \end{pmatrix} \text{ etc.}$$

(The definitions of (ψ), (β), $(1 - \delta)$ and $\left(\dfrac{1}{\kappa_R}\right)$ are analogous.)

(a) $\underline{c}_R$: *the autonomous consumption-pull*
When, in a given period, $\underline{c}_R$ reaches a positive value, then we shall speak of a positive consumption-pull or negative saving pull in the period

concerned. A one-time consumption-pull of 10 can be illustrated as follows:

$$\{\underline{c}_{R_t}\} = \begin{cases} \left\{\begin{bmatrix} 10 \\ 0 \end{bmatrix}\right\} & \text{if } t = 1 \\[2em] \left\{\begin{bmatrix} 0 \\ 0 \end{bmatrix}\right\} & \text{if } t \neq 1 \end{cases}$$

A similar continuous consumption-pull, beginning with period 1 will then be:

$$\{\underline{c}_{R_t}\} = \begin{cases} \left\{\begin{bmatrix} 0 \\ 0 \end{bmatrix}\right\} & \text{if } t < 1 \\[2em] \left\{\begin{bmatrix} 10 \\ 0 \end{bmatrix}\right\} & \text{if } t = 1, 2, \ldots, \infty \end{cases}$$

(b) $\{\underline{i}_t\}$: *the investment-pull and capacity-pull*

The investment-pull has two aspects. In the first place, it affects spendings and at the same time the effective demand which, by means of the investment function sets the endogenous mechanism in motion. In this regard, the effect of the investment-pull does not differ from the consumption-pull.

In the second place, an autonomous investment-pull causes an (also autonomous) increase in capacity (y'). From now on, we shall refer to this aspect of investment-pull as capacity-pull. It can therefore also be said that a capacity-pull is an investment-pull of which the spending effect is neutralised by a comparable saving-pull.

It is easy enough, however, to deduce from the equations of the summary (model 1.2.1) that not only the spending effect, but also the capacity effect of the investment-pull is strongly analogous to the consumption-pull, as far as results are concerned.

In order to limit the length of our presentation, we have paid no further attention to the investment- or capacity-pull in this chapter. To complete the picture, we define a one-time capacity-pull of 10 in region A in period 1 as:

$$\{\underline{i}_t\} = \left\{\begin{bmatrix} 10 \\ 0 \end{bmatrix}\right\} \quad \text{if } t = 1$$

and

$$\{i_t\} = \begin{Bmatrix} 0 \\ 0 \end{Bmatrix} \text{ if } t \neq 1$$

It will be clear, after what we have said about the continuous consumption-pull, how a long term capacity-pull must be illustrated mathematically.

(c) p_l: *the wage-push*
With regard to determination of wages, we distinguish several kinds of autonomous impulses which we consider to be so important that we have given them different names.

The first of these is the *one-time extra wage payment*. This will be the case when, in a given period the endogenous relation is partly neutralised by the addition of the term $\{p_l\}$. This can be illustrated as follows, when there is a one-time wage payment in region A of 10.

$$\{p_{l_t}\} = \begin{cases} \begin{Bmatrix} 10 \\ 0 \end{Bmatrix} \text{ if } t = 1 \\[2em] \begin{Bmatrix} 0 \\ 0 \end{Bmatrix} \text{ if } t \neq 1 \end{cases}$$

More important is perhaps when wages remain at the same level as the previous year, corrected for possible employment mutations. We shall call this the one-time wage-push, and can in fact regard it as a repeated one-time payment.

In the foregoing, we have continually assumed that the indicated autonomous impulses can be manipulated politically. We must realise, however, that in practice, the problems of economic policy do not lie principally in the definition of objectives and instruments related to some economic model, but more in actually obtaining the abovementioned economic political instruments (and others) at the right moment and in the right dose.

But in theory, and our study has not much else to offer, all given instruments can be made effective: the consumption-pull for instance, by the government's budget policy; the capacity-pull indirectly by means of stimulating or slowing down fiscal measures and more directly by

11

manipulation of the government's own investments programme; and finally the wage-push, either influenced by convincing the institutional wage or by the introduction of enforced wage policy measures.

Further, the reader may have noticed that we have not included any autonomous price-push in our observations. However, it is a fact that, especially at the present time, frequent inexplicable price movements do indeed occur. By introducing price impulses into our observations however, we enter the realms of inflation. The problems that then arise are so extensive that their treatment within this thesis would necessarily be too fragmentary. We do believe, however, that the models we have set up (even though some points have not been followed up), can be of some use, not only in studying the well known problem of the inter-national transmission of inflation, but also in throwing some light on the lesser known problem of the international interaction on that point.

1.3 SOLUTION OF THE SYMMETRICAL MODEL

For this simple model we obtain the solution of the model by means of the following equations, which can easily be deduced from model 1.2.1.

$$\{e - m\} = -\left(\frac{\mu'}{1-\lambda_m}\right) \begin{bmatrix} 1 & -1 \\ -1 & 1 \end{bmatrix} \{y_R'\}_{-1} +$$

$$- (\mu_0 y_E \mu \psi) \begin{bmatrix} 1 & -1 \\ -1 & 1 \end{bmatrix} \{\underline{p}_L\}, \tag{1.3.1}$$

Here is:

$$(\mu') \equiv (\mu_0 \eta \psi \beta) \tag{1.3.2}$$

If $\tilde{\gamma}_R + \tilde{\sigma}_R = 1$, it follows from (1), (2) and (3) of model 1.2.1:

$$\{y_R\} = \{y_R'\} + (M) \{e - m\} + (M) \{\underline{x}\}, \tag{1.3.3}$$

where

$$(M) \equiv \left(\frac{1}{1-\zeta\kappa_R}\right) \quad \text{and} \quad \{\underline{x}\} = \{\underline{c}\} + \{\underline{i}\} \tag{1.3.4}$$

Combination of (1.3.4) and (2) of model 1.2.1 produces:

$$\left(\frac{1}{\kappa_R}\right) \{i\} = \left(\frac{\tilde{\sigma}_R}{\kappa_R}\right) \{y_R'\} + (\zeta M) \{e - m\} + (\zeta M) \underline{x} + \left(\frac{1}{\kappa_R}\right) \{\underline{i}\}. \tag{1.3.5}$$

12

If we insert (1.3.5) in the accumulation function (7) and make allowances for (1.3.1), we obtain:

$$\{y_R'\} = \left(1 - \delta + \frac{\tilde{\sigma}_R}{\kappa_R}\right)\{y_R'\}_{-1} - \left(\zeta M \frac{\mu'}{1-\lambda_m}\right)\begin{bmatrix} 1 & -1 \\ -1 & 1 \end{bmatrix}\{y_R'\}_{-2} +$$

$$- (\zeta M \mu_0 y_E \eta \psi)\begin{bmatrix} 1 & -1 \\ -1 & 1 \end{bmatrix}\{\underline{p_l}\}_{-1} + (\zeta m)\{\underline{x}\}_{-1} + \frac{1}{\kappa_R}\{\underline{i}\}_{-1} \quad (1.3.6)$$

The result is thus a fairly simple vector difference equation; the total system is of the 4th order. The endogenous stability of the system is characterised by the eigenvalues of the following matrix (see appendix A 1.2):

$$\begin{bmatrix} \left(1 - \delta + \frac{\tilde{\sigma}_R}{\kappa_R}\right) & 0 & -\zeta M \frac{\mu'}{(1-\lambda_m)} & \zeta M \frac{\mu'}{(1-\lambda_m)} \\ 0 & \left(1 - \delta + \frac{\tilde{\sigma}_R}{\kappa_R}\right) & \zeta M \frac{\mu'}{(1-\lambda_m)} & -\zeta M \frac{\mu'}{(1-\lambda_m)} \\ 1 & 0 & 0 & 0 \\ 0 & 1 & 0 & 0 \end{bmatrix}$$

$$(1.3.7)$$

A system with particularly attractive qualities can be obtained by choosing $\delta = \tilde{\sigma}_R/\kappa_R$. If that is the case, then two eigenvalues of (1.3.7) are 0 and 1, while the remaining two are dependent only on $\zeta M[\mu'/(1-\lambda_m)]$. In the numerical examples we shall use to illustrate the theory expressed in this chapter, the coefficients are chosen in such a way that this quality appears. In this way, the numerical explanation of the model remains manageable, and the interpretation of the results surveyable. Without going further into the details of the matter we note that the system becomes endogenously more unstable the more the formula $\zeta M[\mu'/(1-\lambda_m)]$ increases in value.

To conclude this paragraph, we wish to make one comment about autonomous impulses. The investment-pull occurs twice, once as a spending category and once as a capacity impulse ($\underline{i}$). Moreover, something we mentioned earlier now becomes clear, i.e. that the result of the capacity effect of investments, with reference to the dynamics of the production capacity (apart from quantitative intensity) is practically analogous to the spending impulse. In this exploratory chapter, we shall not therefore treat both pulls separately, but shall limit ourselves to spending or consumption policies.

The effects of the wage-push differ considerably from those of the spending-pull. Formally, this can be expressed in the matrix

$$\begin{bmatrix} 1 & -1 \\ -1 & 1 \end{bmatrix}$$

with which the autonomous wage-push vector p_l is *pre-multiplied*.

In slight anticipation of what follows, we note that the above matrix is responsible for the consequences of a wage-push in the active region being the opposite to those in the passive region. On the other hand the consequences of a unilateral spending-pull, taking place in *one* region only, are to a considerable degree the same in *both* regions.

1.4 DESCRIPTION OF THE BUSINESS CYCLE

As we mentioned before, the cyclical movements which arise after a spending- and investment-pull differ in many respects from those following a wage-push. For this reason we shall examine separately the cyclical course of events after a one-time spending pull and a one-time wage-push.

One of the first assumptions was that the impulses referred to, originate only unilaterally, in one region, i.e. region A. By means of inter-regional contacts, a cyclical movement then arises in both regions. The quantitative results can be found in tables 1.4.1 (spending-pull) and 1.4.2 (wage-push).

Lastly, we record the quantitative values of the coefficients we have used, which are, because of the assumed symmetry, the same for both regions.

$$\alpha = \tfrac{1}{2} \quad \beta = \tfrac{1}{4} \quad \tilde{\gamma}_L = 1 \quad \tilde{\gamma}_R = \tfrac{1}{3} \quad \delta = \tfrac{1}{10} \quad \zeta = \tfrac{1}{10} \quad \eta_e = 4$$

$$\eta_m = 4 \quad \kappa = 4 \quad \lambda_m = \tfrac{1}{2} \quad \mu_0 = \tfrac{1}{2} \quad \tilde{\sigma}_R = \tfrac{4}{3} \quad \psi = 1 \quad g_n = 0$$

Composite expressions:

$$\mu' = \mu_0 \eta \psi \beta = \tfrac{1}{2}$$

$$M = \frac{1}{1 - \zeta\kappa/(1-\lambda_m)} = 5$$

14

Region A

	1	2	3	4	5	6	7	8	Average
c_{R_A}	20	0	0	0	0	0	0	0	0
F.E.[1] y'_{R_A} = l_{v_A}	0	10	10	5	0	0	5	10	5
1. y_{R_A} = $10(y'_{R_{A+1}} - 0{,}9\,y'_{R_A})$	100	10	−40	−45	0	50	55	10	5
2. i_A = $0{,}8\,y'_{R_A} + 0{,}8(y_{R_A} - y'_{R_A})$	80	8	−32	−36	0	40	44	8	4
3. c_{R_A} = $0{,}2\,y'_{R_A} + c_{R_A}$	20	2	2	1	0	0	1	2	1
4. $(e_A - m_A)$ = $-y'_{R_{A-1}} + y'_{R_{B-1}}$	0	0	−10	−10	0	10	10	0	0
5. p_{L_A} = $\dfrac{1}{4}\dfrac{l_{v_{A-1}}}{100}$ (: 100)	0	0	$2\frac{1}{2}$	$2\frac{1}{2}$	$1\frac{1}{4}$	0	0	$1\frac{1}{4}$	$1\frac{1}{4}$

Region B (for the relations, see previous table)

	1	2	3	4	5	6	7	8	Average
F.E.[1] y'_{R_B} = l_B	0	0	0	5	10	10	5	0	5
1. y_{R_B}	0	0	50	55	10	−40	−45	0	5
2. i_B	0	0	40	44	8	−32	−36	0	4
3. c_{R_B}	0	0	0	1	2	2	1	0	1
4. $e_B - m_B$ = $-(e_A - m_A)$	0	0	10	10	0	−10	−10	0	0
5. p_{L_B} (: 100)	0	0	0	0	$1\frac{1}{4}$	$2\frac{1}{2}$	$2\frac{1}{2}$	$1\frac{1}{4}$	$1\frac{1}{4}$

The relations are identical to those of region A

1. F.E. means: final equation.

15

It can be easily verified that with the given coefficients, the four (different) eigenvalues of (1.3.7) assume the following values: 0, 1, $(\frac{1}{2} \pm \frac{1}{2}\sqrt{3}i)$, so that after a one-time impulse, a sinusoide arises with a cycle of six periods.

1.4.1 *One-time spending-pull (see table 1.4.1)*

Period 0
The situation given in table 1.2.1 is the current one (p. 3).

Period 1
An autonomous impulse causes the consumer spendings in region A to increase by an amount of 20 and the actual effective demand out of profit income to be $M \times 20 = 100$ more than would be the case in the equilibrium growth situation. This can be calculated as follows:

$$y_{R_1} = c_R + i = (\tilde{\gamma}_R + \tilde{\sigma}_R) y'_{R_1} + \frac{\zeta\kappa}{1 - \lambda_m}(y_{R_1} - y'_{R_1}) + \underline{c}_{R_1} =$$

$$= 100 + \tfrac{4}{5}(y_{R_1} - 100) + 20$$

$$\therefore\ y_{R_1} = 200 \text{ and } y_{R_1} - y_{R_{1_E}} = 100$$

Investments will then amount to 80 more than normal and consumption 20, as already stated above. For the rest, the variables in region A still reach equilibrium values. There are no repercussions in region A as yet, since the international transmission of the cycle, which always occurs through the balance of the current account, is because of the lag not yet under way.

Period 2
The most important inheritance from the past is the increased production capacity in region A. Expressed in goods, this becomes $(1/\kappa)(160-80) =$ 20 units.

The *actual* overspending out of profit income then amounts to 10. This can be calculated as follows:

$$y_{R_2} = y'_{R_2} + \tfrac{4}{5}(y_{R_2} - y'_{R_2})\ y_{R_2} = y'_{R_2} = 110,$$

so that

$$y_{R_2} - y_{R_{2_E}} = 10$$

Consumption by capitalists is consequently too high, by an amount of $\frac{1}{5} \times 10 = 2$ and gross investments are also still above the normal level, although notably less than in period 1.

16

Because of increased production capacity, demand for labour also increases. But since we have assumed a lagged reaction of wages to stress on the labour market, the wage level and with it the price level remain unchanged, so that still no reaction appears in partner region B, where the situation of equilibrium growth is still maintained, unaltered.

In region A, therefore, the main cycle continues into period 2, although considerably weakened. For example, no net capital accumulation takes place, because the slightly higher gross investments are not sufficient to compensate for the much higher depreciations.

Period 3
In the first place, the same changed production capacity as in period 2 applies. In terms of y'_R, this again amounts to 10 units. In the second place, because of the changed wages and prices in this period, we have a balance on the current account for the first time. This amounts, for region A, to:

$$e_A - m_A = - \mu_0 y_E \eta (p_A - p_B) = -10$$

This amount must, of course, be deducted from domestic spendings, in order to calculate the effective demand out of profit income in region A, thus:

$$y_{R_3} = y'_{R_3} + \tfrac{4}{3}(y_{R_3} - y'_{R_3}) - 10 \ y_{R_{3A}} = y'_{R_{3A}} - 50,$$

$$y_{R_{3A}} - y_{R_{3A_E}} = 60 - 100 = -40$$

There is once again stress in the labour market in region A which will lead to a balance of payments deficit in the next period also. The decline in investment activity continues and leads to a definite decline in net investment volume. In short, there are many signs of an approaching recession in region A.

In region B, on the other hand, the oncoming upward movement begins to be noticeable in period 3. This commences with a surplus of $+10$ in the current account. Consequently, the ex post effective demand out of profit income is higher than normal by an amount of 50.

Period 4
In region A, the recession is well under way: effective demand, in particular investments, reaches a minimum level; production capacity, and with it employment, begins to move towards normal equilibrium growth values. Region A, however, is still struggling with a deficit on current account because the nominal levels are still high there, while

they are still unchanged in region B. While region A is in the depth of a recession, the opposite applies to region B. The boom present there is made up of two components: not only is it caused by the continuing surplus on the balance of payments, but the increased production capacity now has a noticeable effect. Meanwhile, investments too now remain at the same high level as in the previous period.

Period 5
In region A everything has practically settled down, although many disturbing forces remain hidden under the surface. Almost all variables reach their equilibrium values, since the exorbitantly high production capacity at the beginning of the boom has, in the meantime, been called to a halt. The effective demand from abroad is not too high either, since the nominal levels in both regions have, in the meantime, become equal. In region B, a boom situation exists, although much weaker than it was in period 4, because the positive impulse of the surplus on current account is no longer of influence.

On the whole, the economy of region B is relatively stable. The situation does of course become seriously disturbed in the next period because then the enlarged investment activity of period 3 will result in an increased production capacity and therefore an increased demand for labour. Because of the relation between stress on the labour market on the one hand and wages and prices on the other, we can expect in the not too distant future a change for region B as well.

Period 6
In region A, preparations are being made again for a period of prosperity. This is set in motion by both lands changing their places in the competitive relationship: region B has in the meantime become the expensive region. The boom in region A remains of a modest intensity of course, but investment activity is mounting again while, because of an eased labour market, wages and prices can still remain low.

In region B, the recession sets in. It is accompanied by a deficit on current account. The most important result of this is a pronounced decline in both net and gross investments.

Period 7
The endogenous boom reaches its peak in region A; capital forming capacity and also employment reach high values. At the same time, region B reaches the bottom of the depression.

18

Period 8

The process of the weakening of the cycle in region A and a standstill that leads to recovery in region B, repeats itself. In addition to the cyclical consequences of a one-time consumption-pull, as described above, we must pay attention to the structural consequences.

It is, in the first place, striking that the average values spread over the complete business cycle, influenced by a unilateral consumption-pull in region A are absolutely the same for all variables in both regions. This is not surprising, if one keeps in mind that the whole difference in cyclical development between region A and region B lies in the fact that region B is one phase behind. An exception to this is of course the first preliminary period that never comes back again.

It is also worth noting that a one-time spending impulse taking place in one land, is accompanied by permanent structural consequences. This is of course in agreement with our other conclusions, based on the macromodel.

In the model we are dealing with at present, in which the marginal spending quote is equal to 1, it is also implied that a policy of repeated positive consumption (spending) pulls leads to a cumulative dislocation.

Table 1.4.2   One-time negative wage-push in region A. Consequences in region A (the consequences in region B are the opposite, with the exception of wages and prices)

Deviations with regard to equilibrium values	1	2	3	4	5	6	7	8	Average
y'_R	0	10	20	20	10	0	0	10	10
y_R	100	110	20	-80	-90	0	100	110	10
i	80	88	16	-64	-72	0	80	88	8
c_R	0	2	4	4	2	0	0	2	2
$e-m$	20	20	0	-20	-20	0	20	20	0
l	0	10	20	20	10	0	0	10	10
k	0	80	160	160	80	0	0	80	80
d	0	8	16	16	8	0	0	8	8
i_{net}	80	80	0	-80	-80	0	80	80	0
y	100	120	40	-60	-80	0	100	120	20
$p_L = p$									
region A (: 100)	-5	-5	$-2\frac{1}{2}$	0	0	$-2\frac{1}{2}$	-5	-5	$-2\frac{1}{2}$
region B (: 100)	0	0	$-2\frac{1}{2}$	-5	-5	$-2\frac{1}{2}$	0	0	$-2\frac{1}{2}$

1.4.2 *The one-time wage-push (see table 1.4.2)*

Period 1

In region A, wages (and thus prices) decrease for autonomous reasons, with 5% from 1 to 0.95. The wages and prices in region B remain unaltered at first. The changed competitive relationship results in a surplus on current account in region A up to an amount of 20. This can be calculated as follows:

$$(e - m) = \mu_0 y_E \eta (p_A - p_B) = 200$$

Therefore, the effective demand in region A rises by an amount of 100, since the following equation is applicable:

$$y_R = y_R' + 5(e - m) = 20 \therefore y_R - y_{R_E} = 100$$

The consequences in region B are of course exactly the reverse: a deficit on current account and an effective demand out of profit income + abroad, which is 100 lower than normal.

Production capacity and employment still remain at the equilibrium level; investments in region B are 80 higher than normal, because of the increased actual profit income.

Period 2

A second disturbing element now appears in the capacity in region A which, in proportion to the equilibrium growth, is too high, and the related undercapacity in region B. A rise in employment in region A (a drop in region B) is connected with this. Investments in region A remain high, mainly because of a high actual income (and also because of increased capacity).

Period 3

To be brief, we can say that under the influence of a one-time unilateral negative wage-push in region A, the consequences for region B are exactly the reverse of those for region A. The nominal levels form an exception to this. We shall therefore limit our description in future, to the consequences in region A. It is clear that in period 3, wage costs and prices are levelled down in both regions. As a result the current account reaches an equilibrium. In the meantime, overcapacity in region A has increased even more, so that the boom continues there. Net investments now reach however their normal value, so that over-capacity is stabilised. One of the weak spots in the economy of region A becomes visible in this way.

Period 4
In this period, the economy of region *A* shows a clear downward movement. The most important element is that this region has now become expensive in comparison with region *B*, so that the balance of payments equilibrium of period 3 turns into a deficit. This leads to a considerable decline of effective demand and a substantial relapse in investments, whereby the over-capacity which had gradually arisen is decreased by half.

Employment still remains high, so that in the following period the same wages and prices will apply.

Period 5
The economy in region *A* now reaches its lowest point.

Period 6
A situation of equilibrium has practically been reached now, since in period 5 the over-capacity was completely cut off, while international prices reached their equilibrium, resulting in an equilibrium on the current account.

Period 7
The equilibrium is however apparent, since the decline of employment in period 6 causes a decline in wages up to -5 in period 7, after which the procedure repeats itself.

1.4.3 *Comparison of a one-time spending-pull and a one-time wage-push*

The impulses in question have, besides certain similarities, one important difference. The wage-push has an opposite effect in each region, while the ultimate effect of the spending-pull, occurring in *one* region is the same for both regions. The active region is however confronted by the consequences earlier. In this case, it can be assumed that the passive region lags $\frac{1}{2}$ cycle behind the active region.

1.4.4 *The dynamic characteristics*

Now that we have seen how the model works, it seems appropriate to make some comments on the interpretation of its dynamic qualities. We are not satisfied just to refer to the eigenvalues of the matrix (1.3.7) but prefer to study the concrete significance in the economic system.

1. In an integrated model consisting of several regions (lands), the concept 'stability' ('instability') can mean various things. In the first place, we can mean the dynamic qualities of the model as characterised by the abovementioned eigenvalues of the matrix (1.3.7). Since this matrix describes the endogenous working of the total system, we shall speak of 'stability (instability) of the system', according to whether the own roots of (1.3.7) are more or less than 1.

2. We can also consider the dynamic qualities of the aggregates among the various regions. In that case, we are simply dealing with the macromodel as discussed in section 1.2.1.1. We shall indicate the dynamic qualities of the macromodel by the term 'macrostability (instability)'. It goes without saying that macrostability is greater than the systemstability discussed in 1.

3. Finally, the dynamic qualities of each region can be studied separately, disregarding the fact that each region forms a part of an integrated system. In fact, this is the current macroeconomic view. The national economic policies are usually designed and conducted on this basis. When small regions are concerned, this seems to be an acceptable assumption (see, however Appendix A 1.1). When, however, blocks of approximately the same size are closely related, the macroeconomic way of thinking becomes disputable.

Even so, it is possible to define a concept of stability on the basis of the structure coefficients which determine the relations with the partner region. The stability we mean here, which has a macroeconomic character, we shall call *partial stability*. In the foregoing model the *'partial stability'* is greater than the 'system stability'.

In general it would be interesting to examine the possible effects of the partial dynamic qualities on respectively the dynamic qualities of the integrated system and the macrosystem. We will not be doing this in this book.

1.5 ECONOMIC POLICY

In the foregoing, conclusions regarding economic policy have of course already been drawn. Even so, we shall explicitly list a number of relevant inferences in this paragraph. We have limited ourselves to the integrated two-regions model, since the conclusions for the macromodel and thus for the macropolicy can be drawn by simple addition, from the two-regions model.

In summing up, we have not therefore attempted to be systematically complete but have only singled out what we consider to be the most interesting points.

Because of the assumed rigidity of the profit margins (capital income margins) out of all structural problems, we shall treat only those concerned with employment and allocation. Moreover, the rest of this study is devoted to the significance of the flexible profit margins, actually a condition for a changing income distribution, so that we will be able to do justice to the matters related to this.

In addition to the abovementioned (inter-regional) structural problems we shall pay some attention to the possibilities of stabilisation of the cycle arising from the different impulses.

1.5.1 *Employment policy*

1. In theory, *one* land can realise objectives with regard to employment by unilateral application of one of the two given instruments of economic policy, i.e. the consumption-pull (saving-pull) and the autonomous wage-push.

In both of these cases, under the influence of the relations in operation, one single application of the instrument will be sufficient, to achieve the desired results.

We must point out that a unilateral application of the spending or wage impulse in, say region A, has possibly undesirable side effects in the partner region.

2. Despite the effectivity of the instruments in question, in the (regional) international employment policy, striking differences do exist between the effects of the spending-pull on the one hand and the wage-push on the other.

The unilateral application of the former instrument results in fact in an identical development, at least from a structural point of view, in both regions. Seen from a cyclical aspect, however, we note that the passive region lags behind the active region. One can speak therefore of a lagged diffusion effect of the unilateral spending impulse. The diffusion effect referred to here, fails to appear in the case of an autonomous wage-push. On the contrary, in the latter case, practically all aspects of the development in the passive region are the opposite of the development in the active region. A further, formal, explanation of this has been given in the previous paragraph.

3. There is one important exception to this. The opposite effect noted above does not apply for nominal wages and prices. The development of these variables in both regions runs parallel continually, although a lag-difference is present.

4. As we have already stated in 1, unilateral application of only one instrument, in one region is followed by structural repercussions in the passive region (cyclical repercussions as well, of course, but these will be handled in 1.5.2).

A region is not of course expected to await submissively the consequences of the ambitions of its business partner. Obviously, counter measures will be taken to avoid undesired side-effects of the neighbour's campaigns.

When a (large) region does not wish to see its actions crossed by the counter measures of the business partner, it must try to pursue a policy acceptable to its partner. In the present model, this is made possible by choosing a combination of spending-pull on the one hand and wage-push on the other.

This can be illustrated by the following table in which employment in region A is increased by an amount of 20 by simultaneous application of

a. a negative wage-push of 5% and
b. a positive spending-pull of 20.

Only the consequences for employment have been described. If desired, the results for the other variables can be drawn up by using tables 1.4.1 and 1.4.2. We would also like to point out that the processes described are linked with the maintenance of the equilibrium of the balance of payments from a short term as well as a structural point of view.

The consequences for employment of:

a. one-time negative wage-push in region A
b. one-time spending-pull in region A

t	1	2	3	4	5	6	7	8	Average
In region A, of a	0	10	20	20	10	0	0	10	10
b	0	20	20	10	0	0	10	20	10
Total	0	30	40	30	10	0	10	30	20
In region B, of a	0	−10	−20	−20	−10	0	0	−10	−10
b	0	0	0	10	20	20	10	0	10
Total	0	−10	−20	−10	+10	20	10	−10	0

5. In order to achieve a possibly desired reallocation of production factors, a unilateral application of the wage policy instrument is sufficient. It is of course, necessary, in that case, to coordinate the measures on an international basis (see point 4).

If a shift in employment from region A to region B is desired, in actual terms it makes no difference whether this is brought about by means of a negative wage-push in region B or not. In both cases, the abovementioned effect can appear.

In nominal terms, however, both measures have opposite consequences. If we wish to take into consideration the constant value of money then we must of course prescribe a positive wage-push in the first region and a negative wage-push of equal size in the other.

6. A striking factor is that the instruments dealt with here do not evoke any stress. This applies not only to the balance of payments, which is continually in equilibrium, but also to the capacity utilisation degree of the capital goods supply which has the correct capacity utilisation degree with regard to actual production.

1.5.2 Stabilisation policy

The importance of the stabilisation policy depends naturally on the endogenous stability of the model. When all the moduli of the eigenvalues of the model are much smaller than 1, then one need not be concerned about the cyclical stabilisation. The sinusoide that we used as an example has perhaps given a wrong idea of the degree of endogenous instability which appears in reality. However, the following conclusions deserve attention even if only for theoretical reasons. (Unless indicated otherwise, we have continually assumed unilateral impulses in region A.)

1. A one-time negative wage-push in region A can be completely stabilised by a negative wage-push in region B too ('keeping in step'). In actual terms, the effects are then structurally neutral, but in nominal terms a permanent decrease of wage and price level arises. Actually, this issues directly from the (stable) macromodel, in which a one-time wage-push does not evoke any cyclical effects.

2. The consequences of a one-time negative wage-push in period 1 in region A can be countered by a positive spending-pull in period 2 in region B. This is clarified in the following table.

Results for employment development of:

a. one-time wage-push of −5% in region A
b. one-time spending-pull of 20% in region B

	t	1	2	3	4	5	6	7	8	Average
Results in region A,										
of a		0	10	20	20	10	0	0	10	10
b		−	0	0	0	10	20	20	10	10
Total		0	10	20	20	20	20	20	20	20
Results in region B,										
of a		0	−10	−20	−20	−10	0	0	−10	−10
b		−	0	20	20	10	0	0	10	10
Total		0	0	0	0	0	0	0	0	0

We can conclude that region B does region A a great favour, compared with the policy set out in 1, since it not only stabilises the international business cycle by taking the measure, but also reinforces further creation of employment in region A inasmuch as this was intended.

II. Macroeconomics: the closed economy

2.1 INTRODUCTION

In the previous chapter we studied the integrated functioning of a two-regions model, both as a whole and as two separate regions. Although we chose the simplest possible specifications, we still had to introduce rather a lot of mechanisms which dominate the processes of consumption and investment, as well as those of price and income determination.

There are, however, other mechanisms which seem to be of importance in reality, but which have not been considered in Chapter I. Up till now we have assumed unilateral dependence of employment on labour positions available. It is possible that the labour demand is determined not only by the labour positions available but also by the realised degree of capacity utilisation. As we shall see, the introduction of this latter hypothesis has far reaching consequences for the operation of the system.

A second amendment to the assumptions made in Chapter I, concerns the assumed constancy of the expected profit margins. In this new chapter, we shall be working once more with a constant structural distribution of wage and profit incomes, but this is no longer based, for example, on a given degree of monopoly but on the assumption that the economy is in the neighbourhood of 'golden age'. The structural distribution of income, under these circumstances is indeed constant, but cyclically, it can change since the wage costs can differ from the equilibrium level.

This amended assumption enables us, in particular, to abandon the rather unrealistic character of the model described in Chapter I, that an autonomous wage impulse has no cyclical consequences for the macro-economy.

As well as the two points just mentioned, we shall be considering many other matters which are important to the operation of the market system. In order to limit the number of problems somewhat, some restrictions were necessary. Firstly, we made the macroeconomy our starting point, so that the integrated operation of the macrosystems will not be dealt with. The explanations given in this chapter should actually be regarded as preliminary to Chapter IV, where we shall use the model of this chapter as a basis for the analysis of an integrated many-regions model.

2.1.1 *Abstractions*

The remaining abstraction, the most important in our opinion, concerns the assumption that any existing relations with foreign countries have a neutral effect on the endogenous business cycle and structure, so that no disturbing influences on the internal variables arise there. Considered in this way, a 'closed economy' does not necessarily mean that there are absolutely no imports and exports, but only that the balance between these two variables is, by definition, equal to zero. It is even possible to interpret any volume surplus on current account as an autonomous spending impulse.

In Chapter III we shall be dealing in detail with the various mechanisms related to the balance of payments, so that the restrictions just mentioned can be ignored.

A second important postulate concerns the relations between real and money terms. Of these, we have considered only the aspect of, on the one hand transmission of wage costs in prices (wage pressure theory), and on the other hand, the reverse mechanism: transmission of price increases in wage demands (wage indexing).

We shall not be discussing other important aspects of the relations between real terms and money terms, such as the influence of debt ratios on real quantities, the significance of real cash balances or even the classical issue of the influence of interest on investments and accumulation of stocks. An actual integration of both terms is present only to a certain extent.

2.1.2 *Division and content*

We shall begin this chapter with a discussion of the basic model whose structure, in its most important aspects, resembles those usually found in literature and in econometric practice. One important difference from the model in the previous chapter is that spendings now play a main rôle in the labour demand function. The selected specifications continue to be very simple.

28

This basic model will be elaborated by using detailed numerical examples, similar to those used in the previous chapter. In this way we hope to elucidate the characteristics of the model and the way it works, as much as possible. The mathematical structure of the model remains very simple; the mathematics used goes no further than linear difference equations of lower order. It would be possible to describe the characteristics of the model mathematically in a few sentences. However, we consider the significance of the symbols more important than the symbols themselves. For this reason, we have once again emphasised the economic interpretation.

The central problem of this chapter is the question of whether a re-structuring policy for employment, determination of capital and distribution of income is possible within the given, simple scheme, and if so, how this can be done. One condition hereby is that these structural objections must be realised, if possible, without jeopardizing cyclical stability.

In the main part of this chapter we shall be taking into consideration the simplest assumptions in almost all parts of the economic system.

2.1.2.1 *The variables*

In Chapter I, we worked with the absolute values of the variables. In this new chapter, the central variables are considered to be relative deviations from the values, which they would assume in a situation of equilibrium growth (as according to Domar). We express this by adding to the variable the operator g, which for an arbitrary variable z is defined as follows:

$$g_z = \frac{z - z_E}{z_E} \qquad (2.1.1)$$

(Here, the suffix E refers to 'equilibrium'.)

We note hereby, that we may not conclude on these grounds alone, that equilibrium growth is presupposed. We may only ascertain that equilibrium growth is *possible* (constant capital coefficient).

Prices and remuneration rates are exceptions to this rule. The relative deviation of a price level from the equilibrium value is indicated by the following sign ($\vee$), for example:

$$\check{p}_L = \frac{p_L - p_{L_E}}{p_{L_E}} \qquad (2.1.2)$$

We use the same system of symbols that we used in Chapter I, i.e. capital letters represent (money) values and small letters, in general, the corresponding real values (volumina).

In terms of relative deviations, the following apply as (approximate) definition equations for money values.

$$g_z \equiv g_z + \check{p}_z \tag{2.1.3}$$

For an explanatory survey of the most important variables appearing in this chapter, consult the list of symbols at the end of this book.

2.2 BASIC MODEL II

2.2.1 *Comparison with the relations of basic model I*

As already stated, the relations of this model differ from those of the model described in the previous chapter, especially with regard to the specification of the employment function, to which we now add the volume of the actual production as explanatory variable. Although this appears to be only a small alteration, it will become evident that the operation of the model changes radically.

2.2.1.1 *Spending functions and the employment function*
The introduction of production volume into the employment function takes place according to the following formula:

$$g_l = \tilde{\alpha}_k g_k + \tilde{\alpha}_y g_y \tag{2.2.1}$$

A special, but important case of (2.2.1) is obtained if one assumes that employment is the weighted average of labour positions available on the one hand and actual production volume on the other, so that the following equation applies:

$$\tilde{\alpha}_k + \tilde{\alpha}_y = 1.$$

If we remember that for the degree of capacity utilisation of capital goods s_b,

$$s_b \equiv g_k - g_y,$$

applies, then we can also write the following for (2.2.1):

$$g_l = \tilde{\alpha}_k g_k + \tilde{\alpha}_y g_y = (1 - \tilde{\alpha}_y) g_k + \tilde{\alpha}_y g_y =$$
$$= g_k - \tilde{\alpha}_y(g_k - g_y) = g_k - \tilde{\alpha}_y s_b \tag{2.2.2}$$

Therefore, we can interpret the employment function in the latter

30

equation (2.2.2) as follows: at first, demand for labour is determined by the number of labour positions available, to which positive or negative corrections are possible, according to whether the available capital goods are being utilised more than normal or less than normal.

Equation (2.2.1) does not give any insight either into the factors which ultimately determine demand for labour since production volume, which determines employment, is in turn dependent on employment itself. In connection with demand for labour, therefore, a multiplier begins to operate, which allows for the following simple spending function:

$$g_y = g_x = \lambda_0(g_l + \check{w}) + (1 - \lambda_0)\left(g_k + \frac{\check{r}_{-1}}{r_E}\right) \qquad (2.2.3)$$

as labour demand function produces:

$$g_l = M_l\left[\tilde{\alpha}'_k g_k + \tilde{\alpha}_y\left\{\lambda_0\check{w} + (1 - \lambda_0)\frac{\check{r}_{-1}}{r_E}\right\}\right] \qquad (2.2.4)$$

Here

$$M_l \equiv \frac{1}{1 - \tilde{\alpha}_y\lambda_0} \qquad (2.2.5)$$

is the employment-multiplier, and

$$\tilde{\alpha}'_k \equiv \tilde{\alpha}_k + (1 - \lambda_0)\tilde{\alpha}_y \qquad (2.2.6)$$

the corrected marginal employment quote of the capital goods supply.

By substitution of the rate of profit relations (see A 2.1) $\check{r} = -\dfrac{\lambda_0}{\kappa}\check{w}$ and

$r_E = \dfrac{1 - \lambda_0}{\kappa}$ can be simplified (2.2.4) to:

$$g_l = M_l\{\tilde{\alpha}'_k g_k + \tilde{\alpha}_y\lambda_0(\check{w} - \check{w}_{-1})\} \qquad (2.2.7)$$

With the aid of the investment function, in which we assume that investments are wholly dependent on profits (see appendix A 2.1)[1] and passing on to the operator notation, one can, by using (2.2.7) deduce a relationship between the development in time of the demand for labour on the one hand and the development of the real wage rate on the other hand, thus:

1. The investment function is $g_k = g_{k_{-1}} + \sigma_R\check{r}_{-2}$, or $g_k = \sigma_R\dfrac{1}{E^2 - E}\check{r}$.

$$g_l = M_l \left\{ \tilde{\alpha}_y \lambda_0 (I_0 - E^{-1}) - \tilde{\alpha}_k' \sigma_r \frac{\lambda_0}{\kappa} \frac{1}{E^2 - E} \right\} \check{w} \quad (^1) \tag{2.2.8}$$

The interpretation of (2.2.8) deserves some further attention. Although this formula can be regarded as a (dynamic) macroeconomic demand for labour function, the connection with the 'demand for labour' functions referred to in the current publications about macroeconomy, is vague. In these publications, the production function, characterised by decreasing returns of labour, is usually said to be the basis of the demand function. Our way of derivating (2.2.8) differs strongly from the productivity theory, however.

In this specification it cannot even conclusively be determined if the relation between demand for labour on the one hand and the real wage rate on the other will increase or decrease. It depends on the period one wishes to consider. The way in which it all fits together, can easily be discerned by using the following formula instead of (2.2.8):

$$g_l = M_l \tilde{\alpha}_y \lambda_0 \check{w} - 2 M_l \tilde{\alpha}_y \lambda_0 \check{w}_{-1} + M_l \left(\tilde{\alpha}_y \lambda_0 - \tilde{\alpha}_k' \sigma_r \frac{\lambda_0}{\kappa} \right) \check{w}_{-1} + g_{l-1} \tag{2.2.9}$$

Let us suppose that period t has been preceded by an equilibrium growth situation

$$(w_u = g_{l_u} = 0; u < t)$$

and let us assume that a permanent increase of the real wage rate, of $\bar{w}$ takes place in period t. This results in an increase in employment in period t itself up to an amount of $M_l \tilde{\alpha}_y \lambda_0 \bar{w} \%$; in the succeeding period, the *decrease* of employment is also $M_l \tilde{\alpha}_y \lambda_0 \bar{w} \%$, thus bringing the latter variable back to its original, equilibrium level. If, however, the real wage costs remain at the higher level, as we have assumed, then the *change* in employment will be a negative function of the level of the real wage costs, thus:

$$g_l - g_{l-1} = - M_l \tilde{\alpha}_k \sigma_r \frac{\lambda_0}{\kappa} \bar{w} \tag{2.2.10}$$

It must now be obvious that in our view, we must differentiate between the short term connection between wage costs and employment and the long term connection. In the short run, the positive spending effect of the higher real wages is active. In the long run on the other hand, the

1. Here, I_0 is the unit operator and E is the operator defined as $Ex_t \equiv x_{t+1}$.

connection between wage costs and labour demand is clearly negative, because of the induced long term decrease in labour positions available. We can even conclude that in our view a real wage level that is too high affects employment more drastically than is generally supposed.

The unemployment percentage of the model under discussion will continue to grow if a high wage level is maintained for long. It is more often assumed however, that a high wage level maintained for a long period is accompanied only by a constant unemployment percentage.

2.2.1.2 *Determination of price functions*

With regard to the determination of the price function, we assume that prices are determined by wage costs alone. The transmission of wage costs into prices is lagged, in contrast to Chapter I, and occurs according to the formula:

$$\breve{p} = \psi_1 \breve{p}_l + \psi_2 \breve{p}_{l-1} = (\psi_1 + \psi_2 E^{-1}) \breve{p}_l \qquad (2.2.11)$$

In connection with future substitutions, we can deduce from (2.2.11) the following equations for $\breve{p}$ and $\breve{p}_l$ in terms of the real wage rate:

$$\breve{w} \equiv (1 - \psi_1) \breve{p}_l - \psi_2 \breve{p}_{l-1} = \{(1 - \psi_1) - \psi_2 E^{-1}\} \breve{p}_l \Rightarrow \breve{p}_l =$$

$$= \frac{1}{(1-\psi_1)-\psi_2 E^{-1}} \breve{w}, \qquad (2.2.12)$$

so that

$$\breve{p} = \frac{\psi_1 + \psi_2 E^{-1}}{(1-\psi_1)-\psi_2 E^{-1}} \breve{w} \qquad (2.2.13)$$

Finally, a formula used several times is:

$$(\breve{p}_l - \varepsilon \breve{p}) = \frac{(1-\varepsilon\psi_1)-\varepsilon\psi_2 E^{-1}}{(1-\psi_1)-\psi_2 E^{-1}} \breve{w} \qquad (2.2.14)$$

2.2.1.3 *The wage determination function*

Our starting point is a de facto existing wage indexing. The exact formula for the transmission of prices into wages is:

$$\breve{p}_l = \varepsilon \breve{p} + \beta g_l + \underline{\breve{p}_l} \qquad (2.2.15)$$

Of course there is much more to be said about the wage determination function that defines the supply structure of the labour market, than the above simple specification. (For this reason we feel justified in devoting a separate, concise appendix to the theoretical and empirical aspects of the wage determination function.)

Using (2.2.15), and keeping (2.2.12) and (2.2.13) in consideration, we obtain the following equation, showing the relationship between real wage rate on the one hand and the employment situation on the other:

$$\frac{(1-\varepsilon\psi_1)-\varepsilon\psi_2E^{-1}}{(1-\psi_1)-\psi_2E^{-1}}\,\breve{w} = \beta g_l + \breve{p}_l \tag{2.2.16}$$

(2.2.16) vaguely reminds us of the well known labour supply function. In an exceptional case (one that is moreover theoretically important) where $\varepsilon = 1$, (2.2.16) follows the usual rising course. Nevertheless, the interpretation of (2.2.16) is different from that of the usual supply function. In the present theory, a change in the labour supply does not result in a different real wage rate. This does, however, result from a change in labour demand, which is always taken into account in our theory. We have hereby taken into consideration the effect of changed prices on wage demands, on the one hand (2.2.15) and of wage costs on those same prices on the other hand (2.2.9).

We can understand the ultimate development of the real wage rate arising from a certain prolonged level of employment more easily by interpreting (2.2.16) as a simple difference equation. The modulus of this difference equation amounts to $\varepsilon\psi_2/(1-\varepsilon\psi_1)$. The development of the real wage rate as a function of a prolonged rise in the level of employment shall, when we assume a certain starting value, follow a steadily, according to an M.R., falling course as $\varepsilon(\psi_1+\psi_2)<1$, and a continually geometrically rising course in the reverse case that $\varepsilon(\psi_1+\psi_2)>1$. The ratio of the rise/fall is equal to $\varepsilon\psi_2/(1-\varepsilon\psi_1)$.

An important part of the policy of inflation, in particular the 'spiral' effect of wages and prices, can clearly be connected with the above. One last comment on the interpretation of the wage determination function is that although there is clearly a connection with the well known Phillips curve, there is also an important difference. In the original specification of the Phillips curve, it is suggested that real wage costs will change (at least if wages are not fully worked into prices) as long as a situation of full employment has not been realised. In our specification, wage costs stop changing when the employment situation does not change. Our specification is less able to create an equilibrium than the actual Phillips curve is.

Further attention will be paid to this question also in Appendix A 2.2.

2.2.2 *Outline of the model*

In the following survey (model 2.2.1) the most important relations of

34

our basic model have been arranged so that the solution of the model can be obtained in the form of the difference equation by successive substitution. The survey also shows how autonomous development of wages, accumulation of capital and spendings fit into the model.

A further clarification of the operation of the model can be obtained from graph 2.2.1, in which the causality of the model is shown.

The cyclical dynamics arises through expectations and time lags or, in other words, because the present is linked with the past and perhaps also to the (invisible) future. In our basic model, the past affects present economic activity in three respects.

It is affected firstly by the lag in the determination of capital, which is, in turn, based on the gestation period of capital goods, and secondly, by a lag in the spending mechanism which originates, in our model, solely from capitalist spending resulting from the expected relation with respect to the rate of profitability of capital. In the third place, the present determination of prices is also dependent on wage costs in the past, which can also explain the cyclical fluctuations.

Model 2.2.1   Basic model II

Relations	Autonomous impulses
1. $\check{p} = \psi_1 \check{p}_l + \psi_2 \check{p}_{l-1}$	$+\underline{\check{p}}$
2. $\check{w} = \check{p}_l - \check{p}$	
3. $\check{r} = -\dfrac{\lambda_0}{\kappa}\check{w}$	
4. $g_k = g_{k-1} + \sigma_r \check{r}_{-2}$	$+\hat{g}_k$
5. $g_l = M_l\{\lambda_0\tilde{\alpha}_y(\check{w}-\check{w}_{-1}) + \tilde{\alpha}'_k g_k\}$	$+M_l\tilde{\alpha}_y\check{g}_x$
6. $\check{p}_l = \varepsilon\check{p} + \beta\check{g}_l$	$+\underline{\check{p}_l}$

Consequently, we can assume that the total endogenous cyclical movement consists of three components. The first element arises from the changes which occur in the demand for labour as a result of too many or too few labour positions being created in the past; this cause of the total business cycle can be called *labour positions cycle*. The second element also works through the lagged spendings; this cause will be called *spending cycle*. The third reason for cyclical fluctuations, which acts through the wage determination function can be called *prices cycle*.

It is also interesting to note that the labour positions, the spendings and the prices cycles can indeed be distinguished analytically but cannot

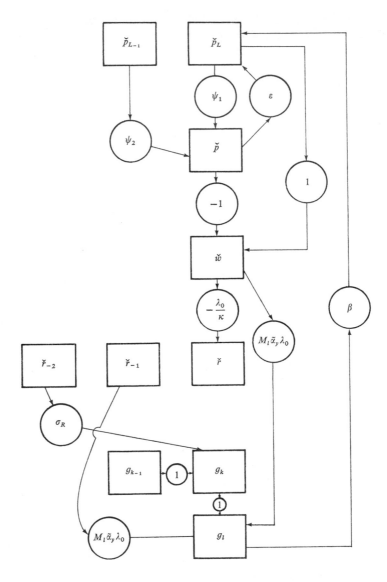

Graph 2.2.1   Diagram of basic model II

be distinguished in the sense that the total cycle would form a simple algebraic addition of the three components. Since the three cycle elements work simultaneously, and therefore influence each other, the labour positions cycle follows a different course when price determination and spending mechanisms are lagged than when these mechanisms are eliminated.

Another observation is that the causality chain of graph 2.2.1 shows some more loops, so that the sequence of successive events cannot be interpreted consecutively. This implies that there are other multipliers at work in the system, apart from the employment multiplier mentioned earlier. One of these, that concerning the large loop, which runs from p_l through w and g_y to g_l, and then returns to p_l through the β coefficient, will particularly require our regular attention. We shall call this the *wage rate multiplier*. The mathematical formula is:

$$M_w \equiv \frac{1}{1 - \beta M_l \lambda_0 \tilde{\alpha}_y}$$

The closed causality chain of graph 2.2.1 shows that the disturbance of the equilibrium development, wherever this occurs in the system, can be transformed into, for instance, a positive or negative pressure on the wage rate.

We can use as an example the case that in period $t-1$ the calculation rate of profit is $\bar{r}_{t-1}$ higher than the equilibrium level so that, for that reason, capitalist spending in period t will be $[\kappa/(1-\lambda_0)]\bar{r}_{t-1}$ higher. Therefore, ex ante total national spending $\kappa\bar{r}_{t-1}$ and ex ante employment $\tilde{\alpha}_y \kappa \bar{r}_{t-1}$ will be higher than the equilibrium. Taking into consideration the employment multiplier discussed earlier, the foregoing implies an initially positive pressure on employment of $M_l \tilde{\alpha}_y \kappa \bar{r}_{t-1}$ which amounts to an initial (induced) wage-push of $M_l \tilde{\alpha}_y \kappa \bar{r}_{t-1}$ (if we follow the causality chain of the model further).

Similarly, a reduced profitability with a lag of two periods can be interpreted as a positive initial wage-push, if we use the appropriate accumulation function.

For the short term course of events it is essentially irrelevant if the positive or negative pushes on the wage rate, or on any other variable, are caused by exogenous factors, in the proper sense of influences coming from outside the system, or by previously fixed variables, which are produced by the system, but in a previous period (in the past).

It is therefore possible to transform all imaginable disturbances in the system into wage impulses, whether induced or not. We can, in a way, compare all the different possible autonomous impulses, in that manner. Furthermore, by doing this, we ensure that when describing the functioning of our models, we can almost suffice with a description of the dynamic consequences of a wage-push.

2.3 THE SOLUTION OF THE MODEL

We can interpret the 'solution' of a dynamic model in various ways. In the first place, we could be referring to the short term solution. We mean then that the variables of a period t are expressed firstly in the well known structural parameters, secondly in the one-time or long-term autonomous impulses and thirdly in variables of the system which have been determined beforehand.

More general, hence more important, because they include the short term solution, are the so-called final equations of the dynamic model, which in our linear system continually arise from linear difference equations with constant coefficients. These describe the cyclical development of the different variables in terms of certain initial values, which are, in turn, determined by autonomous impulses.

Two more aspects of the solution expressed as a difference equation can be distinguished; on the one hand the homogeneous part of the final equation, which determines the endogenous dynamic characteristics of the model and on the other hand the composition of the autonomous impulses. The scheduling of the autonomous impulses is, of course, just as important for the behaviour of a system as the endogenous structural parameters themselves. In this way the rhythm in which exogenous impulses are brought to bear on an originally stable system can cause it to explode. Paragraph 3.6 is also relevant here.

A final possible solution of a dynamic model concerns the structural value of the variables. As we shall see, when determining the average values which the variables will assume as a result of autonomous impulses, both the endogenous structure of the model and the autonomous impulses are of importance.

In the following sections, we will be concerned with all the above-mentioned aspects of the solution of model 2.2.1.

With regard to the autonomous impulses in the relations, we have limited ourselves to those treated in model 2.2.1, i.e.:
a. the wage-push
b. the capacity-pull
c. the spending-pull.

2.3.1 *The short term solution*

In order to obtain the short term solution we determine first the short term labour demand function, in which the autonomous impulses which affect the demand for labour, as well as the factors which are determined beforehand, are expressed. The demand function referred to reads:

$$g_l = M_l \lambda_0 \tilde{\alpha}_y \breve{w} + M_l \{\tilde{\alpha}'_k g_k - \lambda_0 \tilde{\alpha}_y \breve{w}_{-1}\} + M_l \tilde{\alpha}_y \underline{\breve{g}}_x \tag{2.3.1}$$

The Phillips curve for the short term is:

$$\breve{w} = \frac{\beta(1-\psi_1)}{1-\varepsilon\psi_1} g_l + \frac{1}{1-\varepsilon\psi_1} \{(\varepsilon\psi_2 \breve{w}_{-1} - \beta\psi_2 g_{l-1}) +$$

$$+ (1-\psi_1) \underline{\breve{p}}_l - \psi_2 \underline{\breve{p}}_{l-1}\} \tag{2.3.2}$$

Here, we have two equations with two unknown factors, with the following as the solution:

$$w = \frac{\beta \dfrac{1-\psi_1}{1-\varepsilon\psi_1} A_l + A_w}{1 - \beta \dfrac{1-\psi_1}{1-\varepsilon\psi_1} M_l \lambda_0 \tilde{\alpha}_y} \tag{2.3.3}$$

Here is:

$$A_l = M_l \{\tilde{\alpha}'_k g_k - \lambda_0 \tilde{\alpha}_y \breve{w}_{-1}\} + M_l \tilde{\alpha}_y \underline{\breve{g}}_x$$

$$A_w = \frac{1}{1-\varepsilon\psi_1} \{(\varepsilon\psi_2 \breve{w}_{-1} - \beta\psi_2 g_{l-1}) + (1-\psi_1) \underline{\breve{p}}_l - \psi_2 \breve{p}_{l-1}\}$$

Conclusion: in our model, a correction of disturbing influences from the past is possible, by means of a combined short term wage and spending policy. In the short run, real wage policy, as well as employment policy is possible.

These will, however, in general introduce disturbances for the future. If one wishes, therefore, to care for the future in one's economic policy, by pursuing a consistent and more or less constant policy for a not too distant future, then the short term approach outlined above is quite unsuitable and can even lead to serious mistakes (see further paragraph 2.5).

2.3.1.1 *The final equation: the homogeneous part*

A policy for a longer period can be designed only when the characteristics which control developments in time of the model are known. The obvious expedient here, is the so-called 'final equation', which is merely the linear difference equation in which the endogenous dynamic qualities of the model are combined. In fact, there is not just *one* dynamic final equation, but a similar difference equation can be set up for each variable.

In this sub-paragraph, we will deal with the final equation connected with the real wage rate. Since we may be able to learn something about the working of the model from the derivation of the final equation, we shall pause here for a moment.

Our starting point is the labour demand function (the employment multiplier and the corrected marginal labour positions ratio of the capital goods supply have already been taken into account). The demand for labour leads to the following positive (induced) wage impulse:

$$\beta g_l = \beta M_l \lambda_0 \tilde{\alpha}_y \check{w} - \beta M_l \lambda_0 \tilde{\alpha}_y \check{w}_{-1} + \beta M_l \tilde{\alpha}_k' g_k \tag{2.3.4}$$

The components in (2.3.4) can be interpreted as induced impulses, in the following way:

$\beta M_l \lambda_0 \tilde{\alpha}_y \check{w}$: positive wage impulse arising from spendings of wage earners

$-\beta M_l \lambda_0 \tilde{\alpha}_y \check{w}_{-1}$: negative wage impulse arising from spendings of capitalists

$\beta M_l \tilde{\alpha}_k' g_k$: positive wage impulse arising from the labour positions available.

Finally, we present the final equation for the real wage rate. An *ultimate*, complete transmission of wages and prices is hereby assumed.

$$\left(\frac{1 - \varepsilon \psi_1}{1 - \psi_1} - \beta M_l \tilde{\alpha}_y \lambda_0 \right) \check{w} - (\varepsilon + 2 \beta M_l \tilde{\alpha}_y \lambda_0) \check{w}_{-1} +$$

$$+ \left(\beta M_l \tilde{\alpha}_k' \sigma_r \frac{\lambda_0}{\kappa} - \beta M_l \tilde{\alpha}_y \lambda_0 \right) \check{w}_{-2} = 0 \tag{2.3.5}$$

The components of the cycle movement can be clearly recognised in (2.3.5).

2.3.1.2 *The final equation: the autonomous impulses*

Taking into account only the autonomous components in the accumulation-employment function and the wage determination function we arrive at the following final equation of the model:

$$A_0 \breve{w} - A_1 \breve{w}_{-1} + A_2 \breve{w}_{-2} =$$
$$= \beta M_l \tilde{\alpha}'_k \breve{g}_k + \beta M_l \tilde{\alpha}_y (\breve{g}_x) + (1 - \psi_1)(\hat{p}_L) \ (^1) \qquad (2.3.6)$$

A not unimportant variant, one that is used as starting point in a large part of our study is that in which price increases are fully compensated for in real wages, by means of a perfect application of wage indexing.

2.4 DESCRIPTION OF THE BUSINESS CYCLE

A further illustration of the model is given here by using some concrete numerical examples. The results are combined in table 2.4.1. Data used in drawing up this table are:

$\tilde{\alpha}_k = \frac{2}{3}$	$\tilde{\alpha}_y = \frac{1}{3}$	$\beta = \frac{5}{2}$	$\tilde{\gamma}_l = 1$	$\tilde{\gamma}_r + \tilde{\sigma}_r = 1$	
$\varepsilon = 1$	$\kappa = \frac{5}{4}$	$\lambda_0 = \frac{1}{2}$	$\pi = 0$	$\psi_1 = \frac{1}{2}$	$\psi_2 = \frac{1}{2}$

Important composite coefficients are:

$$\tilde{\alpha}_k = \frac{5}{6} \qquad M_l = \frac{6}{5} \qquad M_w = \frac{1}{A_0} = 2 \qquad r_0 = \frac{2}{5}$$

The coefficients have been chosen in such a way that after a one-time autonomous impulse, a sinusoide arises with a period capacity of four periods.

An exceptional quality of the numerical example chosen is that the endogenous working of prices was eliminated, by assuming that $\varepsilon = 1$, thus enabling the study of the real course of events, independently of the nominal transmission of wage costs into prices. For good measure, we have calculated the nominal quantities as well.

In table 2.4.1 we have presented the consequences for several important variables. We note that, despite the identical development of the real wage rate, the other variables do not follow a completely identical course of development, being influenced by various autonomous

---

1. The coefficients A in (2.3.6) represent the earlier derived composite coefficients in the final equation.

Table 2.4.1 The results (in relative deviations with respect to the equilibrium growth value) of several one-time autonomous impulses

a. wage-push; b. spending-pull; c. capacity-pull

Variable	Type of impulse	period $t \to$	1	2	3	4	5	6	average
$\hat{p}_L$	a	$\underline{\hat{p}_L}$	$\tfrac{1}{2}$	0	0	0	0	0	0
	b	$\underline{\hat{g}_x}$	$\tfrac{1}{2}$	0	0	0	0	0	0
	c	$\underline{\hat{g}_k}$	$\tfrac{1}{5}$	0	0	0	0	0	0
$\check{w}$	F.E.[1] $\;A_0\check{w} - A_1\check{w}_{-1} + A_2\check{w}_{-2}$	$= $ a) $\underline{\hat{p}_L}$ $= $ b) $\beta M_1\tilde{\alpha}_y\,\underline{\hat{g}_x}$ $= $ c) $\beta M_1\tilde{\alpha}_k'\,\underline{\hat{g}_k}$	1	0	-1	0	1	0	0
1. $\;\check{r}$	abc	$\check{r} = -\dfrac{\lambda_0}{\kappa}\check{w}$ $= -\tfrac{2}{5}\check{w}$	$-\tfrac{2}{5}$	0	$\tfrac{2}{5}$	0	$-\tfrac{2}{5}$	0	0
2. $\;g_k$	ab	$g_k = g_{k-1} + \sigma_R\check{r}_{-2}$ $= g_{k-1} + \check{r}_{-2}$	0	0	$-\tfrac{2}{5}$	$-\tfrac{2}{5}$	0	0	$-\tfrac{1}{5}$
	c	$g_k = g_{k-1} + \sigma_R\check{r}_{-2} + \underline{\hat{g}_k}$ $= g_{k-1} + \check{r}_{-2} + \underline{\hat{g}_k}$	$\tfrac{1}{5}$	$\tfrac{1}{5}$	$-\tfrac{1}{5}$	$-\tfrac{1}{5}$	$\tfrac{1}{5}$	$\tfrac{1}{5}$	0
3. $\;g_L$	a	$g_L = M_1\{\tilde{\alpha}_k' g_k + \tilde{\alpha}_y\lambda_0(I-E^{-1})\check{w}\}$	$\tfrac{1}{5}$	$-\tfrac{1}{5}$	$-\tfrac{3}{5}$	$-\tfrac{1}{5}$	$\tfrac{1}{5}$	$-\tfrac{1}{5}$	$-\tfrac{1}{5}$
	b	$g_L = M_1\{\tilde{\alpha}_k' g_k + \tilde{\alpha}_y\lambda_0(I-E^{-1})\check{w}\} + M_1\tilde{\alpha}_y\,\underline{\hat{g}_x}$	$\tfrac{2}{5}$	0	$-\tfrac{2}{5}$	0	$\tfrac{2}{5}$	0	0
	c	$g_L = M_1\{\tilde{\alpha}_k' g_k + \tilde{\alpha}_y\lambda_0(I-E^{-1})\check{w}\}$	$\tfrac{2}{5}$	0	$-\tfrac{2}{5}$	0	$\tfrac{2}{5}$	0	0

Table 2.4.1 (cont.)

Variable	Type of impulse	period $t \rightarrow$	1	2	3	4	5	6	average
4. g_y	a	$g_y = \lambda_o(g_L+\check{w})+(1-\lambda_o)\left(g_k+\dfrac{\check{r}_{-1}}{r_E}\right) = \dfrac{1}{2}+(g_L+\check{w})+\dfrac{1}{2}\left(g_k+\dfrac{\check{r}_{-1}}{r_E}\right)+\check{g}_x$	$\frac{3}{5}$	$-\frac{3}{5}$	$-\frac{5}{5}$	$\frac{1}{5}$	$\frac{3}{5}$	$-\frac{3}{5}$	$-\frac{1}{5}$
	b	$g_y =$ idem $\qquad +\check{g}_x =$ idem	$\frac{6}{5}$	0	$-\frac{2}{5}$	$\frac{4}{5}$	$\frac{6}{5}$	0	$\frac{2}{5}$
	c	$g_y =$ idem $\qquad +\check{g}_x =$ $=$	$\frac{4}{5}$	$-\frac{2}{5}$	$-\frac{4}{5}$	$\frac{2}{5}$	$\frac{4}{5}$	$-\frac{2}{5}$	0
5. s_b	a	$s_b \equiv g_k - g_y$	$-\frac{3}{5}$	$\frac{3}{5}$	$\frac{3}{5}$	$-\frac{3}{5}$	$-\frac{3}{5}$	$\frac{3}{5}$	0
	b	$s_b \equiv$ idem	$-\frac{6}{5}$	0	0	$-\frac{6}{5}$	$-\frac{6}{5}$	0	$-\frac{3}{5}$
	c	$s_b \equiv$ idem	$-\frac{3}{5}$	$\frac{3}{5}$	$\frac{3}{5}$	$-\frac{3}{5}$	$-\frac{3}{5}$	$\frac{3}{5}$	0
6. $\check{p}_L$	abc	$\check{p}_L = \dfrac{1}{1-\psi_1}\check{w}+\dfrac{\psi_2}{1-\psi_1}\check{p}_{L-1} = 2\check{w}+\check{p}_{L-1}$	2	2	0	0	2	2	1
7. $\check{p}$	abc	$\check{p} = \psi_1\check{p}_L+\psi_2\check{p}_{L-1} = \tfrac{1}{2}\check{p}_L+\tfrac{1}{2}\check{p}_{L-1}$	1	2	1	0	1	2	1
8. $\check{w}$	abc	$\check{w} = (\varepsilon-1)\check{p}+\beta g_L+\underline{\check{p}_L} = \tfrac{5}{2}g_L+\underline{\check{p}_L}$	1	0	-1	0	1	0	0

43

impulses. The differences are, however, only minor. They concern only the trend levels of the variables; the 'shape' of the development in time is also repeatedly the same.

This large degree of conformity allows us, when describing the business cycle, to confine ourselves to the analysis of the events under the influence of a one-time autonomous wage-push, since it is almost the same story in the other cases, as in the case of a one-time wage-push.

2.4.1 *Description of the periods*

At the beginning of period 1, an autonomous impulse causes nominal wages to reach a level $\frac{1}{2}\%$ higher than would be expected if wage development corresponded with labour productivity. As a result of this, real wages increase further in the same period to 1%, by means of the (real) wage rate multiplier. This is, with the given coefficients, only possible by a nominal wage rate growth of 2%, and a corresponding price increase of 1%.

Further effects of the increased real wage level are: a fall in the rate of profit, with consequences in the short run for capitalist spending and in the more distant future for capital accumulation. In the meantime, employment grows, in the same year as the one-time wage-push, to more than the equilibrium level, because of the increased spendings of the wage earners. At the same time, production volume has increased for the same reason, and since the capital goods supply is still at the equilibrium level, the degree of capacity utilisation increases also. The business cycle is dominated by the spending component.

The increase in real wages is however a short lived joy. In period 2 the economy is submitted to the negative influence of the decreased spendings, because of the lower profitability in period 1. Real wages can just be held at the equilibrium level, because of the autonomous wage increase of the previous period. This means that up to and including period 2, wage earners have profited from the autonomous wage impulse only inasmuch as they are one year ahead in the equilibrium wage development.

However, even this lead will eventually be lost by wage earners if the economic mechanism is allowed to work uninterruptedly. In the meantime, the business cycle is still dominated by the spending component. The introduction of the labour positions cycle is imminent. For this reason, in the *third period* the negative factors are now even larger. Once again capitalist spendings are low – now also because of a shrunken capital goods volume – but above all, pronounced unemployment tendencies, with their wage depressing effect, arise as a result of the shortage of labour positions. The autonomous higher level of real wages is now not even sufficient to keep them at the structural level. Employment and production volume have now been at a low level for two periods in succession. In nominal terms the nominal wage rate has now returned to its equilibrium value. The prices, however, are still high.

The spontaneous slowing down of the wage development in periods 2 and 3 leads to a recovery of the cycle in period 4. Capitalist spendings are now higher than at the structural level. The same applies to the production volume, in close connection with these increased spendings. However, even now, no full employment can be realised because the negative labour positions component exceeds the positive spending component. All things considered, we obtain an equilibrium real wage level in period 4. The nominal quantities also return to their original values; and unemployment reaches a low level. However, the equilibrium situation is only apparent, since in period 5 the autonomously raised wage level behaves as erradically as in period 1, so that the cyclical course of events is resumed.

2.5 ECONOMIC POLICY

We feel it would be useful to follow the pattern of Chapter I and devote this paragraph to a detailed study of the possibilities for policy making. We shall also have the opportunity here of commenting on the difficulties, in practice, of applying the acquired theoretical knowledge to the real situation.

We aim, in our policy of business cycle stabilisation, at eliminating the cyclical fluctuations which arise as a result of autonomous impulses, or at least at stabilising them as much as possible, using as few measures as possible.

The policy referred to here is not to be confused with the usual short term policy. It has, in fact, become obvious from our analyses that it is possible, under certain circumstances and if sufficient instruments are available, to realise a momentary equilibrium, for a definite point of time t. It is however probable, as we have said earlier, that new disequilibriums are thus introduced, which will require other policy measures in the future, etc. In this way we can become involved in a cyclical stop-go-policy which will be virtually never properly timed and dosed.

It is obvious however, that the conditions which must be attached to the execution of a consistent policy are extremely weighty. An accurate diagnosis of past disequilibriums, which cause disturbances at the present time is particularly necessary. At the moment, actual information certainly does not go as far as this. In this context, the speed of reaction of the policy makers is also of importance. The measures to be taken must be adapted to the speed with which the managers react to disturbances. Publications on the matter too often give the impression that those in charge are in agreement about the diagnosis to be given and subsequently, once again unanimously, hasten to take the most appropriate measures. Diagnosis and therapy in economic policy is a lengthy and also often an irrational and controversial process, which in any case progresses differently from the straightforward calculations obtained in a model analysis. For this reason we are concerned, in the following examples, more with an illustration of the many difficulties within the economic policy, than with concrete recommendations for that same policy.

It has appeared several times that one-time autonomous impulses can bring about long-term changes in the structure of the economy. A policy aimed at a long-term re-structuring therefore has, logically, a chance of success.

Structural policy is however in general difficult to create without cyclical oscillations. It is possible, in theory to redress the cyclical disequilibriums, but one must be on guard for new, undesired structural side effects, which can sometimes even imply that the norms of a structural policy, attainable in isolation, are not realised.

Our conclusion is that we can indeed distinguish between the concept of stabilisation policy and the concept of structural policy. In practice however, it will in general be ill advised to actually separate them. Structural policy can be extended logically into stabilisation policy and conversely one must continually be aware, when taking stabilising measures, of possible structural side effects. The following explanation will, we hope, indicate that the cases in question do not exist merely in the mind of the theorist. At this point we shall again assume only a few instruments of economic policy, i.e. wage, investment and spending policies. We shall also make a distinction between stabilisation policy in a narrow sense on the one hand and re-structuring policy on the other.

In the former, the problem posed is simply the stabilisation of cyclical movements arising from autonomous disturbances. In the latter case, the task is to realise long-term objectives while avoiding cyclical instability and as far as possible structural disequilibriums also.

46

2.5.1 *Employment policy*

The way in which certain desirable aspects concerning volume of employment can be realised, can be ascertained from table 2.4.1. The application of the instrument of a one-time wage-push is sufficient in itself to cause long term mutations in employment. The effect which one-time wage measures have on the other variables does not involve lasting tensions. The most important structural alteration, which appears together with the employment mutation, is the alteration in the number of labour positions. Fortunately, in the case of a one-time wage-push, the mutation which occurs in the number of labour positions is exactly that required by the objectives laid down for employment. The change in actual production is also made to measure. The newly employed labourers (in this case the labourers left over after a policy of employment reduction) do not therefore have to work more or less hard than normal. The utilisation of the capital goods supply also reaches structurally normal values.

In order to stabilise the cyclical disequilibriums which have arisen, both the instrument of the one-time capacity-pull and that of the one-time spending-pull can, in theory, be considered. Of these two, the one-time capacity-pull has no structural side effects, and is in that respect preferable to the one-time spending-pull. This latter form of economic policy does not after all have a neutralising action on accumulation of capital or sales development and therefore not on actual production. A positive spending-pull results ultimately in a loss of capital, since the stagnation in investment, induced by the high real wages and the associated low capital yields present at the beginning of the cycle, are not overtaken afterwards. This process is, in this respect, completely analogous to a one-time wage-push. A difference between spending-pull and wage-push exists in the development of actual production. This quantity moves, because of the higher starting value, in the case of a positive spending-pull to a higher level than in the case of a corresponding positive wage-push. The effect is obvious: since, as far as the determination of capital is concerned, the negative wage-push and the positive spending-pull counterbalance each other exactly, but on the other hand a positive spending-pull reinforces even more the stimulating effects of a one-time negative wage-push, then the effect of the combination is: a continuous over-utilisation of the capital goods supply.

Since cyclical stability achieved by a one-time capacity-pull does not possess this fault, this instrument is to be preferred. It may be stated

Table 2.5.1   Employment policy: stabilisation of a:

a. *one-time wage-push through a (also one-time)*
b. *reverse spending-pull and*
c. *reverse capacity-pull*
d. *= a+b trend values if a is stabilised by b*
e. *= a+c trend values if a is stabilised by c*

		t	1	2	3	4	5	6	average
Pushes	$\hat{p}_L$	a	$\frac{1}{2}$	0	0	0	0	0	0
	$\hat{g}_x$	b	$\frac{1}{2}$	0	0	0	0	0	0
	$\hat{g}_K$	c	$\frac{1}{5}$	0	0	0	0	0	0
Results		a	0	0	$-\frac{2}{5}$	$-\frac{2}{5}$	0	0	$-\frac{1}{5}$
		b	0	0	$\frac{2}{5}$	$\frac{2}{5}$	0	0	$\frac{1}{5}$
	g_k	c	$-\frac{1}{5}$	$-\frac{1}{5}$	$\frac{1}{5}$	$\frac{1}{5}$	$-\frac{1}{5}$	$-\frac{1}{5}$	0
		d	0	0	0	0	0	0	0
		e	$-\frac{1}{5}$	$-\frac{1}{5}$	$-\frac{1}{5}$	$-\frac{1}{5}$	$-\frac{1}{5}$	$-\frac{1}{5}$	$-\frac{1}{5}$
		a	$\frac{1}{5}$	$-\frac{1}{5}$	$-\frac{3}{5}$	$-\frac{1}{5}$	$\frac{1}{5}$	$-\frac{1}{5}$	$-\frac{1}{5}$
		b	$-\frac{2}{5}$	0	$\frac{2}{5}$	0	$-\frac{2}{5}$	0	0
	g_L	c	$-\frac{2}{5}$	0	$\frac{2}{5}$	0	$-\frac{2}{5}$	0	0
		d	$-\frac{1}{5}$	$-\frac{1}{5}$	$-\frac{1}{5}$	$-\frac{1}{5}$	$-\frac{1}{5}$	$-\frac{1}{5}$	$-\frac{1}{5}$
		e	$-\frac{1}{5}$	$-\frac{1}{5}$	$-\frac{1}{5}$	$-\frac{1}{5}$	$-\frac{1}{5}$	$-\frac{1}{5}$	$-\frac{1}{5}$
		a	$\frac{3}{5}$	$-\frac{3}{5}$	$-\frac{5}{5}$	$\frac{1}{5}$	$\frac{3}{5}$	$-\frac{3}{5}$	$-\frac{1}{5}$
		b	$-\frac{6}{5}$	0	$\frac{2}{5}$	$-\frac{4}{5}$	$-\frac{6}{5}$	0	$-\frac{2}{5}$
	g_y	c	$-\frac{4}{5}$	$\frac{2}{5}$	$\frac{4}{5}$	$-\frac{2}{5}$	$-\frac{4}{5}$	$\frac{2}{5}$	0
		d	$-\frac{3}{5}$	$-\frac{3}{5}$	$-\frac{3}{5}$	$-\frac{3}{5}$	$-\frac{3}{5}$	$-\frac{3}{5}$	$-\frac{3}{5}$
		e	$-\frac{1}{5}$	$-\frac{1}{5}$	$-\frac{1}{5}$	$-\frac{1}{5}$	$-\frac{1}{5}$	$-\frac{1}{5}$	$-\frac{1}{5}$
		a	$-\frac{3}{5}$	$\frac{3}{5}$	$\frac{3}{5}$	$-\frac{3}{5}$	$-\frac{3}{5}$	$\frac{3}{5}$	0
		b	$\frac{6}{5}$	0	0	$\frac{6}{5}$	$\frac{6}{5}$	0	$\frac{3}{5}$
	s_b	c	$\frac{3}{5}$	$-\frac{3}{5}$	$-\frac{3}{5}$	$\frac{3}{5}$	$\frac{3}{5}$	$-\frac{3}{5}$	0
		d	$\frac{3}{5}$	$\frac{3}{5}$	$\frac{3}{5}$	$\frac{3}{5}$	$\frac{3}{5}$	$\frac{3}{5}$	$\frac{3}{5}$
		e	0	0	0	0	0	0	0

however, that it is much more difficult to put a capacity-pull into practice in actual economic policy than a spending policy which the Government, at least in theory, can handle more quickly and directly than a capacity-pull, by taking fiscal measures. The Government in the present economic organisation is, for the realisation of an intended investment policy, largely dependent on private investment decisions. Moreover, the effect of an investment policy is felt only after a considerable lag.

An exact account of the possibilities of stabilisation in employment (and determination of capital) policy can be found in table 2.5.1.

2.5.2 Income policy: permanent changes in the real wage rate

None of the indicated one-time impulses leads independently to a permanent change in the real wage. On the other hand a permanent rise (or using measures with an opposite effect, a fall) in the real wage can be attained by repeatedly using only one of the three instruments, irrespective of which. It is even possible to acquire a stable development, disregarding a certain preliminary period involving a unilateral use of one of the instruments in question. In the numerical examples given here, it must be remembered that beginning with period 3, the intensity of the given impulse will be double that of the previous periods 1 and 2. All this can be found in the figures.

Table 2.5.2 Stable development of the real wage rate by continual autonomous impulses

	t	t	1	2	3	4	5	6	7	etc.
Arising from	1	1	0	−1	0	1	0	−1	0	etc.
autonomous	2	—	1	0	−1	0	1	0	−1	etc.
impulse in	3	—	—	2	0	−2	0	2	0	etc.
period:	4	—	—	—	2	0	−2	0	−2	etc.
	5	—	—	—	—	2	0	−2	0	etc.
	6	—	—	—	—	—	2	0	−2	etc.
	7	—	—	—	—	—	—	2	0	etc.
	8	—	—	—	—	—	—	—	2	etc.
Total		1	1	1	1	1	1	1	1	etc.

However, it must not be concluded from the foregoing, that from a structural point of view, the relevant instruments are neutral. This can

Table 2.5.3   Development within some other variables

	t	1	2	3	4	5	6	7	8	9
g_k	ab	0	0	$-\frac{2}{5}$	$-\frac{4}{5}$	$-\frac{6}{5}$	$-\frac{8}{5}$	$-\frac{10}{5}$	$-\frac{12}{5}$	etc.
	c	$\frac{1}{5}$	$\frac{2}{5}$	$\frac{2}{5}$	$\frac{2}{5}$	$\frac{2}{5}$	$\frac{2}{5}$	$\frac{2}{5}$	$\frac{2}{5}$	etc.
g_l	a	$\frac{1}{5}$	0	$-\frac{2}{5}$	$-\frac{4}{5}$	$-\frac{6}{5}$	$-\frac{8}{5}$	$-\frac{10}{5}$	$-\frac{12}{5}$	etc.
	bc	$\frac{2}{5}$	$\frac{2}{5}$	$\frac{2}{5}$	$\frac{2}{5}$	$\frac{2}{5}$	$\frac{2}{5}$	$\frac{2}{5}$	$\frac{2}{5}$	etc.
g_y	a	$\frac{3}{5}$	0	$-\frac{2}{5}$	$-\frac{4}{5}$	$-\frac{6}{5}$	$-\frac{8}{5}$	$-\frac{10}{5}$	$-\frac{12}{5}$	etc.
	b	$\frac{6}{5}$	$\frac{6}{5}$	$\frac{10}{5}$	$\frac{14}{5}$	$\frac{18}{5}$	$\frac{22}{5}$	$\frac{26}{5}$	$\frac{30}{5}$	etc.
	c	$\frac{4}{5}$	$\frac{2}{5}$	$\frac{2}{5}$	$\frac{2}{5}$	$\frac{2}{5}$	$\frac{2}{5}$	$\frac{2}{5}$	$\frac{2}{5}$	etc.
s_b	a	$-\frac{2}{5}$	0	0	0	0	0	0	0	etc.
	b	$-\frac{6}{5}$	$-\frac{6}{5}$	$-\frac{12}{5}$	$-\frac{18}{5}$	$-\frac{24}{5}$	$-\frac{30}{5}$	$-\frac{36}{5}$	$-\frac{42}{5}$	etc.
	c	$-\frac{3}{5}$	0	0	0	0	0	0	0	etc.

be deduced from table 2.5.3, where the development of some other central variables is described, under the influence of a series of impulses as defined in table 2.5.2. A study of tables 2.5.2 and 2.5.3 leads to the conclusion that it is indeed possible to obtain a permanent real wage level by forcing a yearly wage increase which exceeds productivity increase. We must then of course ignore the situation on the labour market. This means that the structural wage determination function has been completely set aside. On the other hand, through the decrease in capital profitability and the related decrease in investment burden, the actual income bearers, in this case production capacity are undermined. A structural decrease in employment now appears which is almost parallel to this. It is possible, however, that those who have recommended an over-demanding policy to the trade unions are for a time in the right. They can, in fact, point to an improvement in the real prosperity of the workers as a group up to and including period 5. Up to that period the fall in employment is, it is true, relatively lower than the rise of the real wage rate, so that the real wage sum is higher than it would have been if the equilibrium development had been maintained. When, however the aggressive wage policy effect still continues to operate after period 5, then the prosperity of the professional population, also regarded as a group, will decline rapidly. The unemployment percentage then becomes so large that a continuation of the unaltered original policy is not probable. Nevertheless it will still be period 8 before the initially acquired extra labour incomes are completely 'paid back'. This is illustrated in table 2.5.3a, in which the cumulated extra real wages in the event of a long term policy of wage over-demand in the first two years of $\frac{1}{2}\%$ and thereafter of 1% per year are shown.

Table 2.5.3a   Cumulated extra real wages by a wage determination after the manner of table 2.5.2 (variant a)

t	1	2	3	4	5	6	7	8
$\Sigma\,(g_L+w)$	$\frac{6}{5}$	$\frac{11}{5}$	$\frac{14}{5}$	$\frac{15}{5}$	$\frac{14}{5}$	$\frac{11}{5}$	$\frac{6}{5}$	$-\frac{1}{5}$

It is possible, however, that a more centrally planned wage development can realise the said paying back more gradually. In order to discuss the possibilities involved here, a model of the open economy is necessary. We shall therefore refer to this matter again in Chapter III.

On the other hand, if we wanted to obtain the result of table 2.5.2 by means of a long term spending-pull (b) then the unemployment tendencies will remain absent. The capital goods supply will be affected once again, because of the structurally low rate of profit. No unemployment arises, however, because of the continually rising actual production, which is brought about by demand factors. The result is a rapid rise in the overutilisation of capital goods. In this way, spending policy is labelled as the most unstabilizing policy, since it causes such serious and even continually increasing tensions in the production area, that it is impossible to continue to ascribe the model unlimited influence. The best possibility for a wage policy is finally a continued capacity-pull. In almost all respects this gives the most balanced results if a permanent increase in the real wage is aimed at. Only in the first period is there a certain degree of disequilibrium, with regard to the degree of utilisation of capital goods. For the rest, the development can be steered along the paths of equilibrium forever. A certain degree of stress is however once again unavoidable, since the increase in capital goods supply results in a structurally excessive labour demand.

Table 2.5.4 Balanced policy for a lasting higher real wage rate of 1%

a. positive one-time investment-pull of $\frac{1}{5}$% in period 1
b. positive one-time investment-pull of $\frac{1}{5}$% in period 2
c. positive continuous investment-pull of $\frac{2}{5}$% as from period 3
d. one-time wage-push in period 1 of 2%
e. one-time spending-pull in period 1 of −1%

		1	2	3	4	5	6	average
w	a	1	0	−1	0	1	0	0
	b	—	1	0	−1	0	1	0
	c	—	—	2	2	0	0	1
	Sub total	1	1	1	1	1	1	1
	d	2	0	−2	0	2	0	0
	e	−2	0	2	0	−2	0	0
	Total	1	1	1	1	1	1	1
g_k	a	$\frac{1}{5}$	$\frac{1}{5}$	$-\frac{1}{5}$	$-\frac{1}{5}$	$\frac{1}{5}$	$\frac{1}{5}$	0
	b	—	$\frac{1}{5}$	$\frac{1}{5}$	$-\frac{1}{5}$	$-\frac{1}{5}$	$\frac{1}{5}$	0
	c	—	—	$\frac{2}{5}$	$\frac{4}{5}$	$\frac{2}{5}$	$\frac{2}{5}$	$\frac{2}{5}$
	Sub total	$\frac{1}{5}$	$\frac{2}{5}$	$\frac{2}{5}$	$\frac{2}{5}$	$\frac{2}{5}$	$\frac{2}{5}$	$\frac{2}{5}$
	d	0	0	$-\frac{4}{5}$	$-\frac{4}{5}$	0	0	$-\frac{2}{5}$
	e	0	0	$\frac{4}{5}$	$\frac{4}{5}$	0	0	$\frac{2}{5}$

		1	2	3	4	5	6	average
g_L	a	$\frac{2}{5}$	0	$-\frac{2}{5}$	0	$\frac{2}{5}$	0	0
	b	0	$\frac{2}{5}$	0	$-\frac{2}{5}$	0	$\frac{2}{5}$	0
	c	—	—	$\frac{4}{5}$	$\frac{4}{5}$	0	0	$\frac{2}{5}$
	Sub total	$\frac{2}{5}$	$\frac{2}{5}$	$\frac{2}{5}$	$\frac{2}{5}$	$\frac{2}{5}$	$\frac{2}{5}$	$\frac{2}{5}$
	d	$\frac{2}{5}$	$-\frac{2}{5}$	$-\frac{6}{5}$	$-\frac{2}{5}$	$\frac{2}{5}$	$-\frac{2}{5}$	$-\frac{2}{5}$
	e	$-\frac{4}{5}$	0	$\frac{4}{5}$	0	$-\frac{4}{5}$	0	0
	Total	0	0	0	0	0	0	0
g_y	a	$\frac{4}{5}$	$-\frac{2}{5}$	$-\frac{4}{5}$	$\frac{2}{5}$	$\frac{4}{5}$	$-\frac{2}{5}$	0
	b	—	$\frac{4}{5}$	$-\frac{2}{5}$	$-\frac{4}{5}$	$\frac{2}{5}$	$\frac{4}{5}$	0
	c	—	—	$\frac{8}{5}$	$+\frac{4}{5}$	$\frac{4}{5}$	0	$\frac{2}{5}$
	Sub total	$\frac{4}{5}$	$\frac{2}{5}$	$\frac{2}{5}$	$\frac{2}{5}$	$\frac{2}{5}$	$\frac{2}{5}$	$\frac{2}{5}$
	d	$\frac{6}{5}$	$-\frac{6}{5}$	$-\frac{10}{5}$	$\frac{2}{5}$	$\frac{6}{5}$	$-\frac{6}{5}$	$-\frac{2}{5}$
	e	$-\frac{12}{5}$	0	$\frac{4}{5}$	$-\frac{8}{5}$	$-\frac{12}{5}$	0	$-\frac{4}{5}$

The degree of tension thus caused in the production area depends on the extent to which workers are recruited from new sources (foreign labourers, married women etc.). The extra labour engaged, has only to ensure normal productivity, $(\bar{g}_y = \bar{g}_L)$ while the availability of productive labour positions has been provided for, $(\bar{g}_L = \bar{g}_k)$. When, however, this change in employment is considered undesirable, then an additional employment policy is necessary. In the previous section 2.5.1 we have explained how this can be done in a balanced way. An income policy, combined with an equilibrium employment policy for several variables, has been systematically set out in table 2.5.4.

Our conclusion, in short, is that the core of the income policy is the continual manipulation of the investment instrument. After a preliminary period (including the first two periods), this must be maintained further with a constant intensity. Extra measures to stabilise a cyclical movement are no longer needed. It is possible, if necessary, to eliminate the structural shortage of supply or demand in the labour market in the manner suggested in 2.5.1. If this is to be done, a policy aimed at the structural increase of the real wage of 1% involves:

1. A one-time negative capacity-pull in period 1.
2. A positive capacity-pull in period 2.
3. A long term positive capacity-pull from period 3 (of a considerably stronger intensity than the one-time capacity-pull referred to in 2).
4. A positive one-time wage-push in period 1.

2.5.3

So far we have assumed in our book that the authorities react immediately to disturbances. It is possible, however, that it takes some time before the reaction to the unbalanced developments appears. The conclusions concerning the economic policy to be pursued can change drastically, and even become the contrary, when the reaction time in question alters itself. In the present model, for instance, the results of a one-time positive capacity-pull can be eliminated by means of a one-time negative wage-push in the same period. If, however, a year has passed before the wage measure is taken, then all that is acquired is a continued overemployment while no contribution has been made to the stabilisation of the business cycle.

If there is no reaction, as prescribed above, until period 3, then the effect of the business cycle will only be strengthened, while, in addition the handicap of the structural overemployment is introduced. In the case of such a lengthy reaction time, the operation of the earlier recommended economic policy is pre-eminently procyclic.

If it takes so long before a negative wage-push can be introduced as economic measure, it is better to recommend a reverse policy, i.e. correct the cyclical operation of a one-time positive capacity-pull with a positive wage-push. This has, of course, structural side effects, such as,

Table 2.5.5 Delayed reaction to an autonomous capacity-pull

a. *disturbance of the equilibrium by a positive capacity-pull of $\frac{1}{5}$% in period 1*
b. *stabilisation by a one-time positive wage-push of $\frac{1}{2}$% in period 3*
c. *total of a+b*

	period t	1	2	3	4	5	6	average
	a	1	0	-1	0	1	0	0
w	b	—	—	1	0	-1	0	0
	c	1	0	0	0	0	0	0
	a	$\frac{1}{5}$	$\frac{1}{5}$	$-\frac{1}{5}$	$-\frac{1}{5}$	$\frac{1}{5}$	$\frac{1}{5}$	0
g_k	b	—	—	0	0	$-\frac{2}{5}$	$-\frac{2}{5}$	$-\frac{1}{5}$
	c	$\frac{1}{5}$	$\frac{1}{5}$	$-\frac{1}{5}$	$-\frac{1}{5}$	$-\frac{1}{5}$	$-\frac{1}{5}$	$-\frac{1}{5}$
	a	$\frac{2}{5}$	0	$-\frac{2}{5}$	0	$\frac{2}{5}$	0	0
g_L	b	—	—	$\frac{1}{5}$	$-\frac{1}{5}$	$-\frac{3}{5}$	$-\frac{1}{5}$	$-\frac{1}{5}$
	c	$\frac{2}{5}$	0	$-\frac{1}{5}$	$-\frac{1}{5}$	$-\frac{1}{5}$	$-\frac{1}{5}$	$-\frac{1}{5}$
	a	1	$-\frac{3}{5}$	-1	$\frac{3}{5}$	1	$-\frac{3}{5}$	0
g_y	b	—	—	$\frac{4}{5}$	$-\frac{4}{5}$	$-\frac{6}{5}$	$\frac{2}{5}$	$-\frac{1}{5}$
	c	1	$-\frac{3}{5}$	$-\frac{1}{5}$	$-\frac{1}{5}$	$-\frac{1}{5}$	$-\frac{1}{5}$	$-\frac{1}{5}$
	a	$-\frac{4}{5}$	$\frac{4}{5}$	$\frac{4}{5}$	$-\frac{4}{5}$	$-\frac{4}{5}$	$\frac{4}{5}$	0
s_b	b	—	—	$-\frac{4}{5}$	$\frac{4}{5}$	$-\frac{4}{5}$	$-\frac{4}{5}$	0
	c	$-\frac{4}{5}$	$\frac{4}{5}$	0	0	0	0	0

for instance, a permanent reduction in employment. Table 2.5.1 shows how this can be eliminated, thus implying that on balance, no wage policy should be pursued, while, in view of the stabilisation either a positive spending-pull or a positive capacity-pull will be considered as a possibility. Paragraph 2.5.1 can be consulted for this question.

As soon as speed of reaction enters the picture, a detailed casuistry is of course possible. We shall, however, resist the temptation to do this and shall suffice with these few remarks which are meant merely to call attention to the problem of reaction time. Table 2.5.5 may be consulted for further details.

2.6 SOME TENTATIVE CONCLUSIONS

1. Stimulating measures, applied only once, in the form of creation of extra labour positions, have ultimately no significance for employment. The explanation for this must be sought in the fact that the original, and undoubtedly higher accumulation of capital resulting from a one-time capacity-pull and the creation of labour positions connected with it, are once again annulled some time after, by means of the positive pressure on the wages investments.

2. A policy which includes a permanent repetition of capacity-pulls is not the proper means to attain ultimately a change in employment either. It is more effective to use the instrument of the wage-push, since a negative wage-push given once, will through the lasting higher investment enthusiasm it induces, bring about a permanent higher accumulation of capital.

3. Wage policy and investment policy must not be regarded as rival instruments but more as complements to each other. If they are applied separately, they will, in fact cause a usually undesired business cycle fluctuation. Only a policy consisting of a precisely dosed and timed combination of wage and investment policy measures, with the possible addition of spendings influences, can subdue the cyclical movement completely.

It sounds rather paradoxical in this context, that in a world where profit is a dominant motive for the volume of investment, wage policy is the most obvious means for employment policy, while investment policy, which is of course closely related to the creation of labour positions, has as a function, the redressment of cyclical instability, evoked by the wage policy measures. More complicated assumptions concerning the determination of the price and investment function lead to hardly any new ideas, regarding structural conclusions.

4. The period in which economic-political advices can be followed up is of decisive importance. This applies particularly to the stabilisation policy. Not only is the dosing of the stabilising measures important, but the correct moment of administering is equally important.

5. With reference to point 4, we must bear in mind that the endogenous instability (a sinusoide) chosen by us is probably rather too high, when compared with economic reality. It should be clear that in the case of a high degree of endogenous stability, cyclical policy measures aimed at stabilising, are no longer urgent. This does not mean, of course, that the timing of the cyclical measures is of no great importance.

It can, in fact, be shown that a system with a large degree of endogenous stability, can by way of a resonance effect and through an incorrect timing of economic-political measures be made to explode (see for this, in a rather different context, paragraph 3.6).

III. Macroeconomics: the open economy

3.1 INTRODUCTION

Foreign relations influence the national economic system at many points and in different ways. In Chapter I, this was dealt with briefly, but a rather more detailed study is necessary. In the present chapter however, we shall attempt to include in our model only those international contacts which arise from the international transactions of final products. Transactions resulting from the international movement of production factors are not, therefore, dealt with.

As we shall see, the introduction of international relations means that the general set-up of the model requires hardly any alteration. Once again, by using the procedure described in Chapter II, we shall derive a demand function which, in combination with the 'supply relation' (the Phillips curve) produces solutions similar to those in paragraph 2.4.

In the open economy, the balance of imports and exports, as well as the volume of domestic spendings, determines the effective demand, which in turn helps to determine the labour demand. For this reason, the demand function in particular will undergo some change as a result of the introduction of foreign countries.

A second alteration, also expressed in the labour demand function, can arise through the terms of trade with foreign countries. Changes in this influence in fact the actual rate of profit of capital, which has a rather complicated relationship with employment both in the long and the short run, because of the direct effect on capitalist spendings and also the effect on the accumulation of capital (see appendix A 2.1).

3.1.1 *Some abstractions*

Once again, the most important basic assumptions must be mentioned.

1. We shall ignore the fact that the supply part of the labour market is sometimes directly influenced by developments abroad. This assumption

does not appear to correspond with reality. We are allowed to assume that a certain demonstration effect is active (now and again) in the wage determination process. The osmosis effect among the different national labour markets will increase in proportion to the increase in mobility among them. However interesting this may be, we shall not be including any mechanism in our relations that evokes such an effect. In cases where a demonstration effect is actually operating, we can, if necessary, regard this effect as an autonomous wage-push.

2. The emphasis is again on the real terms side of the economy: in particular we assume that for the supply part of the labour market, it is the real wage rate that matters. Contrary to Chapter ii, certain parts of the price system now have a direct effect on the volume system. Foreign price developments, as well as the determination of export prices by national exporters have indeed an effect on capital profitability and therefore on spendings and accumulation of capital. Because of this, we can no longer avoid all nominal problems. In particular, we must record the effect of changes in import prices on the price level of domestic spendings, and must also postulate a price determination function for export goods. It is well known that the actual functioning of the various transmission mechanisms is not at all simple – and probably cannot yet be sufficiently econometrically identified. However, we shall, for the sake of simplicity, assume in all future cases, the simplest possible un-lagged formulas for the transmission of costs into prices. We assume that the interested reader will be able to carry out the necessary modifications in order to analyse the significance of a more realistic but considerably more complicated transmission structure.

3. We shall not analyse in further detail other influences on real events, of a more monetary nature. We shall therefore disregard the relation between the balance in money terms on the current account of the balance of payments on the one hand and the corresponding available liquid assets for the financing of investments on the other hand. This is perhaps an unexpected assumption in a theory which bases its formulation of the investment function in particular on the available funds hypothesis. We have treated this particular point in preliminary studies but have drawn very few structurally important conclusions.

3.1.2 *Contents*

Because of the similarity between this and the previous chapter with regard to problems and model, we were able to all but copy the pattern of the previous chapter. The most important new basic relations, i.e. the import and export functions as well as the international price determination functions, are introduced first. We begin with a short summary of the empirical material on this subject available in the Netherlands. We have found that it is impracticable to select the 'best' specification of the relations using empirical material.

After choosing the basic model (paragraph 3.3) and giving its solution, we will present a detailed numerical description of the business cycle. In the numerical example we have chosen, we have tried to approximate as closely as possible the numerical example of Chapter II. It was of course not possible to ensure that the development of the different variables was similar if the corresponding behaviour parameters are similar, since the new partial mechanisms contribute to the dynamic behaviour of the system.

We conclude the main text of the chapter with a comment on the possibilities of economic policy.

As in Chapter II we have, in an appendix, discussed briefly the model with changed partial mechanisms (in particular the import and export relations).

3.1.3 *The new economic policy problems*

Although the formal structure of the new model does not differ greatly from what we have already seen, there are rather more problems for economic policy. Concern about the balance of payments has now been added to the objectives concerning employment and division of income. On the other hand however, the arsenal of economic-political instruments is more extended (adaptation to the rate of exchange etc.). It is also possible to use the balance of payments as a safety valve for certain internal tensions.

The difficulties for the 'econocrats' are increased considerably by the many and not always easily foreseen autonomous impulses received by the national economy, through international relations. Resistance to the consequences requires not only a thorough understanding of the structure of one's own economy, but also of the structure of world economy.

A characteristic of autonomous price and volume impulses from abroad is that these reach us by means of a cyclical pattern. It will become obvious that the periodicity of the cycle meant here is, in proportion to the endogenous periodicity, of great importance for the ultimate stability or instability of the national economy. We have placed this point among the problems of economic policy because it is our particular intention to give an outline of the manner in which a country can protect itself against the uprooting action, in certain circumstances, of *'resonant'* cyclical foreign developments.

*

3.2 THE NEW RELATIONS

We commence this chapter with a short summary of the current empirical views in the Netherlands about the proposed relations, import and export functions and price determination functions. We have not, however, carried out any investigation of our own into these topics. We shall therefore base our study mainly on the information on the Central Planning Bureau Model (CPM) appearing in the Central Economic Plan (CEP) for 1971. We shall not however, simply adopt the relations cited there, but will somewhat simplify the theories behind them, give them our interpretation and then integrate them in our own specifications.

3.2.1 *Basic empirical assumptions*

The explanatory notes of the CPM place the development of the world imports relevant to the Netherlands as first in the list of economic factors, which are expected to 'explain' the Dutch export volume. The competitive position takes second place and can be measured in two ways. The first criterion of the competitive position of the Dutch export product is the ratio between the Dutch export price on the one hand and the prices of the competitors on foreign markets on the other hand. Secondly, the solidity of the competitive position can be deduced from the ratio between the domestic costs level, in particular the level of labour costs, with regard to the actual, realised export price.

This latter relationship indicates how much room remains for production costs, before the export becomes unremunerative. In the CPM, both interpretations of the concept competitive position have been included as explanatory variable in the export equation.

The elasticity of the export volume, with regard to the competitive position, would appear to approach 2.5 - 3. It may not, however, be assumed from these not inconsiderable figures that the mutations in the competitive position have in fact been so important for the changes in the Dutch export volume.

It must be borne in mind here that international prices in particular and consequently also the competitive position and the terms of trade during most of the period on which the Central Planning Bureau (CPM) estimations are based, are conspicuously constant. It is also uncertain how the behaviour parameters will act in times of unrest within international prices. We note that at the present time, international prices have begun to change more than in the past, so that estimations of stability in the international price determinations functions must be cautious.

It is important for the structure of the Dutch economy that the exporter behaves on foreign markets most often as a quantity adapter. This can be inferred from the fact that over a long period the development of the Dutch export level is almost the same as that of foreign competitors' prices.

The abovementioned inference is important not only for the specification of the price determination function of export goods but also for the elasticity of exports with regard to domestic costs, particularly wage costs since, if a country's exporters offer a product differentiated to such a degree that they can determine the price on the foreign markets, then they will be in a better position to transmit internal wage costs increases into their prices.

The relative decline in export volume resulting from an internal wage costs increase must then be interpreted as a demand effect arising from the increased ratio between export price and price level of foreign competitors. However, if our exporters adapt to foreign prices, it is possible that the elasticity of export volume with regard to domestic costs is not unimportant. This can be interpreted in such a way that in the case of an increase in domestic costs which cannot be transmitted into export prices, there will be exporters for whom the export is no longer remunerative (marginal firm theory). These employers will concentrate even more than before, if possible, on the internal market but the increase in costs will almost certainly also be followed by a decrease in actual production.

The significance of the foregoing is that a (negative) connection which may have been established between internal costs increases on the one hand and export volume on the other hand, can be interpreted in two ways which we will indicate in future by the following terms which are surely self explanatory: '*monopolistic competition hypothesis*' and '*marginal firm hypothesis*'.

Let us now return to the concrete specification of the export function. The third important explanatory variable is, according to CPM a curvilinear transformation of the unemployment percentage. This variable was formerly described by the CPM as the indicator of the degree of utilisation of capital goods. It is however obvious that neither the unemployment percentage alone, nor any curvilinear transformation has much to do with the degree of utilisation of the capital goods supply. We may assume however, that the CPB has good grounds for using the said variable as a substitute for the degree of under-utilisation. (Probably, under-utilisation and employment have been observed empirically to go hand in hand; but why not publish the degree of utilisation observed in that case, instead of using a substitute for the degree of under-utilisation.) On these grounds it is possible to credit the well known 'home pressure or demand hypothesis'[1] with a certain current interest. The interpretation of this hypothesis is obvious: in times of under-utilisation of the production apparatus, employers look for sales possibilities abroad with more enthusiasm than in times of full utilisation.

Perhaps the most significant explanatory variable in the export function is of an exogenous nature, i.e. the autonomous development of the volume of world imports. During the last few years, the Dutch economy has had to withstand severe shocks, on this exact point.

The dominating explanatory variable in the import function is the actual domestic production. The tie between import volume on the one hand and production volume on the other hand has a strong complementary character; the relevant elasticity amounts to ± 1.

The accumulation of stocks plays a special role in the empirical import function since it is primarily chargeable to imports. The stocks have therefore a sort of buffer function, making it possible to postpone somewhat the imports necessary for the desired production volume. The imports will of course have to be replenished afterwards. Thus, the link in the process formed by the stocks must be regarded as a sort of time-lag in the import function which does not seem to be so important for our main aim, i.e. the elucidation of the structural aspects of some dynamic labour market models.

For this reason we have not included this variable in our further discussion.

The 'home-pressure' of the effective demand is even more important for the import function than it was for the export function. If we again

1. Also called the Zijlstra effect.

take the variable $(\tilde{w}_l)$, included in the CPM, to be indicator of the degree of under-utilisation, then the elasticity of imports with regard to the over-utilisation percentage will be around 2.5 and 3. This behaviour relation can be interpreted in the same way as the export function.

The last important explanatory variable in the import function is once again the competitive position. The elasticities found in the import function are however, considerably smaller than those found in the export function.

In the analysis given in the following paragraphs, we will pay more attention to the balance between import and export functions than to each function separately.

In summing up, we may state that on the grounds of the broad macroeconomic experience, the following should appear as explanatory variables in the balance function in question:

a. The degree of utilisation (lagged for less than one year).
b. The actual production (not lagged).
c. The competitive position ($\pm$ one year lag).
d. World imports (not lagged).

A final comment is that we will only very rarely adopt the exact specification of the CPM. We will also omit any rather rigorous partial mechanisms. This is of course in accordance with our aim of demonstrating in particular the isolated operation of the partial mechanisms.

3.2.1.1 *The actual production*

Foreign influences are all concentrated in the actual production. The changes which, in comparison with Chapter II, must be made can partly be traced to the changed definition of the actual production volume itself. The required adaptations can also partly be attributed to the spendings function in which the terms of trade, as part of the rate of profit are active. The relevant definition of the actual production is:

$$g_y = g_x + s_u = g_x + \mu_0(g_e - g_m) \tag{3.2.1}$$

The foreign volume balances s_u will be split up into three parts, being based on:

1. 'home-pressure' or ω-mechanism (s_{u_1}),
2. the parameter indicated by $\tilde{\mu}$-mechanism, based on the (marginal) complementarity hypothesis between imports on the one hand and actual production on the other hand (s_{u_2}),
3. the balance of trade inasmuch as it arises from price and costs ratios, both domestic and foreign (s_{u_3}).

63

The ω-mechanism

It is assumed that insufficient domestic spendings, compared with available production capacity, ceteris paribus, lead to a decline in imports and a rise in exports. The exact assumption is expressed in the following formulas.

$$g_{e_1} = \frac{1-\omega_e}{\mu_0}(g_k - g_x); \quad g_{m_1} = -\frac{1-\omega_m}{\mu_0}(g_k - g_x) \qquad (3.2.2)$$

A balancing of g_e and g_m, taking into account (3.2.1), produces:

$$s_{u_1} = \{(1-\omega_e) + (1-\omega_m)\}(g_k - g_x) \equiv (1-\omega)(g_k - g_x) \qquad (3.2.3)$$

The composite coefficient $(1-\omega)$ indicates the share of the spending balance that (ex post) is shifted on to foreign countries. The complement is of course that part that is included in an ex post under-utilisation percentage of the capital goods supply.

The μ̃-mechanism

With this, the excess in the structural import volume is, by means of a constant coefficient, made dependent on the higher than normal production volume y, so that we can give the following equation for the relative deviation of the import volume from the trend value.

$$g_m = \frac{\tilde{\mu}}{\mu_0} g_y \qquad (3.2.4)$$

The price mechanism

As we have mentioned briefly in paragraph 3.2.1, two variants concerned with the functioning of prices and costs can be distinguished:
a. The marginal firm theory.
b. The theory of the monopolistic competition.

ref. a. The simplest and perhaps, for the Dutch ratios, most realistic line of thought is that the exporters adapt their export prices to the prices of the competitors on the foreign market. If domestic increases in wage costs occur, then profit margins decrease. Some exporters are then forced to close down. Disregarding the time-lags, this process can be expressed by the following simple function:

$$g_{e_2} = -\eta_{p_L}(\breve{p}_L - \breve{p}_b) \qquad (3.2.5)$$

Here, η_{p_L} = the elasticity of export volume compared with competitive position.

ref. b. Now we postulate a certain margin with regard to the determination of export prices, thus:

$$g_{e_3} = -\eta_e(\breve{p}_e - \underline{\breve{p}_b}),\tag{3.2.6}$$

in which η_e is the usual export elasticity.
A similar formula applies to imports:

$$g_m = \eta_m(\breve{p}_x - \underline{\breve{p}_m})\tag{3.2.7}$$

If we keep in mind the following simple price determination functions:

$$\breve{p}_e = \psi_E\breve{p}_L + \psi_{ME}\underline{\breve{p}_m} + \psi_B\underline{\breve{p}_b}\tag{3.2.8}$$

and

$$\breve{p}_x = \psi_x\breve{p}_l + \psi_{mx}\underline{\breve{p}_m}\tag{3.2.9}$$

then we can give for s_{u_3}:

$$s_{u_3} = -\mu_0\eta_{PL}\left(\frac{1}{1-\psi_x}\breve{w} - \frac{\psi_{mx}}{1-\psi_x}\underline{\breve{p}_m} - \underline{\breve{p}_b}\right) +$$

$$-\mu_0\eta_e\left\{\frac{\psi_E}{1-\psi_x}\breve{w} + \left(\frac{\psi_E\psi_{mx}}{1-\psi_x} + \psi_{me}\right)\underline{\breve{p}_m} - (1-\psi_B)\underline{\breve{p}_b}\right\} +$$

$$-\mu_0\eta_m\left\{\frac{\psi_x}{1-\psi_x}\breve{w} + \left(\frac{\psi_{mx}}{1-\psi_x} - 1\right)\underline{\breve{p}_m}\right\}\tag{3.2.10}$$

This can be summed up in brief as follows:

$$s_{u_3} = -\mu_0\eta_w\breve{w} + \underline{s_{u_3}}\tag{3.2.11}$$

Here,

$$\eta_w \equiv \frac{\eta_{PL} + \eta_e\psi_e + \eta_m\psi_x}{1-\psi_x}\tag{3.2.12}$$

(export elasticity weighed against the real wage rate).

It appears that s_{u_3} possesses a rather complicated totality of positive and negative effects which reflect the influences of foreign prices on the given specific price determination function and demand function.

Finally we add one of the most important components of the ultimate s_u function, i.e. the autonomous development of world imports. The following s_u function then arises, summarising the above equations:

$$s_u = -\mu_0\eta_w\breve{w}_{-1} + (1-\omega)(g_k - g_x) - \tilde{\mu}g_y + \mu_0\breve{g}_e + \underline{s_u}\tag{3.2.13}$$

It will now be clear that in the last relation the variable $\underline{g_e}$ can be related to the excess in structural growth of world imports and $\underline{s_u}$ with all the other autonomous volume impulses on the balance of trade.

A second aspect of foreign relations is, as we have previously stated, localised in the (domestic) spending function. For that reason, we must now take into account the following definition of the calculation rate of profit (see also A 2.1):

$$\check{r} = -\frac{\lambda_0}{\kappa}\check{w} + \frac{\mu_0}{\kappa}(\check{p}_e - \underline{\check{p}_m}) \tag{3.2.14}$$

Because of (3.2.8) and (3.2.9) this becomes:

$$\check{r} = -\frac{\lambda'}{\kappa}\check{w} + \frac{\mu_0}{\kappa}\underline{\check{r}'} \tag{3.2.15}$$

In this is:

$$\check{r}' = \left(\frac{\psi_E\psi_{mx}}{1-\psi_x} + \psi_{mE} - 1\right)\underline{\check{p}_m} + \psi_B\underline{\check{p}_b} \tag{3.2.15a}$$

$$\lambda' \equiv \lambda_0 - \mu_0\psi_w \tag{3.2.16}$$

$$\psi_w \equiv \frac{\psi_E}{1-\psi_x} \tag{3.2.17}$$

3.2.1.2 *The new labour demand function*
The following can easily be deduced, from (3.2.1) and (3.2.13).

$$g_y = M_m\left[\omega\lambda_0 g_l + (1-\omega\lambda_0)\,g_k + \omega\left\{\lambda_0\check{w} - \left(\lambda' + \mu_0\frac{\eta_w}{\omega}\right)\check{w}_{-1}\right\} + \right.$$
$$\left. + \omega\mu_0\underline{\check{r}'_{-1}} + \mu_0\underline{g_e} + \underline{s_u}\right] \tag{3.2.18}$$

Here, $M_m = 1/(1+\check{\mu})$.

Since the fundamental employment hypothesis is still: $g_L = \tilde{\alpha}_y g_y + \tilde{\alpha}_k g_k$, we can easily reduce, as new labour demand function:

$$g_L = M_l\left[\tilde{\alpha}'_k g_k + M_m\tilde{\alpha}_y\omega\left\{\lambda_0\check{w} - \left(\lambda' + \mu_0\frac{\eta_w}{\omega}\right)\check{w}_{-1}\right\} + \right.$$
$$\left. + M_m\tilde{\alpha}_y(\omega\mu_0\underline{\check{r}'_{-1}} + \mu_0\underline{g_E} + \underline{s_u})\right] \tag{3.2.19}$$

Here,

$$M_l = 1/(1-\tilde{\alpha}_y M_m\omega\lambda_0) \tag{3.2.20}$$

$$\tilde{\alpha}'_k = \tilde{\alpha}_k + \tilde{\alpha}_y M_m(1-\omega\lambda_0) \tag{3.2.21}$$

66

3.3 BASIC MODEL III AND ITS SOLUTION

The foregoing can be summarised in the basic model 3.3.1.

Despite the fact that the new model possesses rather more mechanisms than model 2.2.1, its formal structure is essentially the same. The only exception is the second term of the employment function, in which the simple first differentiation of the real wage rate no longer appears. Moreover this difference can still be removed if $\psi_w = \eta_w/\omega$ applies.

In this special case the various domestic effects of both models can be completely eliminated with an adequate choice of β-coefficient which can now be higher, if $\tilde{\mu} > 0$ and $\omega < 1$.

Thus we approach a proposition which can indeed be proved in the present model: a higher marginal import ratio and/or a stronger operation of the 'home pressure' mechanism increase the *endogenous* stability of the system.

3.3.1 *Final equation: the homogeneous sector*

The constant coefficients in the final equation are:

$$
\left.
\begin{aligned}
A_0 &= 1 - \beta M_l \tilde{\alpha}_y M_m \omega \lambda_0 \\[2ex]
A_1 &= 1 - \beta M_l \tilde{\alpha}_y M_m \omega \left\{ 2\lambda_0 - \mu_0 \left(\psi_w - \frac{\eta_w}{\omega} \right) \right\} \\[2ex]
A_2 &= \beta M_l \tilde{\alpha}'_k \sigma_R \frac{\lambda'}{\kappa} - \beta M_l \tilde{\alpha}_y M_m \omega \left(\lambda' + \mu_0 \frac{\eta_w}{\omega} \right)
\end{aligned}
\right\} \tag{3.3.1}
$$

We have previously concluded that the coefficients $\tilde{\mu}$ and $(1-\omega)$ stimulate the endogenous stability of the system. The same can be said of the 'export-elasticity' η_w. In our model, therefore, a general conclusion is that the 'foreign' mechanisms can actually be regarded as a kind of safety valve for domestic tensions.

We have discussed the operation of the cyclical mechanism in detail in Chapter II and can therefore deal very briefly with the functioning of the new model.

The functioning hardly deviates, in fact, from the model discussed earlier. The conclusions remain almost the same. It is perhaps worthwhile noting that a one-time autonomous spending-pull now has an effect on the balance of payments instead of on employment.

Model 3.3.1

Structural relations	Autonomous impulses	
	intern	extern

1. $\check{r} = -\dfrac{\lambda'}{\kappa}\check{w}$

2. $g_k = g_{k-1} + \sigma_R \check{r}_{-2}$ $\qquad +\hat{\underline{g}}_k$ $\qquad +\underline{r}'$

3. $g_L = M_I\left[\tilde{\alpha}'_{k} g_k + M_m \tilde{\alpha}_y \varpi \left(\lambda_o \check{w} - \left\{\lambda' + \mu_o \dfrac{\eta_w}{\varpi}\right\}\check{w}_{-1}\right)\right]$ $\qquad + M_I M_m \tilde{\alpha}_y \varpi \check{\underline{g}}_x$ $\qquad M_I M_m \tilde{\alpha}_y (\varpi\mu_o \check{r}'_{-1} + \mu_o \underline{g}_E + \underline{s}_u)$

4. $\check{w} = \beta g_L +$ $\qquad\qquad\qquad\qquad \check{w}$

Composition: $\qquad M_m = \dfrac{1}{1+\tilde{\mu}}$

$\qquad\qquad\qquad \tilde{\alpha}'_{k} = \tilde{\alpha}_k + \tilde{\alpha}_y(1-\varpi\lambda_o)$

$\qquad\qquad\qquad M_I = \dfrac{1}{(1-\tilde{\alpha}_y M_m \varpi \lambda_o)}$

$\qquad\qquad\qquad \lambda' = \lambda_o - \mu_o \psi_w$

3.4 DESCRIPTION OF THE BUSINESS CYCLE

Before entering into the details of a short description of the business cycle, we will list the data used in our numerical examples:

$$\tilde{\alpha}_y = \tfrac{1}{2} \qquad \omega = \tfrac{1}{2} \qquad \lambda_0 = \tfrac{2}{3} \qquad \psi_w = \tfrac{2}{15}$$

$$\tilde{\alpha}_k = \tfrac{1}{2} \qquad \eta_w = \tfrac{2}{3} \qquad \mu_0 = \tfrac{1}{2} \qquad \psi_E = \tfrac{1}{30}$$

$$\beta = 2 \qquad \tilde{\mu} = 0 \qquad \kappa = 1$$

$$\sigma_R = 1 \qquad \eta_E = 3.$$

Composite expressions:

$$\tilde{\alpha}'_k = \tfrac{5}{6} \qquad \lambda' = \tfrac{3}{5} \qquad M_l = \tfrac{6}{5} \qquad M_w = \tfrac{5}{3}$$

The business cycles of domestic impulses and those of the model of the closed economy can be described analogously. A summary of this can be found in table 3.4.1.

3.5 ECONOMIC POLICY

In the open economy, a major problem of economic policy is how to react to autonomous changes in world trade volume (which also influences internal production volume to a considerable degree) and also how to react to changes in foreign price structure which influence the terms of trade and thereby national spendings and employment on the one hand and the competitive position, which causes a reaction in export volume on the other hand.

In economic policy, not only must the consequences of foreign developments affecting the national economy from the outside and the protection against such consequences be watched intently, but the domestic economic policy must constantly be tested for consequences for the external situation. The task of correct economic policy there, is more important than in a closed economy. On the other hand, the introduction of foreign relations involves an increase in the number of policy instruments. It is also possible, under certain circumstances, to shift internal difficulties, wholly or partly, on to foreign countries.

There is no doubt that the introduction of foreign relations involves the addition of a number of new elements to economic policy. However, it is untrue, as is sometimes claimed, that none of the propositions made for the closed economy, remain intact. On the contrary, the structure

Table 3.4.1 Results of internal impulses (ω mechanism)

a. wage-push; b. spending-pull; c. capacity-pull

		t	1	2	3	4	5	6	average
$\ddot{w}$	a	$\underline{\hat{w}}$	$\frac{3}{5}$	0	0	0	0	0	0
	b	$\underline{\hat{g}_x}$	1	0	0	0	0	0	0
	c	$\underline{\hat{g}_k}$	$-\frac{3}{10}$	0	0	0	0	0	0
		$A_0\ddot{w} - A_1\ddot{w}_{-1} + A_2\ddot{w}_{-2} =$ a) $\underline{\ddot{w}}$							
$\ddot{w}$	F.E.	$\frac{3}{5}\ddot{w} + \frac{3}{5}\ddot{w}_{-2}$ $\quad=$ b) $\beta M_1\bar{\alpha}_y\omega\underline{\hat{g}_x}$	1	0	-1	0	1	0	0
		$\qquad\qquad$ c) $\beta M_1\bar{\alpha}_k\underline{\hat{g}_k}$							
		$(\ddot{w} = \beta g_L + \ddot{w})$							
$\check{r}$	abc	$\check{r} = -\dfrac{\lambda'}{\kappa}\ddot{w} = -\dfrac{3}{5}\ddot{w}$	$-\frac{3}{5}$	0	$\frac{3}{5}$	0	$-\frac{3}{5}$	0	0
g_k	ab	$g_k = g_{k-1} + \bar{\sigma}_R\check{r}_{-2} = g_{k-1} + \check{r}_{-2}$	0	0	$-\frac{3}{5}$	$-\frac{3}{5}$	0	0	$-\frac{3}{10}$
	c	$g_k =$ idem $+ \underline{\hat{g}_k}$	$\frac{3}{10}$	$\frac{3}{10}$	$-\frac{3}{10}$	$-\frac{3}{10}$	$\frac{3}{10}$	$\frac{3}{10}$	0
g_L	a	$= M_1\bar{\alpha}'_k g_k + M_1\bar{\alpha}_y\omega\left\{\lambda_0\ddot{w} - \left(\lambda' + \mu_0\dfrac{\eta_w}{\omega}\right)\ddot{w}_{-1}\right\} =$ $= g_k + \frac{1}{5}\ddot{w} - \frac{3}{10}\ddot{w}_{-1}$	$\frac{1}{5}$	$-\frac{3}{10}$	$-\frac{4}{5}$	$-\frac{3}{10}$	$\frac{1}{5}$	$-\frac{3}{10}$	$-\frac{3}{10}$
	b	$g_L =$ idem $+ M_1\bar{\alpha}_y\omega\underline{\hat{g}_x} =$ idem $+ \frac{3}{10}\hat{g}_x$							
	c	$g_L =$ idem as a	$\frac{1}{2}$	0	$-\frac{1}{2}$	0	$\frac{1}{2}$	0	0
g_x	a	$g_x = \lambda_0(g_L + \ddot{w}) + (1-\lambda_0)g_k + \kappa\check{r}_{-1} =$ $= \frac{2}{3}(g_L + \ddot{w}) + \frac{1}{5}g_k + \check{r}_{-1} =$	$\frac{4}{5}$	$-\frac{4}{5}$	$-\frac{7}{5}$	$\frac{1}{5}$	$\frac{4}{5}$	$-\frac{4}{5}$	$-\frac{3}{10}$
	b	$g_x =$ idem $+ \underline{\hat{g}_x}$	2	$\frac{2}{5}$	$-\frac{2}{5}$	$\frac{7}{5}$	2	$\frac{2}{5}$	$\frac{9}{10}$

		t	1	2	3	4	5	6	average
s	ac	$s = g_k - g_x$	$-\frac{4}{5}$	$\frac{4}{5}$	$\frac{4}{5}$	$-\frac{4}{5}$	$-\frac{4}{5}$	$\frac{4}{5}$	0
	b	$s = $ idem	-2	$-\frac{2}{5}$	$-\frac{2}{5}$	-2	-2	$-\frac{2}{5}$	$-\frac{6}{5}$
$\mu_0 g_E$	abc	$\mu_0 g_E = -\mu_0 \eta_w \breve{w}_{-1} = -\frac{1}{5}\breve{w}_{-1}$	0	$-\frac{1}{5}$	0	$\frac{1}{5}$	0	$-\frac{1}{5}$	0
$\mu_0 g_M$	ac	$\mu_0 g_M = -(1-\omega)s = -\frac{1}{2}s$	$\frac{2}{5}$	$-\frac{2}{5}$	$-\frac{2}{5}$	$\frac{2}{5}$	$\frac{2}{5}$	$-\frac{2}{5}$	0
	b	$\mu_0 g_M = $ idem	1	$\frac{1}{5}$	$\frac{1}{5}$	1	1	$\frac{1}{5}$	$\frac{3}{5}$
s_u	ac	$s_u = \mu_0(g_E - g_M)$	$-\frac{2}{5}$	$\frac{1}{5}$	$\frac{2}{5}$	$-\frac{1}{5}$	$-\frac{2}{5}$	$\frac{1}{5}$	0
	b	$s_u = $ idem	-1	$-\frac{2}{5}$	$-\frac{1}{5}$	$\frac{4}{5}$	-1	$-\frac{2}{5}$	$-\frac{3}{5}$
g_y	a	$g_y = g_x + s_u$	$\frac{2}{5}$	$-\frac{3}{5}$	-1	0	$\frac{2}{5}$	$-\frac{3}{5}$	$-\frac{3}{10}$
	b	$g_y = $ idem	1	0	$-\frac{2}{5}$	$\frac{3}{5}$	1	0	$\frac{3}{10}$
	c	$g_y = $ idem	$\frac{7}{10}$	$-\frac{3}{10}$	$-\frac{7}{10}$	$\frac{3}{10}$	$\frac{7}{10}$	$-\frac{3}{10}$	0
s_b	ac	$g_k - g_y$	$-\frac{2}{5}$	$\frac{3}{5}$	$\frac{2}{5}$	$-\frac{3}{5}$	$-\frac{2}{5}$	$\frac{3}{5}$	0
	b		-1	0	$-\frac{1}{5}$	$-\frac{6}{5}$	-1	0	$-\frac{3}{5}$
S_u	ac	$s_u + \mu_0 \psi_w \breve{w} = s_u + \frac{1}{15}\breve{w}$	$-\frac{1}{3}$	$\frac{1}{5}$	$\frac{1}{3}$	$-\frac{1}{5}$	$-\frac{1}{3}$	$\frac{1}{5}$	0
	b		$-\frac{14}{15}$	$-\frac{6}{15}$	$-\frac{4}{15}$	$-\frac{12}{15}$	$-\frac{14}{15}$	$-\frac{6}{15}$	$-\frac{3}{5}$

of, in particular, internal problems (employment and division of income) is almost the same as in Chapter II.

3.5.1 Employment policy

We can be brief about this. The policy can be enforced exactly as outlined in Chapter II: a one-time wage-push can ensure for the desired employment effect; for stabilisation of the business cycle a capacity-pull in the opposite direction is desired. The ultimate result of such a policy is in balance: employment, capital goods supply, domestic spendings and actual production all undergo the same relative changes, so that neither a domestic utilisation balance nor a spending balance appears. Since domestic costs ratios and prices will show no change, exports will not be put under pressure while at the same time import volume will be maintained at the equilibrium level.

It may now again be possible to stabilise the domestic business cycle originating from the autonomous wage impulse by a spending-pull in the opposite direction. As in the previous chapter, this once again brings about a large number of structural difficulties, one of which is a structural balance of payments surplus. We shall not be referring again to this possibility of the stabilisation policy. If desired, the relevant numerical formulations can be made by referring to table A 3.1.

From table 3.5.1, which has been compiled out of table 3.4.1, we can infer the composition of the structural changes which a number of central variables undergo, under the influence of the impulses mentioned.

3.5.2 Income policy

Essentially, a policy aimed at a long term change in the real wage rate at the expense of the capital yield can be carried out in the same way as in Chapter II, by unilateral application of a long term capacity-pull. Table 3.5.2 illustrates how this occurs in the new context.

An employment effect which can be eliminated according to the lines laid down in par. 3.5.1 reappears now. As well as the positive employment effect occurring as a result of a permanent wage *increase*, a structural balance of payments deficit appears which cannot of course be maintained in the long run. Whilst employment policy, a combination of wage policy and investment policy is not troubled by any concern about the balance of payments, income policy does need to be supplemented by measures aimed at maintaining the balance of payments equilibrium.

72

Table 3.5.1 *Economic policy: employment policy (ω mechanism)*

a. one-time wage-push in period 1 $(+\frac{3}{5}\%)$
b. one-time capacity-pull in period 1 $(-\frac{3}{10}\%)$
c. total

	t	1	2	3	4	5	6	average
g_k	a. wage-push	0	0	$-\frac{3}{5}$	$-\frac{3}{5}$	0	0	$-\frac{3}{10}$
g_k	b. capacity-pull	$-\frac{3}{10}$	$-\frac{3}{10}$	$\frac{3}{10}$	$\frac{3}{10}$	$-\frac{3}{10}$	$-\frac{3}{10}$	0
$\bar{g}_k$	c. total	$-\frac{3}{10}$	$-\frac{3}{10}$	$-\frac{3}{10}$	$-\frac{3}{10}$	$-\frac{3}{10}$	$-\frac{3}{10}$	$-\frac{3}{10}$
g_L	a	$\frac{1}{5}$	$-\frac{3}{10}$	$-\frac{4}{5}$	$-\frac{3}{10}$	$\frac{1}{5}$	$-\frac{3}{10}$	$-\frac{3}{10}$
g_L	b	$-\frac{1}{2}$	0	$\frac{1}{2}$	0	$-\frac{1}{2}$	0	0
$\bar{g}_L$	c	$-\frac{3}{10}$	$-\frac{3}{10}$	$-\frac{3}{10}$	$-\frac{3}{10}$	$-\frac{3}{10}$	$-\frac{3}{10}$	$-\frac{3}{10}$
g_y	a	$\frac{4}{10}$	$-\frac{6}{10}$	-1	0	$\frac{4}{10}$	$-\frac{6}{10}$	$-\frac{3}{10}$
g_y	b	$-\frac{7}{10}$	$+\frac{3}{10}$	$+\frac{7}{10}$	$-\frac{3}{10}$	$-\frac{7}{10}$	$+\frac{3}{10}$	0
$\bar{g}_y$	c	$-\frac{3}{10}$	$-\frac{3}{10}$	$-\frac{3}{10}$	$-\frac{3}{10}$	$-\frac{3}{10}$	$-\frac{3}{10}$	$-\frac{3}{10}$
s_b	a	$-\frac{4}{10}$	$\frac{6}{10}$	$\frac{2}{5}$	$-\frac{3}{5}$	$-\frac{4}{10}$	$\frac{6}{10}$	0
s_b	b	$\frac{4}{10}$	$-\frac{6}{10}$	$-\frac{4}{10}$	$\frac{6}{10}$	$\frac{4}{10}$	$-\frac{6}{10}$	0
$\bar{s}_b$	c	0	0	0	0	0	0	0
s_u	a	$-\frac{2}{5}$	$\frac{1}{5}$	$\frac{2}{5}$	$-\frac{1}{5}$	$-\frac{2}{5}$	$-\frac{1}{5}$	0
s_u	b	$\frac{2}{5}$	$-\frac{1}{5}$	$-\frac{2}{5}$	$\frac{1}{5}$	$\frac{2}{5}$	$\frac{1}{5}$	0
$\bar{s}_u$	c	0	0	0	0	0	0	0
s_u	a $(S_u + \mu_0 \psi_w \breve{w})$	$-\frac{1}{3}$	$\frac{1}{5}$	$\frac{1}{3}$	$-\frac{1}{5}$	$-\frac{1}{3}$	$\frac{1}{5}$	0
s_u	b	$\frac{1}{3}$	$-\frac{1}{5}$	$-\frac{1}{3}$	$\frac{1}{5}$	$\frac{1}{3}$	$-\frac{1}{5}$	0
$\bar{s}_u$	c	0	0	0	0	0	0	0

Table 3.5.2 Economic policy: re-distribution policy

a. one-time capacity-pulls in periods 1 and 2 of $\frac{3}{10}$%
b. long-term capacity-pull in period 3 of $\frac{6}{10}$%
c. total of a and b

	t	1	2	3	4	5	6	average
	a	1	1	-1	-1	1	1	0
w	b	0	0	2	2	0	0	1
	c	1	1	1	1	1	1	1
	a	$\frac{3}{10}$	$\frac{6}{10}$	0	$-\frac{6}{10}$	0	$\frac{6}{10}$	0
g_k	b	0	0	$\frac{6}{10}$	$\frac{12}{10}$	$\frac{6}{10}$	0	
	c	$\frac{3}{10}$	$\frac{6}{10}$	$\frac{6}{10}$	$\frac{6}{10}$	$\frac{6}{10}$	$\frac{6}{10}$	$\frac{6}{10}$
	a	$\frac{1}{2}$	$\frac{1}{2}$	$-\frac{1}{2}$	$-\frac{1}{2}$	$\frac{1}{2}$	$\frac{1}{2}$	0
g_L	b	0	0	1	1	0	0	
	c	$\frac{1}{2}$	$\frac{1}{2}$	$\frac{1}{2}$	$\frac{1}{2}$	$\frac{1}{2}$	$\frac{1}{2}$	$\frac{1}{2}$
	a	$-\frac{2}{5}$	$\frac{1}{5}$	1	$-\frac{1}{5}$	-1	$\frac{1}{5}$	0
s_b	b	0	0	$-\frac{4}{5}$	$\frac{2}{5}$	$\frac{6}{5}$	0	$\frac{1}{5}$
	c	$-\frac{2}{5}$	$\frac{1}{5}$	$\frac{1}{5}$	$\frac{1}{5}$	$\frac{1}{5}$	$\frac{1}{5}$	$\frac{1}{5}$
	a	$-\frac{5}{15}$	$-\frac{2}{15}$	$\frac{8}{15}$	$\frac{2}{15}$	$-\frac{8}{15}$	$-\frac{2}{15}$	0
S_u	b	—	—	$-\frac{10}{15}$	$-\frac{4}{15}$	$\frac{6}{15}$	0	$-\frac{2}{15}$
	c	$-\frac{5}{15}$	$-\frac{2}{15}$	$-\frac{2}{15}$	$-\frac{2}{15}$	$-\frac{2}{15}$	$-\frac{2}{15}$	$-\frac{2}{15}$

3.5.3 Balance of payments policy, by means of spending impulses

We have already stated in paragraph 3.4 that it is possible, in principle, to pursue a balance of payments policy with the aid of the instrument of the spending regulation as well as through changes in the rate of exchange.

We shall deal with the former instrument here, in this sub-paragraph and the alternative, the adaptation of the rate of exchange will be dealt with separately in sub-paragraph 3.5.4.

A balance of payments policy without a business cycle, can be designed fairly easily. In table 3.5.3, an example of a balance of payments surplus of $\frac{3}{5}\%$ of the equilibrium national income has been worked out. This surplus was acquired by a negative spending-pull of -1% in period 1. A positive capacity-pull has again been chosen as stabilising instrument, because of its structural neutrality. The reader is reminded once more that this means in fact that an overdose of an autonomous saving impulse must be administered since a saving impulse is necessary, firstly to finance the balance on current account and secondly to resist the spending effect of an autonomous investment-pull.

Table 3.5.3 Balance of payments policy (ω-mechanism)

a. *negative spending-pull of* -1% *in period 1*
b. *positive investment-pull of* $\frac{3}{10}\%$ *in period 1*
c. *total*

	t	1	2	3	4	5	6	average
g_k	a	0	0	$\frac{3}{5}$	$\frac{3}{5}$	0	0	$\frac{3}{10}$
	b	$\frac{3}{10}$	$\frac{3}{10}$	$-\frac{3}{10}$	$-\frac{3}{10}$	$\frac{3}{10}$	$\frac{3}{10}$	0
	c	$\frac{3}{10}$	$\frac{3}{10}$	$\frac{3}{10}$	$\frac{3}{10}$	$\frac{3}{10}$	$\frac{3}{10}$	$\frac{3}{10}$
g_x	a	-2	$-\frac{2}{5}$	$\frac{1}{5}$	$-\frac{7}{5}$	-2	$-\frac{2}{5}$	$-\frac{9}{10}$
	b	$\frac{11}{10}$	$-\frac{1}{2}$	$-\frac{11}{10}$	$\frac{5}{10}$	$\frac{11}{10}$	$-\frac{5}{10}$	0
	c	$-\frac{9}{10}$	$-\frac{9}{10}$	$-\frac{9}{10}$	$-\frac{9}{10}$	$-\frac{9}{10}$	$-\frac{9}{10}$	$-\frac{9}{10}$
g_y	a	-1	0	$\frac{2}{5}$	$-\frac{3}{5}$	-1	0	$-\frac{3}{10}$
	b	$\frac{7}{10}$	$-\frac{3}{10}$	$-\frac{7}{10}$	$\frac{3}{10}$	$\frac{7}{10}$	$-\frac{3}{10}$	0
	c	$-\frac{3}{10}$	$-\frac{3}{10}$	$-\frac{3}{10}$	$-\frac{3}{10}$	$-\frac{3}{10}$	$-\frac{3}{10}$	$-\frac{3}{10}$
g_L	a	$-\frac{1}{2}$	0	$\frac{1}{2}$	0	$-\frac{1}{2}$	0	0
	b	$\frac{1}{2}$	0	$-\frac{1}{2}$	0	$\frac{1}{2}$	0	0
	c	0	0	0	0	0	0	0

Table 3.5.3   (continued)

	t	1	2	3	4	5	6	average
s	a	2	$\frac{2}{5}$	$\frac{2}{5}$	2	2	$\frac{2}{5}$	$\frac{6}{5}$
	b	$-\frac{4}{5}$	$\frac{4}{5}$	$\frac{4}{5}$	$-\frac{4}{5}$	$-\frac{4}{5}$	$\frac{4}{5}$	0
	c	$\frac{6}{5}$	$\frac{6}{5}$	$\frac{6}{5}$	$\frac{6}{5}$	$\frac{6}{5}$	$\frac{6}{5}$	$\frac{6}{5}$
s_b	a	1	0	$\frac{1}{5}$	$\frac{6}{5}$	1	0	$\frac{3}{5}$
	b	$-\frac{2}{5}$	$\frac{3}{5}$	$\frac{2}{5}$	$-\frac{3}{5}$	$-\frac{2}{5}$	$\frac{3}{5}$	0
	c	$\frac{3}{5}$	$\frac{3}{5}$	$\frac{3}{5}$	$\frac{3}{5}$	$\frac{3}{5}$	$\frac{3}{5}$	$\frac{3}{5}$
s_u	a	1	$\frac{2}{5}$	$\frac{1}{5}$	$\frac{4}{5}$	1	$\frac{2}{5}$	$\frac{3}{5}$
	b	$-\frac{2}{5}$	$\frac{1}{5}$	$\frac{2}{5}$	$-\frac{1}{5}$	$-\frac{2}{5}$	$\frac{1}{5}$	0
	c	$\frac{3}{5}$	$\frac{3}{5}$	$\frac{3}{5}$	$\frac{3}{5}$	$\frac{3}{5}$	$\frac{3}{5}$	$\frac{3}{5}$
S_u	a	$\frac{14}{15}$	$\frac{2}{5}$	$\frac{4}{15}$	$\frac{12}{15}$	$\frac{14}{15}$	$\frac{6}{15}$	$\frac{3}{5}$
	b	$-\frac{1}{3}$	$\frac{1}{5}$	$\frac{1}{3}$	$-\frac{1}{5}$	$-\frac{1}{3}$	$\frac{1}{5}$	0
	c	$\frac{3}{5}$	$\frac{3}{5}$	$\frac{3}{5}$	$\frac{3}{5}$	$\frac{3}{5}$	$\frac{3}{5}$	$\frac{3}{5}$

Although the ultimate aim of the policy, a cyclically stable balance on the balance of payments can be achieved, it cannot be said that the structural situation has no problems. There are, it is true, no tensions on the labour market, at least not as far as employment is concerned, but the rest of the economy is out of equilibrium. The capital goods supply has increased definitely, through the negative spending-pull: the wage-depressing effect appearing immediately after the application of the spending impulse leads after a time to an increased accumulation of capital which is not called to a halt afterwards. Since employment remains constant, the available equipment is undermanned.

National spendings are of course too low, because of the spending-pull itself. (Only a slight correction takes place, resulting from the increased capital goods supply and the associated increase in spendings, out of the capital income.) The lower national spendings are not of course fully accounted for in the form of a decline in actual production, since the excessive capital goods supply on the one hand and the inadequate national spendings on the other hand ensure a spending balance which, in turn, through the action of the Zijlstra effect leads to lower imports. Added to a structurally 'appropriate' volume of exports, this leads to a volume surplus on the balance of payments which can be added on to the insufficient national spendings. Eventually, an insufficient volume of actual production arises.

Full employment can still be realised because the surplus of available capital goods ensures that the labour demand remains up to the mark. There are therefore two reasons for the structural under-utilisation percentage of the capital goods supply: the excessive capital goods volume itself and also the structurally excessive volume of domestic production. It is in fact the labour factor which in a way profits here since the labour productivity required is lower than normal, while the real wage rate remains unaffected. The excess of capital goods, all requiring utilisation, can be interpreted as a wide choice of occupations.

The producers will doubtlessly try to recover from this (inefficient) situation, for instance by no longer manning equipment not used for a long time. This signifies in fact a change in the structural parameters $\tilde{a}'_k$, which however, cannot be analysed within the framework of our linear models.

3.5.4 Balance of payments policy by means of adjustment of the rate of exchange

Changes in the rate of exchange affect structural equations on three important points. Assuming a revaluation, an adjustment of the rate of exchange involves a general decline in foreign prices and in our distinctions in the import price level, as well as the price level of foreign competitors. In this way, revaluation leads to an improvement in the terms of trade, on the one hand and to a deterioration of the competitive position on the other hand. Both aspects have a compensating character with regard to the total effect on the balance of payments. It is even theoretically conceivable that the positive effect of the improvement in the terms of trade is larger than the negative effect of the deterioration in the competitive position, so that the effect on the balance of payments is opposite to that intended. Even so, we shall do what is customary and assume that a revaluation has ultimately a negative effect on the balance of payments; the positive effect of the improvement in the terms of trade is not able to fully counterbalance the negative demand effect.

We must also point out that in reality, the rate of exchange adjustments also affect the *nominal* domestic wages and prices. Since we have taken a real and not the nominal determination of wages as basis, domestic prices have no endogenous effect in the model. The nominal development of wages and prices can once again, as it was in fact in the numerical example cited in Chapter II, be coupled (afterwards) with the real development.

a. *The terms of trade effect*
Using our simple price determination functions a revaluation can be regarded as a one-time positive impulse on the calculation rate of profit. Given the transmission coefficients, the correct size of this impulse can be discovered from equation (3.2.15a), knowing that now $\underline{P_M} = \underline{P_B}$. The profit-rate-push, per percent of revaluation is therefore:

$$\underline{r'} = -\frac{\psi_E \psi_{Mx}}{1-\psi_x} + \psi_{ME} + \psi_B \qquad (3.5.1)$$

We conclude therefore that the positive effect on the rate of profit is decreased the more our exporters have to adapt to the foreign price level (ψ_B), and the more they transmit the decreased import prices into both domestic and foreign prices.

b. *The effect on a competitive position*
We shall explain this according to the interpretation given earlier (costs ratio and price ratio). More important than the competitive effect itself, seems to be the effect on exports and imports. We can express this as an induced S_u-pull (per percent of revaluation), thus:

$$\underline{s'_u} = \mu_0 \left[\eta_{PL}\left(\frac{\psi_{Mx}}{1-\psi_x} + 1\right) - \eta_E\left\{\frac{\psi_E \psi_{Mx}}{1-\psi_x} + \psi_{ME} - (1-\psi_B)\right\} + \right.$$

$$\left. + \eta_M\left(\frac{\psi_{Mx}}{1-\psi_x} - 1\right) \right] \qquad (3.5.2)$$

It can therefore also be concluded that the required cyclical policy *after* a revaluation (devaluation), amounts to that which is also necessary in the case of an autonomous export-pull, or an autonomous change in the rate of profit. For this reason we shall devote the rest of this paragraph to these impulses, in particular to the domestic consequences. The volume balance on current account will also be considered. Theoretically, it would not be difficult to calculate the consequent results for the balance in money terms as well. It would be then necessary, however, to specify the transmission structure. In order to keep our calculations within reasonable limits, we have not done this.

Table 3.5.4   Autonomous changes in the volume of world trade (ω-mechanism)

t	1	2	3	4	5	6	average
$\hat{g}_E$	1	0	0	0	0	0	0
$\begin{aligned}\check{w} &= -\check{w}_{-2} + \dfrac{\beta M_l \tilde{\alpha}_y \mu_0}{A_0}\,\underline{\tilde{g}_E} = \\ &= -\check{w}_{-2} + \tilde{g}_E\end{aligned}$	1	0	-1	0	1	0	0
$\check{r} = -\dfrac{\lambda'}{\kappa}\check{w} = -\tfrac{3}{5}\check{w}$	$-\tfrac{3}{5}$	0	$\tfrac{3}{5}$	0	$-\tfrac{3}{5}$	0	0
$g_k = g_{k-1} + \tilde{\sigma}_R \check{r}_{-2}$	0	0	$-\tfrac{3}{5}$	$-\tfrac{3}{5}$	0	0	$-\tfrac{3}{10}$
$\begin{aligned}g_L &= M_l \tilde{\alpha}'_k g_k + M_l \tilde{\alpha}_y \omega \Big\{ \lambda_0 \check{w} + \\ &\quad -\Big(\lambda' + \mu_0 \dfrac{\eta_\omega}{\omega}\Big)\check{w}_{-1} \Big\} + \\ &\quad + M_l \tilde{\alpha}_y \mu_0 \underline{\check{g}_E}\end{aligned}$	$\tfrac{1}{2}$	0	$-\tfrac{1}{2}$	0	$\tfrac{1}{2}$	0	0
$\begin{aligned}g_x &= \lambda_0(g_L + \check{w}) + \\ &\quad + (1-\lambda_0)g_k + \kappa \check{r}_{-1} = \\ &= \tfrac{2}{3}(g_L + \check{w}) + \tfrac{1}{3}g_k + \check{r}_{-1}\end{aligned}$	1	$-\tfrac{3}{5}$	$-\tfrac{6}{5}$	$\tfrac{2}{5}$	1	$-\tfrac{3}{5}$	$-\tfrac{1}{10}$
$s = g_k - g_x$	-1	$\tfrac{3}{5}$	$\tfrac{3}{5}$	-1	-1	$\tfrac{3}{5}$	$-\tfrac{1}{5}$
$\begin{aligned}\mu_0 g_E &= -\mu_0 \eta_w \check{w}_{-1} + \mu_0 \check{g}_E = \\ &= -\tfrac{1}{5}\check{w}_{-1} + \tfrac{1}{2}\underline{\check{g}_E}\end{aligned}$	$\tfrac{1}{2}$	$\tfrac{3}{10}$	$\tfrac{5}{10}$	$\tfrac{7}{10}$	$\tfrac{5}{10}$	$\tfrac{3}{10}$	$\tfrac{1}{10}$
$\mu_0 g_M = -(1-\omega)s = -\tfrac{1}{2}s$	$\tfrac{1}{2}$	$-\tfrac{3}{10}$	$-\tfrac{3}{10}$	$\tfrac{1}{2}$	$\tfrac{1}{2}$	$-\tfrac{3}{10}$	$\tfrac{1}{10}$
$s_u = \mu_0(g_E - g_M)$	0	$\tfrac{3}{5}$	$\tfrac{4}{5}$	$\tfrac{1}{5}$	0	$\tfrac{3}{5}$	$\tfrac{2}{5}$
$g_y = g_x + s_u$	1	0	$-\tfrac{2}{5}$	$\tfrac{3}{5}$	1	0	$\tfrac{3}{10}$
$s_b = g_k - g_y$	-1	0	$-\tfrac{1}{5}$	$-\tfrac{6}{5}$	-1	0	$-\tfrac{3}{5}$
$S_u = s_u + \tfrac{1}{15}\check{w}$	$\tfrac{1}{15}$	$\tfrac{9}{15}$	$\tfrac{11}{15}$	$\tfrac{3}{15}$	$\tfrac{1}{15}$	$\tfrac{9}{15}$	$\tfrac{6}{15}$

The sequence of the autonomous impulses we have yet to discuss is therefore specified: firstly, an analysis of the export-pull and secondly a study of the autonomous yield-push.

3.5.5 *An autonomous change in the world trade volume*

Table 3.5.4 illustrates the cyclical and structural consequences of a one-time, higher than 'normal' growth rate of the world trade volume. In fact, the pull referred to here, resembles the (domestic) spending-pull, in its effect on several central domestic variables. This is not surprising since the agreement between the autonomous export-pull and the domestic spending-pull lies in the fact that they can each be regarded as an autonomous impulse on the effective demand and thereby (at least in our model, in which the accumulation of stocks is not taken into consideration) on actual production.

The developments of domestic spendings and therefore also of the spending balance are however, because of the influence of the export-pull and spending-pull, divergent. Of course both cyclically and structurally diverging time series arise now after an export-pull or a spending-pull.

It has now become clear, from the above, what the obvious means are for coping with the cyclical disequilibrium resulting from an export-pull; that can be nothing else but a speedily accomplished spending-pull in the opposite direction. After our discussion of the time-lag in economic policy in Chapter II, we need now only add that an extremely deep understanding of the developments of world imports is needed for correct dosing and precise timing. However, in table 3.5.5, we have shown the course of the variables which, influenced by the export-pull, and the corrective spending-pull, undergo structural changes. It would not be wise, although theoretically possible, to react to the export-pull with a negative wage-push. This implies that an attempt would be made to prohibit the higher than normal wage increase in the first period which is a normal accompaniment to the increase in employment. Internal equilibrium could indeed partly be realised in this way, but the major problem that would arise instead, is continued shortage of supply on the labour market. Under these circumstances it is much better to remove at once the cause of the non-motivated wage increase, using the broad measures of the spending policy to prevent the effective demand from increasing with the autonomous extra percentage of increase in world trade. It is also possible, theoretically, to react to a positive export-pull with a negative capital-pull. However, this now has the disadvantage

80

Table 3.5.5   Stabilisation of an export-pull (autonomous increase in world trade by means of an autonomous spending-pull

a. *Export-pull of 1% in period 1*
b. *Spending-pull of −1% in period 1*
c. *Total*

	t	1	2	3	4	5	6	average
$\check{g}_E$	a	1	0	0	0	0	0	0
$\check{g}_x$	b	−1	0	0	0	0	0	0
g_x { a	1	$-\frac{3}{5}$	$-\frac{6}{5}$	$\frac{2}{5}$	1	$-\frac{3}{5}$	$-\frac{3}{10}$
	b	−2	$-\frac{2}{5}$	$\frac{1}{5}$	$-\frac{7}{5}$	−2	$\frac{2}{5}$	$\frac{9}{10}$
$\bar{g}_x$	c	−1	−1	−1	−1	−1	−1	−1
s { a	−1	$\frac{3}{5}$	$\frac{3}{5}$	−1	−1	$\frac{3}{5}$	$-\frac{1}{5}$
	b	2	$\frac{2}{5}$	$\frac{2}{5}$	2	2	$\frac{2}{5}$	$\frac{6}{5}$
$\bar{s}$	c	1	1	1	1	1	1	1
s_u { a	0	$\frac{3}{5}$	$\frac{4}{5}$	$\frac{1}{5}$	0	$\frac{3}{5}$	$\frac{2}{5}$
	b	1	$\frac{2}{5}$	$\frac{1}{5}$	$\frac{4}{5}$	1	$\frac{2}{5}$	0
$\bar{s}_u$	c	1	1	1	1	1	1	1
S_u { a	$\frac{1}{15}$	$\frac{9}{15}$	$\frac{11}{15}$	$\frac{3}{15}$	$\frac{1}{15}$	$\frac{9}{15}$	$\frac{6}{15}$
	b	$\frac{14}{15}$	$\frac{6}{15}$	$\frac{4}{15}$	$\frac{12}{15}$	$\frac{14}{15}$	$\frac{6}{15}$	$\frac{3}{5}$
$\bar{S}_u$	c	1	1	1	1	1	1	1

of a much too neutral structural functioning. In particular, the capacity-pull is no cure for the ultimate decline in the capital goods supply which arises as a result of $\check{g}_E > 0$. Since the actual production volume becomes even higher than normal, this implies a long-term over-utilisation of the available capital goods. It is of course inefficient to maintain this in the long run.

Table 3.5.6 *One-time autonomous decline in the rate of profit of −1% (ω mechanism)*

a. the spending effect; b. capacity effect; c. total

	t	1	2	3	4	5	6	average
$\breve{r}'_{\_}$		−1	0	0	0	0	0	0
$\check{r}'_{\_}$		−1	−1	−1	−1	−1	−1	−1
$\breve{w}$ F.E.	a. Spending effect $\breve{w} = -\breve{w}_{-2} + M_w\beta M_l\tilde{\alpha}_y\omega\kappa(\breve{L}'_{-1} - \breve{L}'_{-2})$	0	−1	0	1	0	−1	0
	b. Capacity effect $\breve{w} = -\breve{w}_{-2} + M_w\beta M_l\tilde{\alpha}_k\tilde{\sigma}_R\breve{L}'_{-2}$	0	0	$-\frac{10}{3}$	$-\frac{10}{3}$	0	0	$-\frac{5}{3}$
	c. Total	0	−1	$-\frac{10}{3}$	$-\frac{7}{3}$	0	−1	$-\frac{5}{3}$
1.	$\breve{r} = -\dfrac{\lambda'}{\kappa}w - \check{r}' = -\dfrac{3}{5}\breve{w} + \check{r}'$	−1	$-\frac{2}{5}$	1	$\frac{2}{5}$	−1	$-\frac{2}{5}$	0
2.	$g_k = g_{k_{-1}} + \tilde{\sigma}_R\check{r}'_{-2} = g_{k_{-1}} + \check{r}'_{-2}$	0	0	−1	$-\frac{7}{5}$	$-\frac{2}{5}$	0	$-\frac{7}{10}$
3.	$g_L = M_l\left[\tilde{\alpha}_k g_k + \alpha_y\omega\left\{\lambda_0 w - \left(\lambda' + \mu_0\dfrac{\eta_w}{\omega}\right)\right\}\breve{w}_{-2}\right] - M_l\tilde{\alpha}_y\omega\kappa\check{r}'_{-1}$ $= g_k + \dfrac{1}{5}\breve{w} - \dfrac{3}{10}\breve{w}_{-1} - \dfrac{3}{10}\check{r}'_{-1}$	0	$-\frac{1}{2}$	$-\frac{5}{3}$	$-\frac{7}{6}$	0	$-\frac{1}{2}$	$-\frac{5}{6}$
4.	$g_x = \lambda_0(g_L + \breve{w}) + (1-\lambda_0)g_k + \kappa\check{r}'_{-1} = \dfrac{2}{3}(g_L + \breve{w}) + \dfrac{1}{3}g_k + \check{r}'_{-1}$	0	−2	$-\frac{61}{15}$	$-\frac{27}{15}$	$\frac{4}{15}$	−2	$-\frac{19}{10}$
5.	$s \equiv g_k - g_x$	0	2	$\frac{46}{15}$	$\frac{6}{15}$	$-\frac{10}{15}$	2	$\frac{6}{5}$
6.	$\mu_0 g_E = -\mu_0\eta_w\breve{w}_{-1} = -\dfrac{1}{5}\breve{w}_{-1}$	0	0	$\frac{1}{5}$	$\frac{2}{3}$	$\frac{7}{15}$	0	$\frac{1}{3}$
7.	$\mu_0 g_M = -(1-\omega)s = -\dfrac{1}{2}s$	0	−1	$-\frac{23}{15}$	$-\frac{3}{15}$	$\frac{5}{15}$	−1	$-\frac{3}{5}$
8.	$s_u = \mu_0(g_E - g_M)$	0	1	$\frac{26}{15}$	$\frac{13}{15}$	$\frac{2}{15}$	1	$\frac{14}{15}$
9.	$g_w = g_x + s_u$		1	3 5	14	6	1	29

3.5.6 *Autonomous changes in foreign prices (induced rate of profit-push)*

We have already stated in par. 3.5.1 that it is possible to distinguish two aspects of changes in foreign prices: 'autonomous profit-rate-push' (the terms of trade aspect) and the 'autonomous export-pull' (the competitive aspect).

A glance at the facts for the Netherlands will reveal two things:

1. The structural development of the import and export price level, and also of the price level of foreign competitors, is slight when compared with other price levels. Periods of quite steep price increases (1954–1956 incl. and 1968–1970 incl.) are followed by a number of years of significant decreases (1967–1971).

2. The very strong bond between the price indexes of imports, exports and competitive goods on the foreign markets. The estimations of the Central Planning Bureau also show the Dutch exporters behaving as price adapters on the foreign markets, so that for the Dutch economy, the simple, marginal-firm theory is probably the one most closely approaching the actual situation.

In any case, it is important for our survey that differences can exist between the development of the import price level on the one hand and that of the foreign competition on the other hand. It is also true that these differences are minor, empirically speaking, especially when considered over a period of several years. We shall not, therefore, be digressing too far from concrete reality, if we assume that the import price level and the price level of the foreign competitors develop in the same way so that competitive position and terms of trade change to the same degree.

By assuming identical $\check{p}_B$- and $\check{p}_m$-developments, the conclusions related to exogenous foreign price developments become of course applicable to a revaluation (devaluation). Thus we kill two birds with the one stone: exogenous foreign price developments can be treated together with the autonomous rate of exchange adjustments.

At this point, we could begin a casuistic detailed discourse by examining all possible quantity equations between $\underline{r}'$ and g'_E. We consider, however, that it is wiser to assume that the export effect (g'_E) of a foreign price mutation clearly dominates the associated induced yield-push ($\underline{r}'$). This is, in any case, the current opinion in the Netherlands. If it is correct, then we can refer to the previous section 3.5.1 for the consequences, also in view of the cyclical stabilisation.

Although the terms of trade effect of a change in foreign price levels does not seem to be so important, we do feel we should pay some attention to it, since changes in the terms of trade have an effect on the balance on current account in money terms. Here it differs from the autonomous export-pull. If we were to give a complete specification of the transmission relations, we could calculate this balance in money terms easily enough.

There is however a second theoretically interesting difference between a foreign price impulse and a volume-pull. We refer here to the influence of the terms of trade on the rate of profit since examination of the model shows us that the most important opponent of an autonomous rate of profit-push is a continual negative capacity-pull.

This gives us the last premise required for the following conclusion with regard to the significance of foreign price developments (in the following, 'revaluation' can also mean 'autonomous definitive decline in foreign price levels'):

A revaluation leads to a continued deficit (or decline in the surplus) on current account of the balance of payments as a result of the demand effect of the revaluation. The deficit referred to here is somewhat reduced, particularly in regard to the balance in current prices as a result of the direct effect of the improved terms of trade. But, apart from this obvious effect, the improved terms of trade imply a rate of profit-push whose effect can be compared to a continual capacity-pull (see table 3.5.6). The stabilising measures are obvious: the demand effect can be stabilised by a positive spending-pull, the direct terms of trade effect can be partly eliminated by an adequate balance of payments policy based on a spending policy, while the cyclical side effects can be countered by a continual negative capacity-pull.

3.6 THE RESONANCE EFFECT

Neither the development of the world trade volume nor the development of foreign prices shows in time, a uniform development, yet they both resemble a cyclical fluctuation. It is striking, in this context, that in the sixties, the foreign volume cycle precedes the price cycle. After ± 1961, the price cycle is almost identical to the volume cycle.

It is known that a system in itself non-explosive, can be induced to explode when subjected to impulses in a non-explosive rhythm. This pattern can be observed in the following discussion, where we have considered the consequences of a number of autonomous impulses produced by world trade, and received in a rhythm identical to the endogenous vibration frequency of our open economy. In table 3.6.1 the relevant results have been set forth.

Table 3.6.1   Resonance effect of a cyclical impulse from world trade volume

	t	1	2	3	4	5	6	7	8	9	10	
Impulse:	$\hat{g}_E$	1	0	-1	0	1	0	-1	0	1	0	etc.
Results:	$\dot{w}$	1	0	-2	0	3	0	-4	0	5	0	etc.
	g_k	0	0	$-\frac{3}{5}$	$-\frac{3}{5}$	$\frac{3}{5}$	$\frac{3}{5}$	$-\frac{6}{5}$	$-\frac{6}{5}$	$\frac{6}{5}$	$\frac{6}{5}$	etc.
	g_x	1	$-\frac{3}{5}$	$-\frac{11}{5}$	1	$\frac{16}{5}$	$-\frac{8}{5}$	$-\frac{22}{5}$	$\frac{10}{5}$	$\frac{27}{5}$	-1	etc.
	S_u	$\frac{1}{15}$	$\frac{9}{15}$	$\frac{10}{15}$	$-\frac{6}{15}$	$-\frac{9}{15}$	$-\frac{15}{15}$	$\frac{20}{15}$	$-\frac{12}{15}$	$-\frac{19}{15}$	$\frac{21}{15}$	etc.

It should be noted that in table 3.6.1 we have taken into consideration only an autonomous volume impulse from world trade, although in reality volume and price impulses have been alternating. It has become clear, however, from the foregoing paragraphs that, apart from a probably small profit-rate-effect from foreign prices, the effect of the price cycle is broadly comparable to the volume-pull from world trade. For this reason we have analysed the resonance effect on the basis of a series of g_E-pulls.

The consequences can be described as follows:

1. Real wages show a fluctuation such that the cyclical deviation, despite the non-explosive character of the g_E-pulls and the likewise non-explosive character of the endogenous system, becomes in both upwards and downwards directions, continually larger. Straight after the autonomous export-pull has completed a four-period turn the real wage decreases to -3%. Because of the proportionality between employment and real wage rate, the former develops parallel to this.

2. Another variable which particularly attracts our attention is the degree of utilisation. Fluctuations in world trade induce, at least in the first seven years of the cycle, an almost continual over-utilisation of the capital goods supply. From the other direction, an almost continual surplus on current account (constant prices) arises. It is, of course,

important in this context, that the cumulative effect with regard to wages, is, on an average, positive, so that structurally an insufficient accumulation of capital results for want of sufficient rate of profit.

Meanwhile, we have not succeeded in explaining verbally the precise structural and cyclical connections in a more or less closely reasoned argumentation. A series of autonomous export-pulls whose periodicity resembles the endogenous system leads to:
- a continual and even increasing balance of payments surplus (constant prices);
- a structurally inadequate accumulation of capital;
- a continuing and similarly increasing over-utilisation of the available capital goods.

3. In the period 1967–1970, the international business cycle has made an almost complete turn except that the ups and downs have alternated in exactly the opposite sequence as in table 3.6.1. We would be the last to want to ascribe a direct empirical and operational significance to analyses such as those appearing in this paragraph. Nevertheless, the foregoing suggests that this hypothesis may be inferred, with regard to the current difficulties (1971–1972) in the business cycle. Regarding this, we can deduce that the effects of the business cycle in 1972 (in a downwards direction) are expected to be more severe than was the case in the Netherlands during the last number of years. The year 1972 would then, at least with altered symbols, roughly correspond to the 5th and 6th periods in table 3.6.1, so that for this reason, the resonance hypothesis could be a fertile starting point for the analysis of the real situation for the years 1972–1973. Other elements have appeared in the actual developments, during the last number of years which ensure that our hypothesis is not rejected without trial. Of these, we mention only the indeed extremely high wage demands and employment in the years 1970 and 1971 (moving upwards), accompanied by a very high accumulation of capital, whilst it is conceivable that capital goods have not been fully utilised.

4. In any case, an excessively varying development in the exogenous factors leads to a cyclical situation which can be described in theory but which in practice gives an impression of chaos. If the resonance does in fact come about along the lines we have suggested, then we must regard a consistent design for economic policy as practically out of the question.

86

IV. Separate labour markets: the significance of the regional demand and price system

4.1 INTRODUCTION

Once again we leave the macroeconomic sphere in order to resume the study of the dynamic problems of the regionally, or in other words, of the internationally separated macrosystems.

The separation between the regional economies is brought about by means of the assumption that the factor labour is absolutely immobile; at least it does not move as a result of regional differences in reward. Clearly, inter-regional wage differentiation can appear under these circumstances both in the long and the short run.

While the above assumptions suggest that the labour markets are not connected on their supply sides, they are definitely connected on their demand sides. We will be assuming that the inter-regional trade proceeds according to relations such as those treated in Chapter III. In this way, a complete interdependence of the effective demand arises through imports and exports, which aims at the different regions and thereby also at the demand for labour in each region. The general design of the previous chapters can be used again: we generalise only the theory of the labour market economy for des-aggregated, but integrated systems.

We were obliged to re-impose important restrictions on ourselves also with regard to the solubility of the concrete numerical examples. Actually, the necessity for simplicity in the specification of our relations is even more urgent than was the case with macrotheory, since we now have to make a survey of the 'home' economy per region while at the same time maintaining the survey of all regions. The most important assumptions on which our observations are based, are summarised in the following section.

4.1.1 *Assumptions*

1. We distinguish only two different regions which together form a closed system in the sense that they have no international relations with third lands. The big advantage of this assumption is of course that the imports of one region are per definition equal to the exports of the other. In a more general model, a distribution mechanism would have to be designed (as already stated in Chapter i), to regulate international demand in the situation with equilibrium growth and in a situation without equilibrium growth.

2. The import/export relations are based on the $\tilde{\mu}$-mechanism on the one hand, while on the other hand a simple price substitution effect is operating between domestic and foreign goods (the $\tilde{\mu}$-mechanism). This latter situation is in complete accordance with Chapter i. (In the following chapter, the import/export relations will be based upon the ω-mechanism.)

3. In order to simplify our explanation even more, we have assumed that the regions under observation are of equal size and are symmetrical on other points as well. (We do not expect that the assumption of differences in size will produce many new wage conclusions, any more than it did in Chapter i.)

4. The more fundamental causes of inter-regional trade are ignored. It can be assumed, if so desired, that both regions produce the same products, to a certain extent. Inter-regional trade can then arise (at least in this chapter) because of differences in price and because of differences in actual production. It is also possible that both regions reveal differences in natural dotation as well. This could explain the 'normal' volume of trade; that which is present in times of equilibrium growth.

5. The accumulation of capital in one region is completely independent of the accumulation of capital in the other region or of the total accumulation in both regions as a whole. The general basic assumption is therefore: regional autarchy (economic self-sufficiency) in the factor markets. Interesting phenomena such as inter-regional (international) wage imitation and the associated problem of the wage leadership do not therefore come into consideration.

4.2 THE RELATIONS

As we have said, in contrast with the previous paragraph, we shall not introduce any really new relations here. We need only provide the relations from Chapter III with an index in order to obtain a complete specification of the new model. It is simpler, however, to work with matrix notation. Thus, for the definitions of effective demand

$$g_{y_A} \equiv g_{x_A} + s_{u_A} \left.\vphantom{\begin{matrix}1\\1\end{matrix}}\right\} \qquad (4.2.1)$$
$$g_{y_B} \equiv g_{x_B} + s_{u_B}$$

we can also write

$$\{g_y\} \equiv \{g_x\} + \{s_u\} \qquad (4.2.2)$$

In matrix and vector notation we have also:

$$\{s_u\} = -\mu_0 \eta_w \begin{bmatrix} 1 & -1 \\ -1 & 1 \end{bmatrix} \{\dot{w}\}_{-1} - \hat{\mu} \begin{bmatrix} 1 & -1 \\ -1 & 1 \end{bmatrix} \{g_y\} \qquad (4.2.3)$$

where η_w is the sum of the import and export elasticities with regard to the real wage costs differences. Keeping in mind the definition for the actual production, as well as the spendings functions used in Chapters II and III, we obtain for the actual production, the following expression:

$$\{g_y\} \equiv \{g_x\} + \{s_u\} = (\lambda_0) \{g_L\} + (1 - \lambda_0) \{g_k\} +$$
$$+ (\lambda_0) \{\dot{w}\} + (\kappa) \{\check{r}\}_{-1} + \{s_u\} \qquad (4.2.4)$$

Since we postulate the following expression as a simple formula for the transmission of wage costs:

$$\{\check{p}\} = (\psi_w) \{\dot{w}\}, \qquad (4.2.5)$$

we obtain for the calculation yield:

$$(\kappa) \{\check{r}\} = - \begin{bmatrix} \lambda_0 - \mu_0\psi_w & \mu_0\psi_w \\ \mu_0\psi_w & \lambda_0 - \mu_0\psi_w \end{bmatrix} \{\dot{w}\} \qquad (4.2.6)$$

Substitution of (4.2.3) and (4.2.5) gives, after elimination of $\{g_y\}$ from the right-hand term:

$$\{g_y\} = [M_m]\left[(\lambda_0)\{g_l\} + (1 - \lambda_0)\{g_k\} + (\lambda_0)\{\tilde{w}\} + \right.$$

$$\left. - \begin{bmatrix} \lambda_0 - \mu_0(\psi_w - \eta_w) & \mu_0(\psi_w - \eta_w) \\ \mu_0(\psi_w - \eta_w) & \lambda_0 - \mu_0(\psi_w - \eta_w) \end{bmatrix} \{\tilde{w}\}_{-1} \right] \qquad (4.2.7)$$

Here, $[M_m]$ is an import multiplier which is analogous to the multiplier M_m in Chapter III, whose exact definition is:

$$[M_m] = \begin{bmatrix} 1 + \tilde{\mu} & -\tilde{\mu} \\ -\tilde{\mu} & 1 + \tilde{\mu} \end{bmatrix}^{-1} = \frac{1}{1 + 2\tilde{\mu}} \begin{bmatrix} 1 + \tilde{\mu} & \tilde{\mu} \\ \tilde{\mu} & 1 + \tilde{\mu} \end{bmatrix} \qquad (4.2.8)$$

Further specification of the demand for labour function is simple and it reads, under the familiar condition:

$$\tilde{\alpha}_{y_i} + \tilde{\alpha}_{k_i} = 1 \qquad (i = A, B):$$

$$\{g_l\} = [M_l]\left[[\alpha'_k]\{g_k\} + (\tilde{\alpha}_y)(\lambda_0)[M_m]\{\tilde{w}\} - (\tilde{\alpha}_y)[M_m] \right.$$

$$\left. \times \begin{bmatrix} \lambda_0 - \mu_0(\psi_w - \eta_w) & \mu_0(\psi_0 - \eta_w) \\ \mu_0(\psi_w - \eta_w) & \lambda_0 - \mu_0(\psi_w - \eta_w) \end{bmatrix} \tilde{w}_{-1} \right] \qquad (4.2.9)$$

In the equation (4.2.9) several important matrix multipliers have been included, which as the reader can easily verify, can be exactly defined as follows:

$$[M_l] = [I - \tilde{\alpha}_y \lambda_0 [M_m]]^{-1} \qquad (4.2.10)$$

(employment multiplier)

$$[\alpha'_k] = [(1 - \tilde{\alpha}_y) + \tilde{\alpha}_y(1 - \lambda_0)[M_m]] \qquad (4.2.11)$$

(corrected marginal employment multiplier of the capital goods supply)

It must be remembered that the employment multiplier $[M_l]$ is a (square) matrix and shows only formal resemblance to the macromultiplier. It can be said that M_l includes the original employment multiplier $(1 - \tilde{\alpha}_y \lambda_0)$, but also the indirect (spendings) effect of the real wage increase in, for example, region B on employment in region A. As well as the own, direct employment multiplier, the real wage rate of the partner regions has an effect on the demand for labour. The connection becomes complicated because own domestic tensions come back again by means of the inter-regional circular effects. A matrix multiplier arises in this way, whose functioning is somewhat similar to the Leontief inverse (the resemblance is however, purely formal; the material interpretation is quite different).

Finally, it can be shown that the average multiplier (for the regions) is the same as that of the macromodel. Something similar applies to the matrix (4.2.11). This illustrates that employment in region A is not wholly dependent on the capital goods supply in A, but that the labour positions available in the partner region are also of importance.

Just as in the foregoing chapters, we shall now summarise the most important relations of the model, including the autonomous impulses as well (see model 4.2.1).

Model 4.2.1

$$\{\check{r}\} = -\left(\frac{1}{\kappa}\right)\begin{bmatrix} \lambda_0 - \mu_0\psi_w & \mu_0\psi_w \\ \mu_0\psi_w & \lambda_0 - \mu_0\psi_w \end{bmatrix}\{\check{w}\} \tag{1}$$

$$\{g_k\} = \{g_{k-1}\} + (\sigma_R)\{\check{r}_{-2}\} + \{\underline{\hat{g}_k}\} \tag{2}$$

$$\{g_l\} = [M_l][\tilde{\alpha}_k']\{g_k\} + (\lambda_0\tilde{\alpha}_y)[M_l][M_m]\{\check{w}\} -$$

$$- \tilde{\alpha}_y[M_l][M_m]\begin{bmatrix} \lambda_0 - \mu_0(\psi_w - \eta_w) & \mu_0(\psi_w - \eta_w) \\ \mu_0(\psi_w - \eta_w) & \lambda_0 - \mu_0(\psi_w - \eta_w) \end{bmatrix}\{\check{w}_{-1}\} +$$

$$+ \tilde{\alpha}_y[M_l][M_m]\{\underline{\check{g}_x}\} \tag{3}$$

$$\{\check{w}\} = (\beta)\{g_L\} + \{\underline{\check{w}}\} \tag{4}$$

The formal structure of the regional model again corresponds completely with that of the macromodel of the closed economy (Chapter II). The *formal* definition of the dynamic characteristics (periodicity, stability, amplitude) presents few formal difficulties.

4.3 THE SOLUTION OF THE MODEL

The solution of model 4.2.1 can be obtained just as easily and directly as those of the macromodels of the foregoing chapters. If we symbolise the homogeneous part of the final equation as follows:

$$[A_0]\{\check{w}\} + [A_1]\{\check{w}_{-1}\} + [A_2]\{\check{w}_{-2}\} = 0 \tag{4.3.1}$$

then the relevant solution can be given as follows:

$$[A_0] = I - (\beta\tilde{\alpha}_y\lambda_0)\,[M_l]\,[M_m]$$

$$[A_1] =$$

$$- \left[I - (\beta\tilde{\alpha}_y)\,[M_l]\,[M_m] \begin{bmatrix} 2\lambda_0 - \mu_0(\psi_w - \eta_w) & \mu_0(\psi_w - \eta_w) \\ \mu_0(\psi_w - \eta_w) & 2\lambda_0 - \mu_0(\psi_w - \eta_w) \end{bmatrix} \right]$$

$$[A_2] = \left(\beta\,\frac{\sigma_R}{\kappa}\right)[M_l]\,[\tilde{\alpha}'_k] \begin{bmatrix} \lambda_0 - \mu_0\psi_w & \mu_0\psi_w \\ \mu_0\psi_w & \lambda_0 - \mu_0\psi_w \end{bmatrix} -$$

$$- (\beta\tilde{\alpha}_y)\,[M_l]\,[M_m] \begin{bmatrix} \lambda_0 - \mu_0(\psi_w - \eta_w) & \mu_0(\psi_w - \eta_w) \\ \mu_0(\psi_w - \eta_w) & \lambda_0 - \mu_0(\psi_w - \eta_w) \end{bmatrix} \qquad (4.3.2)$$

If we also take the autonomous impulses into account, then the complete final equation reads thus:

$$[A_0]\{\tilde{w}\} + [A_1]\{\tilde{w}_{-1}\} + [A_2]\{\tilde{w}_{-2}\} = \underline{\tilde{w}} + (\beta)\,[M_l]\,[\tilde{\alpha}'_k]\,\underline{g}_k +$$

$$+ (\beta\tilde{\alpha}_y)\,[M_l]\,[M_m]\,\underline{g}_x \qquad (4.3.3)$$

The definition of the endogenous dynamic characteristics of an equation such as (4.3.2) is only somewhat more complicated numerically than those of the macromodels of earlier chapters. It can be concluded that if the corresponding macromodels give rise to a difference equation to the mth power, the n-regional model will be to the $n \times m$th power at the most. The purely formal determination of the endogenous dynamic characteristics of (4.3.3) is confined to the calculation of the eigenvalues of the matrix (see Appendix A 1.3):

$$A = \begin{bmatrix} A_0^{-1}A_2 & A_0^{-1}A_2 \\ I & 0 \end{bmatrix} \qquad (4.3.4)$$

We do not intend, however, to discuss the characteristics of (4.3.4) extensively and in general terms. Instead, we prefer to investigate the characteristics and the operation of the model by means of a number of concrete numerical examples. One general observation is that (4.3.3) shows that the differences among wage-push, capacity-pull and spending-pull themselves, are now larger than in the integrated model of Chapter I in which the capacity-pull and spending-pull displayed a considerable degree of analogy and also larger than in the macromodels of Chapters II and III in which the effects of wage-push and capacity-pull strongly resembled each other.

4.4 DESCRIPTION OF THE BUSINESS CYCLE

4.4.1 *General*

We have taken the numerical example of Chapter II as foundation, with regard to the macrosystem. We have also assumed that an excess in actual production (compared with equilibrium growth) leads to an increase in imports equal to half of the excess $\tilde{\mu} = \frac{1}{2}$). The choice of coefficients of the price system ψ_w and η_w is still open. The following matrices of the differential system arise in our numerical example:

$$[A_0] = \frac{1}{22} \begin{bmatrix} 14 & -3 \\ -3 & 14 \end{bmatrix}$$

$$[A_1] = \frac{1}{22} \begin{bmatrix} 6+5(\psi_w-\eta_w) & -6-5(\psi_w-\eta_w) \\ -6-5(\psi_w-\eta_w) & 6+5(\psi_w-\eta_w) \end{bmatrix}$$

$$[A_2] = \frac{1}{22} \begin{bmatrix} 12-13\,\psi_w-5\,\eta_w & -1+13\,\psi_w+5\,\eta_w \\ -1+13\,\psi_w+5\,\eta_w & 12-13\,\psi_w-5\,\eta_w \end{bmatrix} \quad (4.4.1)$$

It can easily be calculated that the characteristic equation of the system, described by the matrices (4.4.1) is as follows:

$$(\lambda^2 + 1)\,\{\lambda^2 - 2a\lambda - (1 + 2b)\} = 0 \ (^1) \quad (4.4.2)$$

Here, a and b stand for, respectively:

$$a = \frac{6+5(\psi_w-\eta)}{17} \qquad b = \frac{-15+13\,\psi_w+5\,\eta}{17} \quad (4.4.3)$$

In equation (4.4.2), the eigenvalues of the macrosystem of Chapter II can be recognised in the solutions produced by the first factor (λ^2+1).

1. This is the characteristic equation of the matrix A of formula (4.3.4).

The values which we obtain by assuming the second factor to be equal to zero arise from the addition of the inter-regional relations. The moduli of these values can be more than, less than, or equal to 1. In the first instance, the inter-regional relations help to make the integral system explode. In the second instance, the influence of the new eigenvalues peters out, so that the system ultimately converges towards the macro-model of Chapter III, when the regions, after an impulse occurring in one of them, will finally keep in step with each other. In our numerical examples, we have restricted ourselves to the, in our opinion instructive, in-between case, where the moduli of the new eigenvalues are again equal to 1. In two cases, simple yet instructive numerical examples are provided; namely if we choose 0 and 1 as values for the λ's. The cases referred to here can be defined as follows:

Case I

$$\left.\begin{array}{l} \lambda_{12} = \pm i \\ \lambda_3 = 0 \\ \lambda_4 = 1 \end{array}\right\} \Rightarrow \eta = 0,\ \psi_w = \tfrac{1}{2}.$$

In this case, the price system operates only half, i.e. through the yields of the accumulation of capital. Volume-demand effects are not considered for the moment. The import and export mechanism is dominated by the effective demand. The final equation is:

$$\{\breve{w}\} = \begin{bmatrix} \tfrac{1}{2} & -\tfrac{1}{2} \\ -\tfrac{1}{2} & \tfrac{1}{2} \end{bmatrix} \breve{w}_{-1} - \begin{bmatrix} \tfrac{1}{2} & \tfrac{1}{2} \\ \tfrac{1}{2} & \tfrac{1}{2} \end{bmatrix} \breve{w}_{-2}.$$

Case II

$$\left.\begin{array}{l} \lambda_{12} = \pm i \\ \lambda_2 = 1 \\ \lambda_3 = -1 \end{array}\right\} \Rightarrow \eta_w = 1{,}7;\ \psi_w = \tfrac{1}{2}.$$

The price system is operating fully here, i.e. the aspects of yield and volume demand are both involved. The $\tilde{\mu}$-mechanism is of course also operating.

We have restricted ourselves in the following description of the operation of the system, to case II, because it is more complete. It should not be difficult for the reader to analyse the first case, as well. The two do not in fact differ greatly.

94

The quantitative expression of the final equation (4.3.3) is, therefore:

$$\frac{1}{22}\begin{bmatrix} 14 & -3 \\ -3 & 14 \end{bmatrix}\{\check{w}\} - [0]\{\check{w}_{-1}\} + \frac{1}{22}\begin{bmatrix} -3 & 14 \\ 14 & -3 \end{bmatrix}\{\check{w}_{-2}\} =$$

$$= \underline{\check{w}} + \frac{5}{22}\begin{bmatrix} 10 & 1 \\ 1 & 10 \end{bmatrix}\underline{\hat{g}_k} + \frac{1}{11}\begin{bmatrix} 8 & 3 \\ 3 & 8 \end{bmatrix}\underline{\hat{g}_x} \qquad (4.4.4)$$

After continued multiplication with

$$A_0^{-1} = \frac{2}{17}\begin{bmatrix} 14 & 3 \\ 3 & 14 \end{bmatrix}$$

the following equation arises:

$$\{\check{w}\} = [0]\{\check{w}_{-1}\} - \begin{bmatrix} 0 & 1 \\ 1 & 0 \end{bmatrix}\{\check{w}_{-2}\} +$$

$$+ \frac{2}{17}\begin{bmatrix} 14 & 3 \\ 3 & 14 \end{bmatrix}\{\check{w}\} + \frac{5}{17}\begin{bmatrix} 13 & 4 \\ 4 & 13 \end{bmatrix}\{\underline{\hat{g}_k}\} + \frac{2}{17}\begin{bmatrix} 11 & 6 \\ 6 & 11 \end{bmatrix}\{\underline{\hat{g}_x}\}$$
$$(4.4.5)$$

We can, therefore, ascertain, as we have stated at the end of paragraph 4.3, that the differences between the effects of wage-push, capacity-pull and spending-pull are now larger than they were in the macroeconomy. The relative similarity between wage-push and capacity-pull, for instance, has now partly disappeared. The macrostructure ultimately acquired is identical to the example in Chapter II.

Because of the differences existing between them, we will now discuss briefly the consequences of respectively, a one-time wage-push, a one-time capacity-pull and a one-time spending-pull, which all took place unilaterally in region A in period 1.

The list of coefficients, used in the following examples as well, can be found in Chapter II. In addition, we have used:

$$\eta_w = \frac{17}{10}, \quad \psi_w = \frac{1}{2} \text{ and } \tilde{\mu} = \frac{1}{2}.$$

Table 4.4.1   One-time wage-push of 1% in region A in period 1

$t \rightarrow$	1	2	3	4	5	6	average
Region A							
Push $\hat{\underline{w}}_A$	1	0	0	0	0	0	0
F.E. $\check{w}_A$	$\frac{28}{17}$	0	$-\frac{6}{17}$	0	$\frac{28}{17}$	0	$\frac{11}{34}$
1. $\check{r}_A = -\frac{\lambda_0}{\kappa}\check{w}_A + \frac{\mu_0\psi_w}{\kappa}(\check{w}_A - \check{w}_B)$	$-\frac{2}{5}$	0	$\frac{2}{5}$	0	$-\frac{2}{5}$	0	0
2. $g_{KA} = g_{KA-1} + \sigma_R \check{r}_{A-2}$	0	0	$-\frac{2}{5}$	$-\frac{2}{5}$	0	0	$-\frac{1}{5}$
3. $g_{LA} = \frac{1}{\beta}\check{w}_A - \frac{1}{\beta}\underline{\check{w}}_A$	$\frac{22}{85}$	$-\frac{34}{85}$	$-\frac{46}{85}$	$-\frac{34}{85}$	$\frac{22}{85}$	$-\frac{34}{85}$	$-\frac{23}{85}$
4. $g_{yA} = \lambda_0 g_{LA} + (1-\lambda_0)g_{KA} + \lambda_0\check{w}_A + \kappa\check{r}_{A-1} + s_{uA}$	$\frac{66}{85}$	$-\frac{102}{85}$	$-\frac{70}{85}$	$-\frac{34}{85}$	$\frac{66}{85}$	$-\frac{102}{85}$	$-\frac{35}{85}$
5. $s_{bA} = g_{KA} - g_{yA}$	$-\frac{66}{85}$	$\frac{102}{85}$	$\frac{36}{85}$	0	$-\frac{66}{85}$	$\frac{102}{85}$	$\frac{16}{85}$

Table 4.4.1 (continued)

$t \rightarrow$	1	2	3	4	5	6	average
Region B							
F.E. $\breve{w}_B$	$\frac{6}{17}$	0	$-\frac{28}{17}$	0	$\frac{6}{17}$	0	$-\frac{11}{34}$
1. $\breve{r}_B$	$-\frac{2}{5}$	0	$\frac{2}{5}$	0	$-\frac{2}{5}$	0	0
2. g_{k_B}	0	0	$-\frac{2}{5}$	$-\frac{2}{5}$	0	0	$-\frac{1}{5}$
3. g_{L_B}	$+\frac{12}{85}$	0	$-\frac{56}{85}$	0	$\frac{12}{85}$	0	$-\frac{11}{85}$
4. g_{y_B}	$\frac{36}{85}$	0	$-\frac{100}{85}$	$\frac{68}{85}$	$\frac{36}{85}$	0	$\frac{1}{85}$
5. s_{b_B}	$-\frac{36}{85}$	0	$\frac{66}{85}$	$-\frac{102}{85}$	$-\frac{36}{85}$	0	$-\frac{16}{85}$
General							
1. $\breve{w}_A - \breve{w}_B$	$\frac{22}{17}$	0	$\frac{22}{17}$	0	$\frac{22}{17}$	0	$\frac{22}{34}$
2. $\breve{g}_{yA} - \breve{g}_{yB}$	$\frac{30}{85}$	$-\frac{102}{85}$	$\frac{30}{85}$	$-\frac{102}{85}$	$\frac{30}{85}$	$-\frac{102}{85}$	$-\frac{36}{85}$
3. $\breve{s}_{u_A}$	$-\frac{15}{85}$	$-\frac{1}{2}$	$-\frac{15}{85}$	$-\frac{1}{2}$	$-\frac{15}{85}$	$-\frac{1}{2}$	$-\frac{23}{68}$

4.4.1.1 *The unilateral wage-push*

The consequences of a one-time wage-push, effected in region *A* in period 1 are presented in table 4.4.1. By aggregating the corresponding variables in both regions, the results of Chapter II, table 2.4.1 can be obtained.

It is also interesting to compare these with the results of a one-time, unilateral wage-push in the integrated model in Chapter I. An important conclusion there, was that the consequences in the passive region were the exact opposite of those in the active region (with the exception of nominal wages and prices). A study of table 4.4.1 reveals that in the new model the dissimilarity in line of development (at least with regard to structure) is indeed partly continued (real wages, degree of utilisation and of course the balance of payments), but that there is no sign of this contrast in development in other aspects. The yields development and the accumulation of capital, for instance, advance in both regions under the influence of a unilateral wage-push given in one of the two, even parallel.

It is perhaps useful to elucidate the operation of the model even further by giving a detailed account of events from period to period.

Period 1

In region *A*, the wage-push causes a strong over-spending. This leads to over-employment of labour and over-utilisation of the capital goods supply. The increased demand for labour results in an increase in real wages ex-post, which exceeds the intensity of the original impulse.

The over-spending in region *A* causes the deficit on the balance of payments occurring there. A part of the over-spending is thus transferred to region *B*, where wage increases occur just as in region *A*, although to a lesser degree, as a result of the functioning of the Phillips curve.

The high wage costs in both regions are of course accompanied by yield decreases. In this case, the yield decrease is exactly the same in both regions. The wage cost increase is indeed higher in region *A* than in region *B* but this is counterbalanced by an improvement in the terms of trade.

Period 2

Period 2 is characterised by the under-spending of region *A*. This originates partly internally from the decreased yield in period 1 and partly from the negative competitive effect from period 1 which has now become active as a result of the lag in export relations. The under-spending in region *A* is accompanied by an 'equilibrium' wage level, unemployment and a deficit on current account, even larger than that in period 1, in the region itself. In *B*, all variables reach equilibrium values, except of course the current account which displays a surplus even larger than that in period 1.

Period 3
Period 3 is characterised by the (negative) labour positions cycle becoming effective for the first time. Since in period 1 the yields in both regions decreased to the same degree, the effect in both regions will be theoretically the same. Nevertheless, the slump in region *B* with regard to employment and under-spending, is more significant than in *A*, because in the latter region, given the same level of employment, wages are higher as a result of the autonomous impulse in period 1. These higher wages partly reduce the under-spending.

Period 4
Period 4 ushers in the recovery. The available capital goods supply and thus the available labour positions are indeed still low but a general recovery in spendings does occur, caused in particular by the high yields in period 3. The wage rate reaches equilibrium level; in region *A* through the autonomous element in the wage rate, and in region *B* through the relatively high spendings in region *A* as a result of which the surplus on current account remains at a high level.

Period 5
Period 5 is an exact replica of period 1 and with period 6 the cycle just described, begins again.

Summary
A one-time positive wage-push has diverging results in active and passive regions. The general climate in the active region is characterised by a lack of effective demand (caused especially by continual deficits on the balance of payments, while the passive region has a surplus effective demand (resulting here from the structural surpluses on the balance of payments).

In region *A*, real wages are high despite the under-utilisation and in region *B*, low real wages accompany the over-utilisation.

On an average, we have unemployment in both regions, although it is twice as high in the active region as in the passive region.

It is also worth of note, that the positive wage-push given in region *A* causes deterioration of the capital goods supply to the same extent in both regions.

Finally, we must point out what we consider to be an important difference from the macroeconomy. In the macroeconomy, a one-time wage-push had no structural effects on the real wage rate, but in the des-aggregated model, a one-time wage-push causes a continued increase in real wages in the active region and a corresponding decrease in wages in the passive region. The proposition that a one-time wage-push has a neutral effect on real wages applies therefore only for the regions as a community but definitely not for each region separately.

4.4.1.2 *The consumption (spending)-pull*
In this and the following paragraphs, we will not describe in detail the course of events arising after an exogenous impulse such as, for example, a positive spending-pull. We shall limit ourselves to a number of general comments. In the macroeconomy, the effects of a one-time wage-push and a one-time capacity-pull on wage developments, were identical, but this can no longer be said of unilateral impulses. The ups and downs do indeed occur at the same moment, but the amplitudes are different for each region. The difference in structural development of the real wage rate is important, however. While in the macroeconomy we could conclude that a spending-pull was important for the average value of the real wage, this is no longer the case with our integrated model;

Table 4.4.2 Consumption-pull of 1% in region A

	1	2	3	4	5	6	average
Region A							
$\check{g}_x$	1	1	1	1	1	1	1
F.E. $\check{w}$	$\frac{22}{17}$	0	$-\frac{12}{17}$	0	$\frac{22}{17}$	0	$\frac{5}{34}$
1. $\check{r}$	$-\frac{2}{5}$	0	$+\frac{2}{5}$	0	$-\frac{2}{5}$	0	0
2. g_k	0	0	$-\frac{2}{5}$	$-\frac{2}{5}$	0	0	$-\frac{1}{5}$
3. g_L	$\frac{44}{85}$	0	$-\frac{24}{85}$	0	$\frac{44}{85}$	0	$\frac{5}{85}$
4. g_y	$\frac{132}{85}$	0	$-\frac{4}{85}$	$\frac{68}{85}$	$\frac{132}{85}$	0	$\frac{49}{85}$
5. s_b	$-\frac{132}{85}$	0	$-\frac{30}{85}$	$-\frac{102}{85}$	$-\frac{132}{85}$	0	$-\frac{66}{85}$

Table 4.4.2   (continued)

	1	2	3	4	5	6	average
Region B							
F.E. $\breve{w}$	$\frac{12}{17}$	0	$-\frac{22}{17}$	0	$\frac{12}{17}$	0	$-\frac{5}{34}$
1. $\breve{r}$	$-\frac{2}{5}$	0	$\frac{2}{5}$	0	$-\frac{2}{5}$		0
2. g_k	0	0	$-\frac{2}{5}$	$-\frac{2}{5}$	0	0	$-\frac{1}{5}$
3. g_L	$\frac{24}{85}$	0	$-\frac{44}{85}$	0	$\frac{24}{85}$	0	$-\frac{5}{85}$
4. g_y	$\frac{72}{85}$	0	$-\frac{64}{85}$	$\frac{68}{85}$	$\frac{72}{85}$	0	$\frac{19}{85}$
5. s_b	$-\frac{72}{85}$	0	$\frac{30}{85}$	$-\frac{102}{85}$	$-\frac{72}{85}$	0	$-\frac{36}{85}$
General							
1. $\breve{w}_A - \breve{w}_B$	$\frac{10}{17}$	0	$\frac{10}{17}$	0	$\frac{10}{17}$	0	$\frac{5}{17}$
2. $g_{y_A} - g_{y_B}$	$\frac{60}{85}$	0	$\frac{60}{85}$	0	$\frac{60}{85}$	0	$\frac{30}{85}$
3. s_{u_A}	$-\frac{30}{85}$	$-\frac{1}{2}$	$-\frac{30}{85}$	$-\frac{1}{2}$	$-\frac{30}{85}$	$-\frac{1}{2}$	$-\frac{29}{68}$

a positive spending-pull leads to a structural wage increase in the active region whereas the passive region experiences a structural wage decrease.

We are dealing here with a distinction similar to that observed in the case of the one-time wage-push. We can comment on employment in a similar fashion.

The situation following a unilateral positive consumption-pull will be characterised by:
- overspending in both regions; in region A because of the autonomous impulse and in region B because of the presence of the surplus on current account;
- decrease in the capital goods supply because the deterioration of capital appearing in period 3 is not compensated for afterwards;
- over-utilisation of the available capital goods; in the active region to a larger and in the passive region to a lesser degree.

Once again, by reason of the above, we may conclude that a spending-pull evokes numerous tensions in the terms of production and accumulation at a number of places in the economy.

4.4.1.3 *The one-time capacity-pull*

It is striking that the capacity-pull and the wage-push (if of comparable intensity) had an identical effect on almost all variables in the macro-economy. In the des-aggregated model now at hand, this is true to a much lesser degree.

Table 4.4.3   *One-time capacity-pull of $\frac{2}{5}$% in region A in period 1*

	1	2	3	4	5	6	average
Region A							
$\hat{g}_{k_A}$	$\frac{2}{5}$	0	0	0	0	0	0
F.E. $\breve{w}_A$	$\frac{26}{17}$	0	$-\frac{8}{17}$	0	$\frac{26}{17}$	0	$\frac{9}{34}$
1. $\breve{r}_A$	$-\frac{2}{5}$	0	$\frac{2}{5}$	0	$-\frac{2}{5}$	0	0
2. g_{k_A}	$\frac{2}{5}$	$\frac{2}{5}$	0	0	$\frac{2}{5}$	$\frac{2}{5}$	$+\frac{1}{5}$
3. g_{L_A}	$\frac{52}{85}$	0	$-\frac{16}{85}$	0	$\frac{52}{85}$	0	$\frac{9}{85}$
4. g_{y_A}	$\frac{88}{85}$	$-\frac{68}{85}$	$-\frac{48}{85}$	0	$\frac{88}{85}$	$-\frac{68}{85}$	$-\frac{7}{85}$
5. s_{b_A}	$-\frac{54}{85}$	$\frac{102}{85}$	$\frac{48}{85}$	0	$-\frac{54}{85}$	$\frac{102}{85}$	$\frac{24}{85}$
Region B							
F.E. $\breve{w}_B$	$\frac{8}{17}$	0	$-\frac{26}{17}$	0	$\frac{8}{17}$	0	$-\frac{9}{34}$
1. r_B	$-\frac{2}{5}$	0	$\frac{2}{5}$	0	$-\frac{2}{5}$	0	0
2. g_{k_B}	0	0	$-\frac{2}{5}$	$-\frac{2}{5}$	0	0	$-\frac{1}{5}$
3. g_{L_B}	$\frac{16}{85}$	0	$-\frac{52}{85}$	0	$\frac{16}{85}$	0	$-\frac{9}{85}$
4. g_{y_B}	$\frac{48}{85}$	0	$-\frac{88}{85}$	$\frac{68}{85}$	$\frac{48}{85}$	0	$\frac{7}{85}$
5. s_{b_B}	$-\frac{48}{85}$	0	$\frac{54}{85}$	$-\frac{102}{85}$	$-\frac{48}{85}$	0	$-\frac{24}{85}$
General							
1. $\breve{w}_A - \breve{w}_B$	$\frac{18}{17}$	0	$\frac{18}{17}$	0	$\frac{18}{17}$	0	$\frac{9}{17}$
2. $g_{y_A} - g_{y_B}$	$\frac{46}{85}$	$-\frac{68}{85}$	$\frac{40}{85}$	$-\frac{68}{85}$	$\frac{40}{85}$	$-\frac{68}{85}$	$-\frac{14}{85}$
3. s_{u_A}	$-\frac{20}{85}$	$-\frac{1}{2}$	$-\frac{20}{85}$	$-\frac{1}{2}$	$-\frac{20}{85}$	$-\frac{1}{2}$	$-\frac{25}{68}$

While in the rest of the macroeconomy, the capacity-pull had a neutral effect in nearly all respects (at least in real terms), even a one-time capacity-pull now evokes not only a short-term business cycle fluctuation, but at the same time, important structural consequences. It may be inferred though, that the consequences referred to are, in the two regions, opposite to each other: in the active region real wage increase, in the passive region wage decrease; in the active region over-employment and over-utilisation of the capital goods supply, in region B the reverse; in region A the accumulation of capital increases while it decreases in the passive region; in the active region A a deficit on current account and of course in B the corresponding surplus.

It is interesting to compare the wage-push and the capacity-pull on these points. It strikes us immediately that under the influence of the former impulse, the contrast in development – except of course with regard to the balance on current account – concerns only the real wage rate and to a lesser extent the actual production, while the development of the other variables (accumulation of capital and employment) in the active and passive regions, although not identical, does go in the same direction. The above observations seem to require an attempt at further explanation. Model 4.2.1 provides us with the means to do this, as follows.

From equation (2) of model 4.2.1 (page 91) follows that in the case of a one-time wage-push as well as in the case of a one-time capacity-pull, the trend value of $\{\bar{r}\}$ is equal to $\{0\}$. Taking this into consideration in equation (1) it becomes immediately obvious that the real wage rates in both regions must be opposite to each other. (The yield loss caused by an excessive real internal wage is exactly counterbalanced by a positive terms of trade profit.) We can indeed find this divergent wage rate development in the foregoing tables.

From equation (4) we can easily conclude that in the case of a capacity-pull (so that in equation (4), $\{\tilde{w}\} = \{0\}$ applies), the trend values of the g_L's must also be in opposition, since there is then the same degree of proportionality between wage rate and employment development in each region.

If, however, there is a wage-push in action (so that $\{\tilde{w}\} \neq \{0\}$), the proportionality in region A which we have just mentioned, is destroyed. We can now explain why, in the case of a unilateral wage-push, despite the opposite wage rate development in both regions, a similar employment development (and accumulation of capital) exists.

Problems of employment and income policy which we have discussed in detail in previous chapters, can now be treated in a similar way. (We have confined ourselves to problems of employment solely because of the limited space available.)

There are, however, from the des-aggregated point of view, some additional problems to be solved. Firstly, policy objectives will have to be specified per region. It is once again of importance to consider if it is in fact possible for each region to follow its own separate policy in order to realise its own objectives, without interfering with the course of events in the other regions. If this does not as a rule appear to be possible, then counter-measures can be expected. An escalation of action and reaction may then follow, which can only result in chaos and inexpediency.

Whether or not an inter-regional or international policy coordination is desirable depends of course on the answer to this, and similar questions. However, we consider it permissible to conclude in advance that in view of the different possible interpretations of the concept stability (see paragraph 1.4), 'co-ordination' will have to mean more than a policy which is imitative and has the same aims in all regions.

A further comment is that realisation of internal and external equilibrium within a region does not, by itself, give sufficient guarantees for the inter-regional neutrality of the measures taken. It is conceivable, for example, that the external equilibrium has been stabilised upon a higher/lower level of imports and exports, so that the passive region is confronted by an altered structural datum, involving all the consequences outlined in Chapter III.

The problems already discussed, show a clear affinity with the problems of the macroeconomy. However, problems which apply specifically to the regional economy also exist. Of these, we shall be dealing with the forced re-allocation of production means from one region to another.

Such problems are extremely urgent in the Netherlands at the present time, and are also becoming more pronounced within the Common Market countries. We are perhaps justified in concluding that our views are supported empirically more in the situation in Europe as a whole than in the situation in the Netherlands, since more clear-cut differences exist among wage determination in the different members of the Common Market than among the economic regions within the Netherlands.

4.5.1 *Employment policy*

Assume that an increase in employment in region A is aimed at, whereby the level of employment in region B must remain constant. Assume also that the business cycle should hereby remain stable. We must immediately distinguish two important facts:

A. The cyclical stabilisation is achieved by the active region A itself.

B. Region A takes measures to obtain its structural objective, but region B, confronted not only by the cyclical, but also by the structural side effects of A's actions, attempts to avoid these by counter-actions, regardless of whether these are effective or not.

A. *Cyclical stabilisation by region A*

It is at first possible for A to increase its employment level in the long run by applying each of the three instruments.

Table 4.5.1   Employment policy: partial stabilisation by A

a. *one-time negative wage-push in region A of* -1%
b. *one-time positive capacity-pull in region A of* $\frac{2}{5}\%$
c. *total of a and b*

	$t \rightarrow$	1	2	3	4	5	6	average
Region A								
g_{L_A}	a	$-\frac{22}{85}$	$+\frac{34}{85}$	$+\frac{46}{85}$	$+\frac{34}{85}$	$-\frac{22}{85}$	$\frac{34}{85}$	$\frac{23}{85}$
	b	$\frac{52}{85}$	0	$-\frac{16}{85}$	0	$\frac{52}{85}$	0	$\frac{9}{85}$
	c	$\frac{30}{85}$	$\frac{34}{85}$	$\frac{30}{85}$	$\frac{34}{85}$	$\frac{30}{85}$	$\frac{34}{85}$	$\frac{32}{85}$
$S_{u_A} = -S_{u_B}$	a	$\frac{15}{85}$	$\frac{1}{2}$	$\frac{15}{85}$	$\frac{1}{2}$	$\frac{15}{85}$	$\frac{1}{2}$	$\frac{23}{68}$
	b	$-\frac{20}{85}$	$-\frac{1}{2}$	$-\frac{20}{85}$	$-\frac{1}{2}$	$-\frac{20}{85}$	$-\frac{1}{2}$	$-\frac{25}{68}$
	c	$-\frac{5}{85}$	0	$-\frac{5}{85}$	0	$-\frac{5}{85}$	0	$-\frac{2}{68}$
Region B								
g_{L_B}	a	$-\frac{12}{85}$	0	$-\frac{56}{85}$	0	$-\frac{12}{85}$	0	$\frac{11}{85}$
	b	$\frac{16}{85}$	0	$-\frac{52}{85}$	0	$\frac{16}{85}$	0	$-\frac{9}{85}$
	c	$\frac{4}{85}$	0	$\frac{4}{85}$	0	$\frac{4}{85}$	0	$\frac{2}{85}$

Table 4.5.1 illustrates the situation in which region A attempts to increase employment according to the principles of macroeconomics; a negative one-time wage-push for the employment effect and a positive capacity-pull to counteract the induced cyclical instability.

We can conclude that the set objective can be largely achieved by using the correct combination of both these instruments. Employment in region A increases, because of both wage-push and capacity-pull and the cyclical movement is subdued to a large extent because of the 'similarity' of capacity-pull and wage-push. Moreover, the employment acquired as a result of the negative wage-push in region B is largely lost as a result of the capacity-pull. We may conclude that although the measures taken by A have almost the same results, the combination of instruments used is not 100% satisfactory, since we are left with a small degree of over-employment in the passive region and a structural shortage on the balance of payments in the active region A.

The question then arises if it is possible to have a combination of instruments for one region which not only achieves the proposed employment objective in region A but also ensures that no tension appears either from a cyclical or a structural point of view.

This question must be answered in the affirmative. The results of table 4.5.1 indicate the answer. The reason for the remaining disequilibrium is of course the (small) structural demand surplus in region A. It is however possible to eliminate the demand shortage induced by the negative wage-push, both cyclically and structurally, by using a correctly balanced combination of capacity-pull and spending-pull. A comparison of the results in relation to the balance of payments, using tables 4.4.1–4.4.3, shows that the above can occur if a factor of $\frac{3}{2}$ is used for the capacity-pull and a factor of $-\frac{1}{2}$ for the spending-pull.

This view is applied in table 4.5.2 in which an equilibrium employment policy is outlined.

We can conclude, that an equilibrium employment policy can be realised by one single region without causing either cyclical or structural disturbances within the activities of the trade partners.

The only aspect that could possibly cause tensions is if the actual production in region A remains unchanged, although employment has increased. This implies of course a decrease in the actual average productivity of labour.

Table 4.5.2 Employment policy: complete stabilisation of the negative wage-push

a. negative one-time wage-push of 1% in region A
b. positive capacity-pull of $\frac{3}{5}$% in region A
c. negative consumption-pull of $-\frac{1}{2}$% in region A
d. total

$t \rightarrow$		1	2	3	4	5	6	average
Region A								
$\breve{w}_A$	a	$-\frac{28}{17}$	0	$\frac{6}{17}$	0	$-\frac{28}{17}$	0	$-\frac{11}{34}$
	b	$\frac{39}{17}$	0	$-\frac{12}{17}$	0	$\frac{39}{17}$	0	$\frac{29}{68}$
	c	$-\frac{11}{17}$	0	$-\frac{6}{17}$	0	$-\frac{11}{17}$	0	$-\frac{5}{68}$
	d	0	0	0	0	0	0	0
g_{L_A}	a	$-\frac{22}{85}$	$\frac{34}{85}$	$+\frac{46}{85}$	$\frac{34}{85}$	$-\frac{22}{85}$	$\frac{34}{85}$	$\frac{23}{85}$
	b	$\frac{78}{85}$	0	$-\frac{24}{85}$	0	$\frac{78}{85}$	0	$\frac{27}{170}$
	c	$-\frac{22}{85}$	0	$\frac{12}{85}$	0	$-\frac{22}{85}$	0	$-\frac{5}{170}$
	d	$\frac{34}{85}$	$\frac{34}{85}$	$\frac{34}{85}$	$\frac{34}{85}$	$\frac{34}{85}$	$\frac{34}{85}$	$\frac{34}{85}$
g_{y_A}	a	$-\frac{66}{85}$	$\frac{102}{85}$	$\frac{70}{85}$	$\frac{34}{85}$	$-\frac{66}{85}$	$\frac{102}{85}$	$\frac{35}{85}$
	b	$\frac{132}{85}$	$-\frac{102}{85}$	$\frac{72}{85}$	0	$\frac{132}{85}$	$-\frac{102}{85}$	$\frac{21}{170}$
	c	$-\frac{66}{85}$	0	$-\frac{2}{85}$	$-\frac{34}{85}$	$-\frac{66}{85}$	0	$-\frac{24}{170}$
	d	0	0	0	0	0	0	0
Region B								
$\breve{w}_B$	a	$-\frac{6}{17}$	0	$\frac{28}{17}$	0	$-\frac{6}{17}$	0	$\frac{11}{34}$
	b	$\frac{12}{17}$	0	$-\frac{39}{17}$	0	$\frac{12}{17}$	0	$-\frac{27}{68}$
	c	$-\frac{6}{17}$	0	$\frac{11}{17}$	0	$-\frac{6}{17}$	0	$\frac{5}{68}$
	d	0	0	0	0	0	0	0

Table 4.5.2   (continued)

	t→	1	2	3	4	5	6	*average*
g_{L_B}	a	$-\frac{12}{85}$	0	$\frac{56}{85}$	0	$-\frac{12}{85}$	0	$\frac{11}{85}$
	b	$\frac{24}{85}$	0	$-\frac{78}{85}$	0	$\frac{24}{85}$	0	$-\frac{27}{170}$
	c	$-\frac{62}{85}$	0	$\frac{22}{85}$	0	$-\frac{12}{85}$	0	$\frac{5}{170}$
	d	0	0	0	0	0	0	0
g_y	a	$-\frac{36}{85}$	0	$\frac{100}{85}$	$-\frac{68}{85}$	$-\frac{36}{85}$	0	$-\frac{1}{85}$
	b	$\frac{72}{85}$	0	$-\frac{132}{85}$	$\frac{102}{85}$	$\frac{72}{85}$	0	$\frac{21}{170}$
	c	$-\frac{36}{85}$	0	$\frac{32}{85}$	$-\frac{34}{85}$	$-\frac{36}{85}$	0	$-\frac{19}{170}$
	d	0	0	0	0	0	0	0
$s_{u_A} = -s_{u_B}$	a	$\frac{15}{85}$	$\frac{1}{2}$	$\frac{15}{85}$	$\frac{1}{2}$	$\frac{15}{85}$	$\frac{1}{2}$	$\frac{23}{68}$
	b	$-\frac{30}{85}$	$-\frac{3}{4}$	$-\frac{30}{85}$	$-\frac{3}{4}$	$-\frac{30}{85}$	$-\frac{5}{4}$	$-\frac{75}{136}$
	c	$\frac{15}{85}$	$\frac{1}{4}$	$\frac{15}{85}$	$\frac{1}{4}$	$\frac{15}{85}$	$\frac{1}{4}$	$\frac{29}{136}$
	d	0	0	0	0	0	0	0

B. *Employment policy in region A: neutralisation in region B*

We shall now assume that region A is aiming at a long-term increase in employment of $\frac{23}{85}$%. Table 4.4.1 indicates that such a structural change can be effected by the unilateral application of a one-time wage-push of 1% in period 1.

If the alternative region then fails to redress the cyclical and structural effects of its actions, then the question arises if region B can successfully defend itself against the consequences of A's actions. A second problem is the possibility of B's resistance, interfering in turn with the objectives of A's policy.

When dealing with these questions, we shall distinguish between a structural and a cyclical aspect.

We shall begin with the structural aspect. Using tables 4.4.1–4.4.3 we can calculate that region B can eliminate the structural consequences of a one-time negative wage-push by applying:

– a one-time negative capacity-pull of $-\frac{20}{21} \times \frac{2}{5}$%.

108

- a one-time positive wage-push of $\frac{2}{21}\times1\%$.
- a one-time negative consumption-pull of $-\frac{1}{21}\times1\%$.

If region B operates according to this scheme, a structural development arises, such as is reproduced in table 4.5.3.

We can conclude from table 4.5.3 that it is indeed possible for B to cope successfully with the consequences of A's intervention (at least from a structural point of view). If B uses the proposed combination of measures, then an equilibrium capital goods supply and equilibrium employment in region B arise while the equilibrium on current account is maintained.

Table 4.5.3 Structural consequences of:

a. one-time negative wage-push in region A of -1%
b. one-time negative capacity-pull in region B of $-\frac{20}{21}\times\frac{2}{5}\%$
c. negative spending-pull in region B of $\frac{1}{21}\times1\%$
d. one-time positive wage-push in region B of $\frac{2}{21}\times1\%$
e. total

Structural consequences for:		$\breve{w}$	g_k	g_L	S_u
Region A	a	$-\frac{11}{34}$	$\frac{1}{5}$	$\frac{23}{85}$	$\frac{23}{68}$
	b	$\frac{20}{21}\cdot\frac{9}{34}$	$\frac{20}{21}\cdot\frac{1}{5}$	$\frac{20}{21}\cdot\frac{9}{85}$	$-\frac{20}{21}\cdot\frac{25}{68}$
	c	$\frac{1}{21}\cdot\frac{5}{34}$	$\frac{1}{21}\cdot\frac{1}{5}$	$\frac{1}{21}\cdot\frac{5}{85}$	$-\frac{1}{21}\cdot\frac{29}{68}$
	d	$-\frac{2}{21}\cdot\frac{11}{34}$	$-\frac{2}{21}\cdot\frac{1}{5}$	$-\frac{2}{21}\cdot\frac{11}{85}$	$\frac{2}{21}\cdot\frac{23}{68}$
Total	e	$-\frac{68}{714}$	$\frac{40}{105}$	$\frac{646}{1785}$	0
Region B	a	$\frac{11}{34}$	$\frac{1}{5}$	$\frac{11}{85}$	$-\frac{23}{68}$
	b	$-\frac{20}{21}\cdot\frac{9}{34}$	$-\frac{20}{21}\cdot\frac{1}{5}$	$-\frac{20}{21}\cdot\frac{9}{85}$	$\frac{20}{21}\cdot\frac{25}{68}$
	c	$-\frac{1}{21}\cdot\frac{5}{34}$	$\frac{1}{21}\cdot\frac{1}{5}$	$-\frac{1}{21}\cdot\frac{5}{85}$	$\frac{1}{21}\cdot\frac{29}{68}$
	d	$\frac{2}{21}\cdot\frac{11}{34}$	$-\frac{2}{21}\cdot\frac{1}{5}$	$-\frac{2}{21}\cdot\frac{23}{85}$	$-\frac{2}{21}\cdot\frac{23}{68}$
Total	e	$\frac{68}{714}$	0	0	0

The counter-measures in region B do not interfere with A's policy. On the contrary, the creation of employment in region A which is a direct result of B's actions is hereafter the same size as the creation of employment resulting from A's own intervention. B's resistance thus plays right into A's hands, with regard to the desired creation of employment.

It may also be concluded that the required counter-measures are aimed more at 'keeping in step' than providing counter-pressure since the main element in the combination of defence measures is a *negative* capacity-pull in B as a reaction to an also *negative* wage-push in A.

We will leave the structural aspect for a moment to devote a few lines to the cyclical stability. It can be proved that the indicated combination of policy measures, if precisely timed, is sufficient to neutralise not only the structural consequences but the cyclical as well.

In table 4.5.4 we have not attempted to achieve perfection regarding this but have investigated the consequences of the combination of a one-time negative wage-push in region A (the employment policy) and the most important stabilisation instrument for region B as a reaction to this: a negative capacity-pull. It appears then that an almost complete stabilisation of the business cycle can thus be obtained with almost a structural equilibrium for all important variables of the economy. Timing must of course be precise: the negative capacity-pull in B must succeed the negative wage-push of region A, with a delay of two periods.

We note that the creation of labour positions in region A is partly debited to its wage-earners (decrease in the real wage-rate) but on the other hand we see an improvement in labour as a group, since the increased demand for labour more than compensates for the decrease in real wages.

It is worth mentioning that the decreased real wage-rate in region A is accompanied by an increase of that quantity in region B, while in this latter region the employment (in table 4.5.4 almost) remains constant, so that the factor labour in region B profits from the increased employment in region A.

To conclude this paragraph we will comment briefly on the political attainability of the measures presented in table 4.5.4.

We may assume that a policy will be more inclined to win approval if the expected short-term effects are less unfavourable. If a negative wage-push is applied, these effects are very unfavourable: in the active region A, not only does the wage rate fall even further than the autonomous impulse of -1%, because of the relevant multiplier but a severe decrease in employment must also be expected in the first period.

It is possible however to spread the burden of the policy rather more simply among the regions: for this purpose, a positive capacity-pull

110

Table 4.5.4 Partial stabilisation by region B

a. one-time negative wage-push of -1% in region A in period 1
b. one-time positive capacity-pull of $-\frac{2}{5}\%$ in region B in period 3

		1	2	3	4	5	6	average
Region A								
$\breve{w}_A$	a	$-\frac{28}{17}$	0	$+\frac{6}{17}$	0	$-\frac{28}{17}$	0	$-\frac{11}{34}$
	b	—	—	$-\frac{8}{17}$	0	$+\frac{26}{17}$	0	$+\frac{9}{34}$
	Total	$-\frac{28}{17}$	0	$-\frac{2}{17}$	0	$-\frac{2}{17}$	0	$-\frac{1}{17}$
g_{K_A}	a	0	0	$+\frac{2}{5}$	$+\frac{2}{5}$	0	0	$+\frac{1}{5}$
	b	—	—	0	0	$+\frac{2}{5}$	$+\frac{2}{5}$	$+\frac{1}{5}$
	Total	0	0	$+\frac{2}{5}$	$+\frac{2}{5}$	$+\frac{2}{5}$	$+\frac{2}{5}$	$+\frac{2}{5}$
g_{L_A}	a	$-\frac{22}{85}$	$+\frac{34}{85}$	$+\frac{46}{85}$	$+\frac{34}{85}$	$-\frac{22}{85}$	$+\frac{34}{85}$	$+\frac{23}{85}$
	b	—	—	$-\frac{16}{85}$	0	$+\frac{52}{85}$	0	$+\frac{9}{85}$
	Total	$-\frac{22}{85}$	$+\frac{34}{85}$	$+\frac{30}{85}$	$+\frac{34}{85}$	$+\frac{30}{85}$	$+\frac{34}{85}$	$+\frac{32}{85}$
s_{u_A}	a	$+\frac{15}{85}$	$+\frac{1}{2}$	$+\frac{15}{85}$	$+\frac{1}{2}$	$+\frac{15}{85}$	$+\frac{1}{2}$	$+\frac{23}{68}$
	b	—	—	$-\frac{20}{85}$	$-\frac{1}{2}$	$-\frac{20}{85}$	$-\frac{1}{2}$	$-\frac{25}{68}$
	Total	$+\frac{15}{85}$	$+\frac{1}{2}$	$-\frac{5}{85}$	0	$-\frac{5}{85}$	0	$-\frac{1}{34}$
Region B								
$\breve{w}_B$	a	$-\frac{6}{17}$	0	$+\frac{28}{17}$	0	$-\frac{6}{17}$	0	$+\frac{11}{34}$
	b	—	—	$-\frac{26}{17}$	0	$+\frac{8}{17}$	0	$-\frac{9}{34}$
	Total	$-\frac{6}{17}$	0	$+\frac{2}{17}$	0	$+\frac{2}{17}$	0	$+\frac{1}{17}$
g_{K_B}	a	0	0	$+\frac{2}{5}$	$+\frac{2}{5}$	0	0	$+\frac{1}{5}$
	b	—	—	$-\frac{2}{5}$	$-\frac{2}{5}$	0	0	$-\frac{1}{5}$
	Total	0	0	0	0	0	0	0

Table 4.5.4   (continued)

		1	2	3	4	5	6	average
g_{L_B}	a	$-\frac{12}{85}$	0	$+\frac{56}{85}$	0	$-\frac{12}{85}$	0	$+\frac{11}{85}$
	b	—	—	$-\frac{52}{85}$	0	$+\frac{16}{85}$	0	$-\frac{9}{85}$
	Total	$-\frac{12}{85}$	0	$+\frac{4}{85}$	0	$+\frac{4}{85}$	0	$+\frac{2}{85}$
s_{u_B}	a	$-\frac{15}{85}$	$-\frac{1}{2}$	$-\frac{15}{85}$	$-\frac{1}{2}$	$-\frac{15}{85}$	$-\frac{1}{2}$	$-\frac{23}{68}$
	b	—	—	$+\frac{20}{85}$	$+\frac{1}{2}$	$+\frac{20}{85}$	$+\frac{1}{2}$	$+\frac{25}{68}$
	Total	$-\frac{15}{85}$	$-\frac{1}{2}$	$+\frac{5}{85}$	0	$+\frac{5}{85}$	0	$+\frac{1}{34}$

should be given (for example, in the form of a gift of capital goods) accompanied by a negative spending-pull.

An increase in employment in region A will thus be obtained, as early as period 1. The measures we have indicated must be annulled after a time; in period 3 in fact. This has been elaborated in a concrete fashion in table 4.5.5. The specific measures are shown to have a virtually neutral effect, except in period 1.

Table 4.5.5

a. one-time positive capacity-pull in region A of $\frac{2}{5}\%$ in period 1
b. one-time negative consumption-pull in region A of -1% in period 1
c. total of a and b
d. the reverse of c from period 3
e. total of c and a

		1	2	3	4	5	6	average
Region A								
$\breve{w}_A$	a	$\frac{26}{17}$	0	$-\frac{8}{17}$	0	$\frac{26}{17}$	0	$\frac{9}{34}$
	b	$-\frac{22}{17}$	0	$\frac{12}{17}$	0	$-\frac{22}{17}$	0	$-\frac{5}{34}$
	c	$\frac{4}{17}$	0	$\frac{4}{17}$	0	$\frac{4}{17}$	0	$\frac{4}{34}$
	d	—	—	$\frac{4}{17}$	0	$-\frac{4}{17}$	0	$-\frac{4}{34}$
	e	$\frac{4}{17}$	0	0	0	0	0	0

Table 4.5.5 (continued)

		1	2	3	4	5	6	average
g_{L_A}	a	$\frac{52}{85}$	0	$-\frac{16}{85}$	0	$\frac{52}{85}$	0	$\frac{9}{85}$
	b	$-\frac{44}{85}$	0	$\frac{24}{85}$	0	$-\frac{44}{85}$	0	$-\frac{5}{85}$
	c	$\frac{8}{85}$	0	$\frac{8}{85}$	0	$\frac{8}{85}$	0	$\frac{4}{85}$
	d	—	—	$-\frac{8}{85}$	0	$-\frac{8}{85}$	0	$-\frac{4}{85}$
	e	$\frac{8}{85}$	0	0	0	0	0	0
S_{u_A}	a	$-\frac{20}{85}$	$-\frac{1}{2}$	$-\frac{20}{85}$	$-\frac{1}{2}$	$-\frac{20}{85}$	$-\frac{1}{2}$	$-\frac{25}{68}$
	b	$\frac{30}{85}$	$\frac{1}{2}$	$\frac{30}{85}$	$\frac{1}{2}$	$\frac{30}{85}$	$\frac{1}{2}$	$\frac{29}{68}$
	c	$\frac{10}{85}$	0	$\frac{10}{85}$	0	$\frac{10}{85}$	0	$\frac{4}{68}$
	d	—	—	$-\frac{10}{85}$	0	$-\frac{10}{85}$	0	$-\frac{4}{68}$
	e	$\frac{10}{85}$	0	0	0	0	0	0

Region B

		1	2	3	4	5	6	average
$\check{w}_B$	a	$\frac{8}{17}$	0	$-\frac{26}{17}$	0	$\frac{8}{17}$	0	$-\frac{9}{34}$
	b	$-\frac{12}{17}$	0	$\frac{22}{17}$	0	$-\frac{12}{17}$	0	$\frac{5}{34}$
	c	$-\frac{4}{17}$	0	$-\frac{4}{17}$	0	$-\frac{4}{17}$	0	$-\frac{4}{34}$
	d	—	—	$\frac{4}{17}$	0	$\frac{4}{17}$	0	$\frac{4}{34}$
	e	$-\frac{4}{17}$	0	0	0	0	0	0
g_{L_B}	a	$\frac{16}{85}$	0	$-\frac{52}{85}$	0	$\frac{16}{85}$	0	$-\frac{9}{85}$
	b	$-\frac{24}{85}$	0	$\frac{44}{85}$	0	$-\frac{24}{85}$	0	$\frac{5}{85}$
	c	$-\frac{8}{85}$	0	$-\frac{8}{85}$	0	$-\frac{8}{85}$	0	$-\frac{4}{85}$
	d	—	—	$\frac{8}{85}$	0	$\frac{8}{85}$	0	$\frac{4}{85}$
	e	$-\frac{8}{85}$	0	0	0	0	0	0

The resulting unemployment in region B can present a problem. It is however possible that B considers itself united with A with regard to the pursuit of objectives, so that *B* could accept the sacrifice of the unemployment as being rational.

4.5.2 *Some further comments*

In the previous paragraph we obtained some probably surprising results relating to the inter-regional (international) employment (or rather the reallocation policy of the means of production in a broader sense). These deserve further comment.

In both cases we have observed, a policy of low wages in the region where employment (and accumulation of capital) had to be stimulated was an important, necessary element of the general policy. This is not surprising in a theoretical context, where profitability is the explanatory variable for investment.

However, the matter is not done with yet, not only because an isolated wage-push would result in less desired cyclical phenomena, but even more because of the structural side effects:
1. a surplus on current account of the active region (in both current and constant prices);
2. over-employment in the passive region *B* where the basic equilibrium situation was regarded as the most desirable in our hypotheses.

There is also a striking resemblance between compensating policies in the case where the active region *A* is itself responsible for a development which approaches the equilibrium as much as possible, c.q. where *A* relies on *B* to redress the structural and cyclical disturbances in the equilibrium induced by the wage-push. That is to say, in both these cases the essence of the neutralisation policy is: a one-time capacity-pull 'in favour' of the region in which employment has to be increased.

In both cases, the capacity-pull does strengthen in fact the effect of the low wage policy in the region where this is desired, while on the other hand the undesired structural side effect of the wage policy in region *A*, regarding employment and the balance of payments in *B* is eliminated.

The central point in this conclusion is of course the characteristic of the model that a given one-time wage-push in one of the regions has a similar effect in both regions with regard to the allocation of the production factors; while the effect of a unilateral one-time capacity-pull in one region is exactly the opposite to that in the other region. A further explanation of this difference between the effects of wage-push and capacity-pull can be found in par. 4.4.1.3.

114

V. Separate labour markets: the significance of the regional supply balance

5.1 INTRODUCTION

Our basic assumptions in this chapter are exactly the same as in Chapter IV, except for the import and export equations, where we have replaced the η- and $\tilde{\mu}$-mechanisms by the ω-mechanism. We shall see that this has far-reaching consequences for the cyclical functioning of the system in particular and more especially for the length of the cycle.

5.2 THE RELATIONS

In the matrix and vector notations we now obtain for the balance on current account:

$$\{s_u\} = (1 - \omega) \begin{bmatrix} 1 & -1 \\ -1 & 1 \end{bmatrix} \{g_k - g_x\} \qquad (5.2.1)$$

The equation for the actual production is:

$$\{g_y\} = \begin{bmatrix} \omega & 1-\omega \\ 1-\omega & \omega \end{bmatrix} \{g_x\} + (1 - \omega) \begin{bmatrix} 1 & -1 \\ -1 & 1 \end{bmatrix} \{g_k\} \qquad (5.2.2)$$

Subsequently we introduce:

$$[\Omega] = \begin{bmatrix} \omega & 1-\omega \\ 1-\omega & \omega \end{bmatrix} \qquad (5.2.3)$$

so that for (5.2.2) we obtain the following manageable form:

$$\{g_y\} = [\Omega] \{g_x\} + [I - \Omega] \{g_k\} \qquad (5.2.4)$$

115

The further specification of the demand for labour function is simple and, on the familiar condition that:

$$\tilde{\alpha}_{y_i} + \tilde{\alpha}_{k_i} = 1 \quad (i = A, B)$$

reads as follows:

$$\{g_L\} = \{g_k\} + [(\hat{\alpha}_y \lambda_0) M_l \Omega] \{w - w_{-1}\} \tag{5.2.5}$$

(We ignore all price effects. $\{\check{r}\} = -(\lambda_0/k)\{\check{w}\}$ is taken to be the yield function.)

It must be borne in mind, however, that the employment multiplier M_l is now a (square) matrix and resembles the macro-multiplier only formally.

The relevant algebraic formula reads as follows:

$$[M_l] = [I - (\hat{\alpha}_y \lambda_0^\Omega \dots \lambda_0 \Omega)]^{-1} \tag{5.2.6}$$

Summarising, we obtain the following model, including the autonomous impulses.

Model 5.2.1   Basic model IV

$$\{\check{r}\} = \left(-\frac{\lambda_0}{\kappa}\right)\{\check{w}\} \tag{1}$$

$$\{g_k\} = \{g_{k_{-1}}\} + (\sigma_R)\{\check{r}_{-2}\} + \{\hat{g}_k\} \tag{2}$$

$$\{g_L\} = \{g_k\} + [(\hat{\alpha}_y \lambda_0) M_l \Omega]\{w - w_{-1}\} + |\hat{\alpha}_y M_l \Omega|\{\underline{\check{g}}_x\} \tag{3}$$

$$\{w\} = (\beta)\{g_L\} + \{\check{w}\} \tag{4}$$

N.B. As well as the volume-balance of the balance of payments, an important distinction from Chapter IV is that the relation with prices has now been severed. This new model is completely dominated by effective demand and degree of utilisation.

5.3 THE SOLUTION OF THE MODEL

The most important results are:

$$[A_0] = [I - (\beta\hat{\alpha}_y\lambda_0) M_l \Omega]$$
$$[A_1] = [I - 2(\beta\hat{\alpha}_y\lambda_0) M_l \Omega]$$
$$[A_2] = \left[\left(\beta\sigma \frac{\lambda_0}{\kappa}\right) - (\beta\hat{\sigma}_y\lambda_0) M_l \Omega\right] \tag{5.3.1}$$

116

The final equation in the matrix notation is (taking into account the definitions (5.3.1)):

$$[A_0] \{w\} - [A_1] \{w_{-1}\} + [A_2] \{w_{-2}\} =$$
$$= \{\hat{w}\} + (\beta) \{\hat{g}_k\} + [\beta \hat{a}_y M_l \Omega] \{\hat{g}_x\} \qquad (5.3.2)$$

As in the macroeconomy of Chapter II, we define a (matrix) wage multiplier in the form:

$$(M_w) = [A_0]^{-1} = [1 - \beta \hat{a}_y \lambda_0 M_l \Omega]^{-1} \qquad (5.3.3)$$

5.4 DESCRIPTION OF THE BUSINESS CYCLE

5.4.1 *Introduction*

As in Chapter I, the cyclical movements, which arise under the influence of, respectively, an autonomous wage development, a capacity-pull and a spending-pull, differ to a not unimportant extent. As may be expected on the grounds of the basic model of Chapter II (since the macrostructure of the new model is identical to this model), the one-time wage-push and one-time capacity-pull exhibit a certain degree of similarity, while the results of the one-time spending-pull differ greatly from them. In this respect, the new model deviates significantly from that of Chapter IV. Only the most characteristic difference will be indicated here i.e. the diffusion effect previously discussed in par. 1.4.3 which characterises the spending impulse in contrast to the wage-push and capacity-pull.

The above provides us with a motive for treating the wage- and capacity-pulls together in the descriptive analysis of the one-time (instrumental) impulses which now follows. A separate sub-paragraph will be devoted to the spending impulse.

Moreover, the cyclical movement in this new model is no longer as simple as in the macroeconomy, and also somewhat more complicated than in the integral model of Chapter IV. The reason for this is that the new two-region model is characterised by more eigenvalues than we have previously had. For this reason the total cyclical movement is made up of four different components.

It is therefore not surprising that it generally takes longer to complete a full business cycle than it does in the macroeconomy.

In order to maintain a link with the foregoing, we have used the structural parameters of Chapter II, slightly enlarged by a number of parameters describing inter-regional contacts, i.e. μ_0 and ω.

The complete list of quantitative values of the data is:

$$\tilde{\alpha}_k = \tfrac{2}{3} \qquad \tilde{\alpha}_y = \tfrac{1}{3} \qquad \beta = \tfrac{5}{2} \qquad \tilde{\gamma}_L = 1 \qquad \tilde{\gamma}_R = 0 \qquad \delta = \tfrac{2}{3}$$

$$\varepsilon = 1 \qquad \kappa = \tfrac{5}{4} \qquad \lambda_0 = \tfrac{1}{2} \qquad \mu_0 = \tfrac{1}{2} \qquad \omega = \tfrac{1}{2}$$

In the new model, the cyclical situation is characterised by two things; the spendings situation and the labour positions situation. Insufficient ex ante spendings have their negative effect on the demand for labour and subsequently, through the supply relation on the supply market, on wages. A shortage of available labour positions is also accompanied by a certain initial wage depressing effect. We can therefore regard the total cyclical movement as being composed of a labour positions component and a spending component (this has already been touched on in Chapters II and III). It is useful to remember this distinction, because of the relative complexity of the cyclical movement we are to describe. It has at least given us a greater understanding of the matter as a whole. The distinction we have made is also of practical significance, because an undesired cyclical development can only be properly withstood after it has been determined whether the causes of a decline for instance can be found within labour positions or within spendings.

5.4.2 *The wage-push and the capacity-pull*

The results of a one-time wage-push and capacity-pull are summarised in tables 5.4.1 and 5.4.2. In table 5.4.1, the results are calculated for unilateral impulses, i.e. impulses initiated in one region only (region A). In table 5.4.2, we see the situation that arises if the impulses are given in both regions at the same time and to the same degree. The outcome, in that case, is of course (because of the symmetry) identical to that of the macroeconomy.

Let us firstly, however, confine ourselves to unilateral impulses. Before passing on to a detailed description of the periods, a few general remarks will be made.

We can ascertain that the cycle, compared with the macroeconomic model has become considerably longer. Although we began with the same structural parameters as those present in the numerical example produced in Chapter II, the periodicity of the model has increased, in comparison with the situation in that chapter, from 4 to no less than 12 years.

Furthermore we can deduce from the analysis given in table 5.4.1 that the consequences of a unilateral wage-push in region A are

Table 5.4.1

a. one-time wage-push in region A; b. one-time capacity-pull in region A

		1	2	3	4	5	6	7	8	9	10	11	12	13	14	average
Region A																
Push: $\breve{w}_A$	a	$\frac{1}{2}$	0	0	0	0	0	0	0	0	0	0	0	0	0	0
Pull: $\hat{g}_{k_A}$	c	$\frac{1}{5}$	0	0	0	0	0	0	0	0	0	0	0	0	0	0
F.E. $\hat{w}_A$	a c	$\frac{3}{4}$	$\frac{1}{4}$	$-\frac{2}{4}$	$-\frac{1}{4}$	$\frac{1}{4}$	0	$-\frac{1}{4}$	$\frac{1}{4}$	$\frac{2}{4}$	$-\frac{1}{4}$	$-\frac{3}{4}$	0	$\frac{3}{4}$	$\frac{1}{4}$	0
1. $\hat{r}_A$	a c	$-\frac{3}{10}$	$-\frac{1}{10}$	$\frac{2}{10}$	$\frac{1}{10}$	$-\frac{1}{10}$	0	$\frac{1}{10}$	$-\frac{1}{10}$	$-\frac{2}{10}$	$\frac{1}{10}$	$\frac{3}{10}$	0	$-\frac{3}{10}$	$-\frac{1}{10}$	0
2. g_{k_A}	a	0	0	$-\frac{3}{10}$	$-\frac{4}{10}$	$-\frac{2}{10}$	$-\frac{1}{10}$	$-\frac{2}{10}$	$-\frac{2}{10}$	$-\frac{1}{10}$	$-\frac{2}{10}$	$-\frac{4}{10}$	$-\frac{3}{10}$	0	0	$-\frac{2}{10}$
	c	$\frac{2}{10}$	$\frac{2}{10}$	$-\frac{1}{10}$	$-\frac{2}{10}$	0	$\frac{1}{10}$	0	0	$\frac{1}{10}$	0	$-\frac{2}{10}$	$-\frac{1}{10}$	$\frac{2}{10}$	$\frac{2}{10}$	0
3. g_{L_A}	a	$\frac{1}{10}$	$-\frac{1}{10}$	$-\frac{4}{10}$	$-\frac{3}{10}$	$-\frac{1}{10}$	$-\frac{2}{10}$	$-\frac{3}{10}$	$-\frac{1}{10}$	0	$-\frac{3}{10}$	$-\frac{5}{10}$	$-\frac{2}{10}$	$\frac{1}{10}$	$-\frac{1}{10}$	$-\frac{2}{10}$
	c	$\frac{3}{10}$	$\frac{1}{10}$	$-\frac{2}{10}$	$-\frac{1}{10}$	$\frac{1}{10}$	0	$-\frac{1}{10}$	$\frac{1}{10}$	$\frac{2}{10}$	$-\frac{1}{10}$	$-\frac{3}{10}$	0	$\frac{3}{10}$	$\frac{1}{10}$	0
4. g_{x_A}	a	$\frac{17}{30}$	$-\frac{12}{30}$	$-\frac{26}{30}$	$-\frac{5}{30}$	$\frac{6}{30}$	$-\frac{10}{30}$	$-\frac{13}{30}$	$\frac{6}{30}$	$\frac{4}{30}$	$-\frac{23}{30}$	$-\frac{24}{30}$	$\frac{8}{30}$	$\frac{17}{30}$	$-\frac{12}{30}$	$-\frac{6}{30}$
	c	$\frac{23}{30}$	$-\frac{6}{30}$	$-\frac{20}{30}$	$\frac{1}{30}$	$\frac{12}{30}$	$-\frac{4}{30}$	$-\frac{7}{30}$	$\frac{12}{30}$	$\frac{10}{30}$	$-\frac{17}{30}$	$-\frac{18}{30}$	$\frac{14}{30}$	$\frac{23}{30}$	$-\frac{6}{30}$	0
5. s_A	a c	$-\frac{17}{30}$	$\frac{12}{30}$	$\frac{17}{30}$	$-\frac{7}{30}$	$-\frac{12}{30}$	$\frac{7}{30}$	$\frac{7}{30}$	$-\frac{12}{30}$	$-\frac{7}{30}$	$\frac{17}{30}$	$\frac{12}{30}$	$-\frac{17}{30}$	$-\frac{17}{30}$	$\frac{12}{30}$	0

Table 5.4.1 (continued)

		1	2	3	4	5	6	7	8	9	10	11	12	13	14	average
Region A (cont.)																
6. g_{y_A}	a	$\frac{3}{10}$	$-\frac{3}{10}$	$-\frac{6}{10}$	$-\frac{1}{10}$	$\frac{1}{10}$	$-\frac{4}{10}$	$-\frac{5}{10}$	$\frac{1}{10}$	$\frac{2}{10}$	$-\frac{5}{10}$	$-\frac{7}{10}$	$\frac{0}{10}$	$\frac{3}{10}$	$-\frac{3}{10}$	$-\frac{2}{10}$
	c	$\frac{5}{10}$	$-\frac{1}{10}$	$-\frac{4}{10}$	$\frac{1}{10}$	$\frac{3}{10}$	$-\frac{2}{10}$	$-\frac{3}{10}$	$\frac{3}{10}$	$\frac{4}{10}$	$-\frac{3}{10}$	$-\frac{5}{10}$	$\frac{2}{10}$	$\frac{5}{10}$	$-\frac{1}{10}$	0
Region B																
F.E. $\check{w}_B$	a c	$\frac{1}{4}$	$-\frac{1}{4}$	$\frac{1}{4}$	$\frac{1}{4}$	$\frac{3}{4}$	0	$-\frac{3}{4}$	$-\frac{1}{4}$	$\frac{2}{4}$	$\frac{1}{4}$	$-\frac{1}{4}$	0	$\frac{1}{4}$	$-\frac{1}{4}$	0
1. $\check{r}_B$	a c	$-\frac{1}{10}$	$\frac{1}{10}$	$\frac{2}{10}$	$-\frac{1}{10}$	$-\frac{3}{10}$	0	$\frac{3}{10}$	$\frac{1}{10}$	$-\frac{2}{10}$	$-\frac{1}{10}$	$\frac{1}{10}$	0	$-\frac{1}{10}$	$\frac{1}{10}$	0
2. g_{k_B}	a c	0	0	$-\frac{1}{10}$	0	$\frac{2}{10}$	$\frac{1}{10}$	$-\frac{2}{10}$	$-\frac{2}{10}$	$\frac{1}{10}$	$\frac{2}{10}$	0	$-\frac{1}{10}$	0	0	0
3. g_{L_B}	a c	$\frac{1}{10}$	$-\frac{1}{10}$	$-\frac{2}{10}$	$\frac{1}{10}$	$\frac{3}{10}$	0	$-\frac{3}{10}$	$-\frac{1}{10}$	$\frac{2}{10}$	$\frac{1}{10}$	$-\frac{1}{10}$	0	$\frac{1}{10}$	$-\frac{1}{10}$	0
4. g_{x_B}	a c	$\frac{7}{30}$	$-\frac{12}{30}$	$-\frac{10}{30}$	$\frac{17}{30}$	$\frac{18}{30}$	$-\frac{14}{30}$	$-\frac{23}{30}$	$\frac{6}{30}$	$\frac{20}{30}$	$-\frac{1}{30}$	$-\frac{12}{30}$	$\frac{4}{30}$	$\frac{7}{30}$	$-\frac{12}{30}$	0
5. s_B	a c	$-\frac{7}{30}$	$\frac{12}{30}$	$\frac{7}{30}$	$-\frac{17}{30}$	$-\frac{12}{30}$	$\frac{17}{30}$	$\frac{17}{30}$	$-\frac{12}{30}$	$\frac{7}{30}$	$\frac{7}{30}$	$\frac{12}{30}$	$-\frac{7}{30}$	$-\frac{7}{30}$	$\frac{12}{30}$	0
6. g_{y_B}	a c	$\frac{3}{10}$	$-\frac{3}{10}$	$-\frac{4}{10}$	$\frac{3}{10}$	$\frac{5}{10}$	$-\frac{2}{10}$	$-\frac{5}{10}$	$\frac{1}{10}$	$\frac{4}{10}$	$-\frac{1}{10}$	$-\frac{3}{10}$	$\frac{2}{10}$	$\frac{3}{10}$	$-\frac{3}{10}$	0
Inter-regional																
$s_{u_A} = -s_{u_B}$	a c	$-\frac{5}{30}$	0	$\frac{5}{30}$	$\frac{5}{30}$	0	$-\frac{5}{30}$	$-\frac{5}{30}$	0	$\frac{5}{30}$	$\frac{5}{30}$	0	$-\frac{5}{30}$	$-\frac{5}{30}$	0	0

Table 5.4.2 One-time wage-push in region A of 1% in region A (see table 2.4.1)

a. results in region A; b. results in region B; c. (a+b)/2: consequences for the macroeconomy

		1	2	3	4	5	6	7	8	9	10	11	12	13	14	average
1.	$\check{w}$															
	a	$\frac{6}{4}$	$\frac{2}{4}$	$-\frac{4}{4}$	$-\frac{2}{4}$	$\frac{2}{4}$	0	$-\frac{2}{4}$	$\frac{2}{4}$	$\frac{4}{4}$	$-\frac{2}{4}$	$-\frac{6}{4}$	0	$\frac{6}{4}$	$\frac{2}{4}$	0
	b	$\frac{2}{4}$	$-\frac{2}{4}$	$-\frac{4}{4}$	$\frac{2}{4}$	$\frac{6}{4}$	0	$-\frac{6}{4}$	$-\frac{2}{4}$	$\frac{4}{4}$	$\frac{2}{4}$	$-\frac{2}{4}$	0	$\frac{2}{4}$	$-\frac{2}{4}$	0
	c	$\frac{4}{4}$	0	$-\frac{4}{4}$	0	$\frac{4}{4}$	0	$-\frac{4}{4}$	0	$\frac{4}{4}$	0	$-\frac{4}{4}$	0	$\frac{4}{4}$	0	0
2.	g_k															
	a	0	0	$-\frac{6}{10}$	$-\frac{8}{10}$	$-\frac{4}{10}$	$-\frac{2}{10}$	$-\frac{4}{10}$	$-\frac{4}{10}$	$-\frac{2}{10}$	$-\frac{4}{10}$	$-\frac{8}{10}$	$-\frac{6}{10}$	0	0	$-\frac{4}{10}$
	b	0	0	$-\frac{2}{10}$	0	$\frac{4}{10}$	$\frac{2}{10}$	$-\frac{4}{10}$	$-\frac{4}{10}$	$\frac{2}{10}$	$\frac{4}{10}$	0	$-\frac{2}{10}$	0	0	0
	c	0	0	$-\frac{4}{10}$	$-\frac{4}{10}$	0	0	$-\frac{4}{10}$	$-\frac{4}{10}$	0	0	$-\frac{4}{10}$	$-\frac{4}{10}$	0	0	$-\frac{2}{10}$
3.	g_l															
	a	$\frac{2}{10}$	$-\frac{2}{10}$	$-\frac{8}{10}$	$-\frac{6}{10}$	$-\frac{2}{10}$	$-\frac{4}{10}$	$-\frac{6}{10}$	$-\frac{2}{10}$	0	$-\frac{6}{10}$	$-\frac{10}{10}$	$-\frac{4}{10}$	$-\frac{2}{10}$	$-\frac{2}{10}$	$-\frac{4}{10}$
	b	$\frac{2}{10}$	$-\frac{2}{10}$	$-\frac{4}{10}$	$\frac{2}{10}$	$\frac{6}{10}$	0	$-\frac{6}{10}$	$-\frac{2}{10}$	$\frac{4}{10}$	$\frac{2}{10}$	$-\frac{2}{10}$	0	$-\frac{2}{10}$	$-\frac{2}{10}$	0
	c	$\frac{2}{10}$	$-\frac{2}{10}$	$-\frac{6}{10}$	$-\frac{2}{10}$	$\frac{2}{10}$	$-\frac{2}{10}$	$-\frac{6}{10}$	$-\frac{2}{10}$	$\frac{2}{10}$	$-\frac{2}{10}$	$-\frac{6}{10}$	$-\frac{2}{10}$	$-\frac{2}{10}$	$-\frac{2}{10}$	$-\frac{2}{10}$
4.	g_y															
	a	$\frac{8}{10}$	$-\frac{8}{10}$	$-\frac{14}{10}$	0	$\frac{4}{10}$	$-\frac{10}{10}$	$-\frac{12}{10}$	$\frac{4}{10}$	$\frac{6}{10}$	$-\frac{12}{10}$	$-\frac{16}{10}$	$\frac{2}{10}$	$\frac{8}{10}$	$-\frac{8}{10}$	$-\frac{4}{10}$
	b	$\frac{8}{10}$	$-\frac{8}{10}$	$-\frac{10}{10}$	$\frac{8}{10}$	$\frac{12}{10}$	$-\frac{6}{10}$	$-\frac{12}{10}$	$\frac{4}{10}$	$\frac{10}{10}$	$-\frac{4}{10}$	$-\frac{8}{10}$	$\frac{6}{10}$	$\frac{8}{10}$	$-\frac{8}{10}$	0
	c	$\frac{8}{10}$	$-\frac{8}{10}$	$-\frac{12}{10}$	$\frac{4}{10}$	$\frac{8}{10}$	$-\frac{8}{10}$	$-\frac{12}{10}$	$\frac{4}{10}$	$\frac{8}{10}$	$-\frac{8}{10}$	$-\frac{12}{10}$	$\frac{4}{10}$	$\frac{8}{10}$	$-\frac{8}{10}$	$-\frac{2}{10}$

completely different there than in region B. In Chapter I the situations in the two regions were opposite to each other. This is definitely not the case here. It is more probable that the general cyclical situation in both regions is moving roughly in the same direction, in the sense that the situations of boom and depression and of growth and decline, appear in both regions simultaneously. After a one-time wage-push, however, in region A the general impression is one of insufficient employment (while from a *structural* point of view the other variables are in equilibrium). In region B on the other hand, there is even an equilibrium structural development for all variables. However, we will now give our attention to each period separately.

Period 1

Our description begins with the introduction of an ex ante nominal wage increase of $\frac{1}{2}$% in region A. As macroanalysis has taught us, the real wage rate subsequently increases in both regions together, with 1%, since the macroeconomic wage rate multiplier is two. The distribution of this wage pressure between the regions can be calculated by means of the wage rate multiplier, whose quantitative value amounts to:

$$[M_w] = [I - \beta \hat{\alpha}_y \lambda_0 M_l \Omega]^{-1} = \begin{bmatrix} \frac{3}{4} & -\frac{1}{4} \\ -\frac{1}{4} & \frac{3}{4} \end{bmatrix}^{-1} = \frac{1}{2} \begin{bmatrix} 3 & 1 \\ 1 & 3 \end{bmatrix} \quad (5.4.1)$$

The interpretation of (5.4.1) must be that the initial wage pressure will discharge for 75% in a real wage increase in region A and for 25% in region B. With this, the first period has been explained sufficiently. In both regions, yields are low and spendings high, but not however, to the same extent in each region. A deficit on current account arises in region A as a result of this inequality.

Period 2

The inter-regional cyclical situation is dominated by the under-spending caused by the inadequate yields in period 1. Consequently, a negative pressure on employment arises which can be calculated according to:

$$-[(\hat{\alpha}_y \lambda_0) M_l \Omega] \{ \breve{w}_{-1} \} = -\frac{1}{10} \begin{bmatrix} 1 & 1 \\ 1 & 1 \end{bmatrix} \begin{Bmatrix} \frac{3}{4} \\ \frac{1}{4} \end{Bmatrix} = -\begin{Bmatrix} \frac{1}{10} \\ \frac{1}{10} \end{Bmatrix} \quad (5.4.2)$$

If we allow for *one* β of $\frac{2}{5}$, an ex ante pressure on the real wage rate of $-\frac{1}{4}$% then arises, which is furthermore the same for both regions. This alone would lead to a reduced real wage level of $-\frac{1}{2}$% in both regions.

122

However, since the autonomous wage-push in period 1 resulted in an excessive wage level of $\frac{3}{4}$% in region A and $\frac{1}{4}$% in region B, the ultimate result of $+\frac{1}{4}$% in region A and $-\frac{1}{4}$% in region B is explained sufficiently. This outcome is acceptable only if employment is identical in both regions, since the endogenous wage deviation (with regard to the *equilibrium situation*) is in fact the same in both regions. The deficiency in demand is also the same in both regions although it is brought about in region A despite spending out of wage income, while the situation is the reverse in region B. In the meantime, the identical spending situation guarantees that there is equilibrium on the balance of payments in this period.

Period 3

In this period, the labour positions cycle becomes noticeable for the first time. The associated initial pressure on employment amounts to $-\frac{3}{10}$% for region A and $-\frac{1}{10}$% for region B. This can be transformed into an ex ante (induced) wage impulse of $-\frac{3}{4}$% and $-\frac{1}{4}$%, respectively, by means of the Phillips curve. If we apply the wage rate multiplier (5.4.1) to this, the effect on the wage level is:

$$\frac{1}{2} \begin{vmatrix} 3 & 1 \\ 1 & 3 \end{vmatrix} \left\{ \begin{matrix} -\frac{3}{4} \\ -\frac{1}{4} \end{matrix} \right\} = - \left\{ \begin{matrix} \frac{5}{4} \\ \frac{3}{4} \end{matrix} \right\}$$

As well as the labour positions cycle just described, the spending cycle is also operating (at least in the beginning). However, because of the now familiar 'diffusion effect' and since the spending impulses arising from period 2 are in opposition, the influence of wages on the spending cycle in period 3 is zero.

Finally we still have the autonomous element in the wage level, originating from period 1, which produces $+\frac{3}{4}$% for region A and $+\frac{1}{4}$% for region B, after application of the wage rate multiplier. On balance, therefore, the wage rate $(-\frac{5}{4}\% + \frac{3}{4}\%) = -\frac{1}{2}$% in region A is too low, while in B the same wage level is reached, thus: $(-\frac{3}{4} + \frac{1}{4})\% = -\frac{1}{2}$%.

Since the under-spending in region A is of a much more serious nature than in B, a surplus on current account arises in region A.

Table 5.4.1 provides an explanation of the other variables.

Period 3 reflects the deepest point of the depression, since both under-spending and shortage of labour positions are intensely active.

Period 4

Period 4 is characterised by a general recovery, resulting in particular from the increase of spendings out of non-wage incomes.

The influence of this, expressed in terms of the initial wage impulse is $+\frac{1}{4}\%$ and is of course the same in both regions. The contribution towards the real wage rate amounts to $+\frac{1}{2}\%$.

The general situation concerning the available labour positions, has not deteriorated since period 2, although there is still a slight decline in region A, which is compensated by a rise in B. This results finally in an inadequate real wage rate in A of $-\frac{3}{2}\%$ and in region B of $+\frac{1}{2}\%$.

If we add the autonomous part from period 1 to the above endogenous (although originating from the past) wage elements, then we obtain a too low real wage rate of $(\frac{2}{4}-\frac{6}{4}+\frac{3}{4})\% = -\frac{1}{4}\%$ for region A in period 1. In the same way we can calculate an excessively high real wage of $+\frac{1}{4}$ for region B.

In region B in particular, the under-spending has turned into a considerable over-spending. In A, however, the spendings are well on the way to an equilibrium. Because of this, the surplus on current account of A still remains.

Period 5

Period 5 contains a new cyclical peak which is followed firstly by an unavoidable crisis and then by a decline.

The general situation is one of over-spending; in region A rather less than in B. The allied tension on the labour market, and consequent increase in wages is not tempered by a shortage of labour positions. The capital goods supply in region A has taken a large step towards an equilibrium in comparison with period 4, while the relevant variable in region B even exceeds the equilibrium and is stimulating the spending boom there even more.

Although the overspending in region A is slightly less than in B, we still have an equilibrium on the balance of payments, because the capital goods supply in A is lower than in B. This compensates for the difference in spendings.

It is unnecessary to describe in detail the complete cycle of 12 periods. We consider it more advisable to concentrate on a few essentials.

We can then ascertain that the total cycle of 12 periods is composed of 4 sub-cycles, each consisting of 4 periods (apparently some of the periodicity of Chapter II is still present).[1] The peaks of the business

1. Strictly speaking, this is an expression of the characteristic of the model that the average business cycle in the regions (i.e. the macrocycle) is of course identical to the movement of Chapter II.

cycle are found in periods 1, 5, 9 and 13. Both regions continue to share in the boom but with a different intensity. If we consider employment only, we can ascertain that in period 1, the intensity of the boom is the same in both regions. In period 5 on the other hand, the boom in region B reaches an absolute top, while the boom is barely noticeable in the active region A. Although employment is higher than in the periods immediately before and after, there is still no full employment.

Period 9

In period 9, once again a top year, the boom is higher in region A (even the unemployment disappears) but lower in region B than in period 5. Finally, in period 13, the levelling tendency of the business cycle has continued further, so that regarding employment the regions revert to the situation of period 1 which was identical for both regions.

After period 13 there is no similarity between the regions since the recent past of region A is not identical to that of region B.

Obviously similar remarks can be made about the lowest points of periods 3, 7 and 11 and also about the intervening periods of growth and decline.

The foregoing description can, without doubt help to clarify the business cycle. The following analysis is nevertheless indispensable for a fuller understanding.

The basis of the analysis is the view that the business cycle in the present model, is made up of a spending component, a labour positions component and an autonomous impulse component. We shall now attempt to unravel these three components in figures also in the case of the autonomous wage-push.

In formal terms this boils down to the splitting-up (of, for example $\tilde{w}$ at any point of time) into a part that corresponds to the spendings of capitalists ($\check{r}_{-1}$), a part that corresponds to the present production capacity (g_k) and finally the autonomous wage-push ($\underline{\tilde{w}}$) according to the formula:

$$\{\tilde{w}\} = [\beta M_w]\{g_k\} + [\beta\tilde{\alpha}_y\kappa M_w M_l\Omega]\{\check{r}_{-1}\} + [M_w]\{\underline{\tilde{w}}\} \qquad (5.4.3)$$

To be more specific, the quantitative values of the matrices M_l and $M_w M_l\Omega$ are given.

$$M_l = \tfrac{1}{10}\begin{bmatrix} 11 & 1 \\ 1 & 11 \end{bmatrix} \qquad (5.4.4)$$

125

Table 5.4.3 Analysis of the labour positions cycle and spendings cycle ($\{\check{w}\}$) after a one-time wage-push in region A)

t		1	2	3	4	5	6	7	8	9	10	11	12	13	14
1. Labour positions cycle															
$[\beta M_w]\{g_k\}$ — Region A		0	0	$-\frac{12,5}{10}$	$-\frac{1,5}{10}$	$-\frac{5}{10}$	$\frac{2,5}{10}$	$-\frac{1,0}{10}$	$-\frac{1,0}{10}$	$-\frac{2,5}{10}$	$-\frac{5}{10}$	$-\frac{1,5}{10}$	$-\frac{12,5}{100}$	0	0
Region B		0	0	$-\frac{7,5}{10}$	$-\frac{5}{10}$	$-\frac{5}{10}$	$-\frac{2,5}{10}$	$-\frac{1,0}{10}$	$-\frac{1,0}{10}$	$-\frac{2,5}{10}$	$-\frac{5}{10}$	$-\frac{5}{10}$	$-\frac{7,5}{10}$	0	0
2. Spendings cycle															
$[\beta\tilde{z}_y\kappa M_w M_i\Omega]\{\check{r}_{-1}\}$		0	$-\frac{5}{10}$	0	$\frac{5}{10}$	0	$-\frac{5}{10}$	0	$\frac{5}{10}$	0	$-\frac{5}{10}$	0	$\frac{5}{10}$	0	$-\frac{5}{10}$
Region A = Region B															
3. Autonomous element															
$[M_w]\{\underline{\check{w}}\}$ — Region A		$\frac{7,5}{10}$	$\frac{7,5}{10}$	$\frac{7,5}{10}$	$\frac{7,5}{10}$	$\frac{7,5}{10}$	$\frac{7,5}{10}$	$\frac{7,5}{10}$	$\frac{7,5}{10}$	$\frac{7,5}{10}$	$\frac{7,5}{10}$	$\frac{7,5}{10}$	$\frac{7,5}{10}$	$\frac{7,5}{10}$	$\frac{7,5}{10}$
Region B		$\frac{2,5}{10}$	$\frac{2,5}{10}$	$\frac{2,5}{10}$	$\frac{2,5}{10}$	$\frac{2,5}{10}$	$\frac{2,5}{10}$	$\frac{2,5}{10}$	$\frac{2,5}{10}$	$\frac{2,5}{10}$	$\frac{2,5}{10}$	$\frac{2,5}{10}$	$\frac{2,5}{10}$	$\frac{2,5}{10}$	$\frac{2,5}{10}$
4. Total $1+2+3$															
$\check{w}$ — Region A		$\frac{7,5}{10}$	$\frac{2,5}{10}$	$\frac{7,5}{10}$	$-\frac{2,5}{10}$	$\frac{2,5}{10}$	0	$-\frac{2,5}{10}$	$\frac{2,5}{10}$	$\frac{5}{10}$	$-\frac{2,5}{10}$	$-\frac{7,5}{10}$	0	$\frac{7,5}{10}$	$\frac{2,5}{10}$
Region B		$\frac{2,5}{10}$	$-\frac{2,5}{10}$	$\frac{2,5}{10}$	$\frac{2,5}{10}$	$\frac{7,5}{10}$	0	$-\frac{7,5}{10}$	$-\frac{2,5}{10}$	$\frac{5}{10}$	$\frac{2,5}{10}$	$-\frac{2,5}{10}$	0	$\frac{2,5}{10}$	$-\frac{2,5}{10}$

Table 5.4.4   One-time spending-pull in region A of $\frac{4}{3}\%$

t	1	2	3	4	5	6	average
Region A							
F.E. $\breve{w}_A$	1	0	-1	0	1	0	0
1. $\breve{r}_A = \dfrac{\lambda_0}{\kappa}\breve{w}_A$	$-\frac{2}{5}$	0	$\frac{2}{5}$	0	$-\frac{2}{5}$	0	0
2. $g_{kA} = g_{kA-1}+\sigma_R\breve{r}_{A-2}$	0	0	$-\frac{2}{5}$	$-\frac{2}{5}$	0	0	$-\frac{1}{5}$
3. g_{1A}	$\frac{2}{5}$	0	$-\frac{2}{5}$	0	$\frac{2}{5}$	0	0
4. $g_{xA} = \lambda_0(g_{1A}+\breve{w}_A)+(1-\lambda_0)g_{kA}+$	$\frac{34}{15}$	$\frac{10}{15}$	$\frac{4}{15}$	$\frac{28}{15}$	$\frac{34}{15}$	$\frac{10}{15}$	$\frac{19}{15}$
$+\kappa\breve{r}_{A-1}+\underline{\breve{g}}_{xA}$	$\frac{19}{15}$	$-\frac{10}{15}$	$-\frac{16}{15}$	$\frac{8}{15}$	$\frac{14}{15}$	$-\frac{10}{15}$	$-\frac{1}{15}$
5. $s_A-s_B \equiv g_{xB}-g_{xA}$	$-\frac{20}{15}$	$-\frac{20}{15}$	$-\frac{20}{15}$	$-\frac{20}{15}$	$-\frac{20}{15}$	$-\frac{20}{15}$	$-\frac{20}{15}$
6. $s_{uA} = -s_{uB} = (1-\omega)(s_A-s_B)$	$-\frac{10}{15}$	$-\frac{10}{15}$	$-\frac{10}{15}$	$-\frac{10}{15}$	$-\frac{10}{15}$	$-\frac{10}{15}$	$-\frac{10}{15}$
7. $g_{yA} = g_{xA}+s_{uA}$	$\frac{24}{15}$	0	$-\frac{6}{15}$	$\frac{18}{15}$	$\frac{24}{15}$	0	$\frac{9}{15}$
Region B							
F.E. $\breve{w}_B$							
1. $\breve{r}_B = -\frac{2}{5}\breve{w}_B$							
2. $g_{kB} = g_{kB-1}+\breve{r}_{B-2}$							
3. g_{1B}							
4. $g_{xB} = \frac{2}{3}(g_{1B}+\breve{w}_B)+\frac{1}{3}g_{kB}+$							
$+\frac{5}{3}\breve{r}_{B-1}$							
8. $g_{yB} = g_{xB}+s_{uB}$							

127

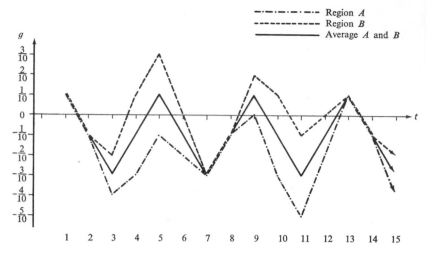

Graph 5.4.1   One-time unilateral wage-push in region A: employment

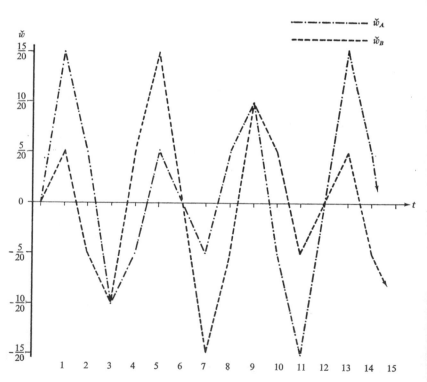

Graph 5.4.2   One-time unilateral wage-push in region A: the real wage rate

$$M_w M_l \Omega = \tfrac{6}{5} \begin{bmatrix} 1 & 1 \\ 1 & 1 \end{bmatrix} \qquad\qquad (5.4.5)$$

Taking into account the above expressions, we can formulate table 5.4.4 (page 127). Graph 5.4.1 and graph 5.4.2 provide a more detailed explanation of the results.

5.4.3 *The unilateral spending-pull*

We refer the reader to table 5.4.4 for a summary of the results. We assume that the interpretation of the table will now be clear.

The striking difference between the wage-push and the capacity-pull is that the consequences of a *unilateral* impulse from region *A* are, in the case at hand, spread evenly between the regions. The formal explanation of this can be found in the matrix $[\beta \tilde{\alpha}_y M_l \Omega]$ (see formula 5.3.2), which of course comprises the results of the impulse vector $\{\tilde{g}_x\}$.

5.5 ECONOMIC POLICY

Income policy has been added to the general problems dealt with in paragraph 4.5. For the rest, we have been guided by the system used in Chapters II–IV.

5.5.1 *Employment policy (including cyclical stabilisation)*

As mentioned earlier, the objectives of employment should now be indicated for each region separately. We shall concentrate firstly on our first objective – the unilateral growth of employment (and production) in region *A* while maintaining a constant employment in region *B*. Summing up, we can draw the following conclusions:

1. The instrument of the one-time wage-push in region *A* is sufficient to realise structural objectives regarding employment in that region. If a negative wage-push of $\tfrac{1}{2}\%$ is introduced in region *A*, a structural employment increase of $\tfrac{1}{4}\%$ will arise. The cyclical stabilisation of such a policy produces in itself few problems: a positive one-time capacity-pull in period 1 is sufficient.

2. In the case discussed above in 1, we assumed that region *A* would

129

itself attend to the cyclical neutralisation of its activities. However, the question again arises whether region B can withstand the cyclical consequences of A's intervention without frustrating A's intentions.

It is also assumed that complete equilibrium must be maintained in the rest of region B, so that a structurally neutral instrument or combination of instruments must be employed.

If we consult tables 5.4.1 and 5.4.2, we see that a stabilisation policy by region B is certainly partly possible. If a positive capacity-pull, causing an autonomous increase of capital goods in period 1 is organised in B in time, the business cycle will be reduced to 4 periods and will thereby become more comprehensible. The table set out below, illustrates this.

The remainder of the business cycle can be eliminated by means of a one-time negative spending-pull in region B of $-\frac{4}{3}\%$ (see table 5.4.3). The spending variables and all associated factors (production, spendings, balance of payments and degree of utilisation) do however then become structurally out of equilibrium.

The general structural situation, after all the changes, can be summarised as follows:

	Region A	*Region B*
real wage rate:	in equilibrium	id.
employment:	decreased	in equilibrium
production:	decreased	decreased
spendings:	slightly increased	severely decreased
balance of payments:	deficit	surplus

It has, in the meantime, become impossible to realise the desired objectives in the model at hand while at the same time maintaining the equilibrium production and (internal and external) sales relations.

The case discussed here can be regarded to some degree as the 'keeping in step' that we touched on in paragraph 1.5.2, with the exception that a positive wage-push in region A must not in this new model be answered with a similarly positive wage-push but with a positive capacity-pull, which does of course have an indirect wage-increasing effect. The replacement of wage-push by capacity-pull is necessary because of the structural neutrality of the abovementioned impulse (see also page 110).

130

a. one-time positive wage-push in region A of ½% in period 1
b. one-time positive capacity-pull in region B of ⅓% in period 1
c. a+b

		1	2	3	4	5	6	7	8	9	10	11	12	13	14	average
Region A																
$\dot{w}$	a	$\frac{3}{4}$	$\frac{1}{4}$	$-\frac{1}{2}$	$\frac{1}{4}$	$\frac{1}{4}$	0	$-\frac{1}{4}$	$\frac{1}{4}$	$\frac{1}{2}$	$-\frac{1}{4}$	$-\frac{3}{4}$	0	$\frac{3}{4}$	$\frac{1}{4}$	0
	b	$\frac{1}{4}$	$-\frac{1}{4}$	$-\frac{1}{2}$	$\frac{1}{4}$	$\frac{3}{4}$	0	$-\frac{3}{4}$	$-\frac{1}{4}$	$\frac{1}{2}$	$\frac{1}{4}$	$-\frac{1}{4}$	0	$\frac{1}{4}$	$-\frac{1}{4}$	0
	c	1	0	-1	0	1	0	-1	0	1	0	-1	0	1	0	0
g_l	a	$\frac{1}{10}$	$-\frac{1}{10}$	$-\frac{4}{10}$	$-\frac{3}{10}$	$-\frac{1}{10}$	$-\frac{2}{10}$	$-\frac{3}{10}$	$-\frac{1}{10}$	0	$-\frac{3}{10}$	$-\frac{5}{10}$	$-\frac{2}{10}$	$\frac{1}{10}$	$-\frac{1}{10}$	$\frac{2}{10}$
	b	$\frac{1}{10}$	$-\frac{1}{10}$	$-\frac{2}{10}$	$\frac{1}{10}$	$\frac{3}{10}$	0	$-\frac{3}{10}$	$-\frac{1}{10}$	$\frac{2}{10}$	$\frac{1}{10}$	$-\frac{1}{10}$	0	$\frac{1}{10}$	$-\frac{1}{10}$	0
	c	$\frac{2}{10}$	$-\frac{2}{10}$	$-\frac{6}{10}$	$-\frac{2}{10}$	$\frac{2}{10}$	$-\frac{2}{10}$	$-\frac{6}{10}$	$-\frac{2}{10}$	$\frac{2}{10}$	$-\frac{2}{10}$	$-\frac{6}{10}$	$-\frac{2}{10}$	$\frac{2}{10}$	$-\frac{2}{10}$	$\frac{2}{10}$
Region B																
$\dot{w}$	a	$\frac{1}{4}$	$-\frac{1}{4}$	$-\frac{1}{2}$	$\frac{1}{4}$	$\frac{3}{4}$	0	$-\frac{3}{4}$	$-\frac{1}{4}$	$\frac{1}{2}$	$\frac{1}{4}$	$-\frac{1}{4}$	0	$\frac{1}{4}$	$-\frac{1}{4}$	0
	b	$\frac{3}{4}$	$\frac{1}{4}$	$-\frac{1}{2}$	$-\frac{1}{4}$	$\frac{1}{4}$	0	$-\frac{1}{4}$	$\frac{1}{4}$	$\frac{1}{2}$	$-\frac{1}{4}$	$-\frac{3}{4}$	0	$\frac{3}{4}$	$\frac{1}{4}$	0
	c	1	0	-1	0	1	0	-1	0	1	0	-1	0	1	0	0
g_l	a	$\frac{1}{10}$	$-\frac{1}{10}$	$-\frac{2}{10}$	$\frac{1}{10}$	$\frac{3}{10}$	0	$-\frac{3}{10}$	$\frac{1}{10}$	$\frac{2}{10}$	$\frac{1}{10}$	$-\frac{1}{10}$	0	$\frac{1}{10}$	$-\frac{1}{10}$	0
	b	$\frac{3}{10}$	$\frac{1}{10}$	$-\frac{2}{10}$	$-\frac{1}{10}$	$\frac{1}{10}$	0	$-\frac{1}{10}$	$-\frac{1}{10}$	$\frac{2}{10}$	$-\frac{1}{10}$	$-\frac{3}{10}$	0	$\frac{3}{10}$	$\frac{1}{10}$	0
	c	$\frac{4}{10}$	0	$-\frac{4}{10}$	0	$\frac{4}{10}$	0	$-\frac{4}{10}$	0	$\frac{4}{10}$	0	$-\frac{4}{10}$	0	$\frac{4}{10}$	0	0

3. In Chapter I (paragraph 1.5.2) it was possible, not only to 'keep in step' but also to react with counter-pressure to the negative wage-push from the partner region by a positive impulse, which should have appeared after some delay.

Such a policy was possible there because an autonomous wage-push placed both regions in phases cyclically opposite to each other. Stabilisation was then possible, either by 'keeping in step' from the beginning, or by waiting half a cycle and then answering the original impulse with a contrary measure.

In the present model, there is no question of an opposite business cycle. On the contrary, both regions are continually in the same cycle fluctuation. For this reason, a 'counter-pressure' would seem at first to be the obvious means. However, the course of the business cycle is not *identical* in both active and passive regions and a 'counter-pressure' alone does not therefore produce the desired result. The actual ratio of the 'keeping in step' capacity-pull now becomes clear: it ensures that the business cycle proceeds identically in many respects, in both regions. The situation is thus prepared for the counter-thrust of the negative spending-pull, whose important effects are divided evenly between the two regions (see further tables 5.5.1 and 5.4.4).

5.5.2 *Regional income policy*

We will be discussing only the situation where region A experiences a permanent increase in real wages while in region B the distribution of income is supposed to remain at an equilibrium. Once again, we demand cyclical stability and also avoidance of structural tensions with regard to the degree of utilisation of capital goods, employment and the balance of payments between the regions.

In table 5.5.2 we have shown how a policy that satisfies the above demands can be carried out. As in Chapter II, the core of this is a continual capacity-pull. This is naturally more suitable than a continual wage-push because of the capital destroying effect of the latter measure. It is therefore difficult to achieve a stable development except for the first three periods. The continual capacity-pull results in a permanent increase in employment which can, if desired, be eliminated according to the results of paragraph 5.5.1.

We may conclude that objectives related to the distribution of income per region, can also be achieved by means of an individual policy of one of the regions.

Regional coordination of economic policy is unnecessary, either for

132

Table 5.5.2 Regional income policy (un-coordinated)

a. continued capacity-pull of $+\frac{1}{3}\%$ in region A of period 1
b. one-time opposite capacity-pull of $-\frac{1}{3}\%$ in region A of period 2
c. total of a and b
d. repetition of a and b in period 3
e. total of c and d

Region A^1

Pull: $\hat{g}_{k_A}$

		1	2	3	4	5	6	7	8	9	10	11	12	13	14	average
$\hat{w}_A$	a	$\frac{3}{15}$	0	$\frac{6}{15}$	$\frac{3}{15}$	$\frac{6}{15}$	$\frac{6}{15}$	$\frac{6}{15}$	$\frac{6}{15}$	$\frac{6}{15}$	$\frac{6}{15}$	$\frac{6}{15}$	$\frac{6}{15}$	$\frac{6}{15}$	$\frac{6}{15}$	$\frac{6}{15}$
	b	$-$	$-\frac{15}{20}$	$-\frac{5}{20}$	$+\frac{10}{20}$	$+\frac{5}{20}$	$-\frac{5}{20}$	0	$+\frac{15}{20}$	$-\frac{5}{20}$	$-\frac{10}{20}$	$+\frac{5}{20}$	$+\frac{15}{20}$	0	$-\frac{15}{20}$	0
	c	$\frac{15}{20}$	$\frac{20}{20}$	$\frac{10}{20}$	$\frac{5}{20}$	$\frac{10}{20}$	$\frac{10}{20}$	$\frac{5}{20}$	$\frac{10}{20}$	$\frac{20}{20}$	$\frac{15}{20}$	0	0	$\frac{15}{20}$	$\frac{20}{20}$	$\frac{30}{60}$
	d	$-$	$-$	$\frac{15}{20}$	$\frac{5}{20}$	$\frac{5}{20}$	$\frac{15}{20}$	$\frac{15}{20}$	$\frac{5}{20}$	$\frac{5}{20}$	$\frac{15}{20}$	$\frac{15}{20}$	$\frac{5}{20}$	$\frac{5}{20}$	$\frac{15}{20}$	$\frac{30}{60}$
	e	$\frac{15}{20}$	$\frac{5}{20}$	$\frac{15}{20}$	$\frac{5}{20}$	$\frac{20}{20}$	$\frac{15}{20}$	$\frac{20}{20}$	$\frac{20}{20}$	$\frac{20}{20}$	$\frac{20}{20}$	$\frac{20}{20}$	$\frac{20}{20}$	$\frac{20}{20}$	$\frac{20}{20}$	$\frac{60}{60}$
g_{k_A}	a	$\frac{4}{20}$	$\frac{8}{20}$	$\frac{6}{20}$	$\frac{2}{20}$	$\frac{2}{20}$	$\frac{4}{20}$	$\frac{4}{20}$	$\frac{4}{20}$	$\frac{6}{20}$	$\frac{6}{20}$	$\frac{2}{20}$	0	$\frac{4}{20}$	$\frac{8}{20}$	$\frac{60}{300}$
	b	$-$	$-\frac{4}{20}$	$-\frac{4}{20}$	$+\frac{2}{20}+\frac{2}{20}$	$+\frac{4}{20}$	0	$-\frac{2}{20}$	0	0	$-\frac{2}{20}$	0	$+\frac{4}{20}+\frac{2}{20}$	$+\frac{2}{20}$	$-\frac{4}{20}$	0
	c	$\frac{4}{20}$	$\frac{4}{20}$	$\frac{2}{20}$	$\frac{4}{20}$	$\frac{6}{20}$	$\frac{4}{20}$	$\frac{2}{20}$	$\frac{4}{20}$	$\frac{6}{20}$	$\frac{4}{20}$	$\frac{2}{20}$	$\frac{4}{20}$	$\frac{6}{20}$	$\frac{4}{20}$	$\frac{60}{300}$

1. In region B, all variables are in equilibrium.

133

Table 5.5.2 (continued)

		1	2	3	4	5	6	7	8	9	10	11	12	13	14	average
	d	—	—	$\frac{4}{20}$	$\frac{4}{20}$	$\frac{2}{20}$	$\frac{4}{20}$	$\frac{6}{20}$	$\frac{4}{20}$	$\frac{2}{20}$	$\frac{4}{20}$	$\frac{6}{20}$	$\frac{4}{20}$	$\frac{2}{20}$	$\frac{4}{20}$	$\frac{60}{300}$
	e	$\frac{4}{20}$	$\frac{4}{20}$	$\frac{6}{20}$	$\frac{8}{20}$	$\frac{8}{20}$	$\frac{8}{20}$	$\frac{8}{20}$	$\frac{8}{20}$	$\frac{8}{20}$	$\frac{8}{20}$	$\frac{8}{20}$	$\frac{8}{20}$	$\frac{8}{20}$	$\frac{8}{20}$	$\frac{120}{300}$
g_{1_A}	a	$\frac{6}{20}$	$\frac{86}{20}$	$\frac{4}{20}$	$\frac{2}{20}$	$\frac{4}{20}$	$\frac{4}{20}$	$\frac{2}{20}$	$\frac{4}{20}$	$\frac{8}{20}$	$\frac{6}{20}$	0	0	$\frac{6}{20}$	$\frac{8}{20}$	$\frac{60}{300}$
	b	—	$-\frac{6}{20}$	$-\frac{2}{20}$	$+\frac{4}{20}$	$+\frac{2}{20}$	$-\frac{2}{20}$	0	$+\frac{2}{20}$	$-\frac{2}{20}$	$-\frac{4}{20}$	$+\frac{2}{20}$	$+\frac{6}{20}$	0	$-\frac{6}{20}$	0
	c	$\frac{6}{20}$	$\frac{2}{20}$	$\frac{2}{20}$	$\frac{2}{20}$	$\frac{6}{20}$	$\frac{2}{20}$	$\frac{2}{20}$	$\frac{6}{20}$	$\frac{6}{20}$	$\frac{2}{20}$	$\frac{2}{20}$	$\frac{2}{20}$	$\frac{6}{20}$	$\frac{2}{20}$	$\frac{60}{300}$
	d	—	—	$\frac{6}{20}$	$\frac{2}{20}$	$\frac{2}{20}$	$\frac{6}{20}$	$\frac{6}{20}$	$\frac{2}{20}$	$\frac{2}{20}$	$\frac{6}{20}$	$\frac{6}{20}$	$\frac{2}{20}$	$\frac{2}{20}$	$\frac{6}{20}$	$\frac{60}{300}$
	e	$\frac{6}{20}$	$\frac{2}{20}$	$\frac{8}{20}$	$\frac{8}{20}$	$\frac{8}{20}$	$\frac{8}{20}$	$\frac{8}{20}$	$\frac{8}{20}$	$\frac{8}{20}$	$\frac{8}{20}$	$\frac{8}{20}$	$\frac{8}{20}$	$\frac{8}{20}$	$\frac{8}{20}$	$\frac{120}{300}$
g_{x_A}	a	$\frac{46}{60}$	$\frac{34}{60}$	$\frac{6}{60}$	$-\frac{4}{60}$	$\frac{20}{60}$	$\frac{12}{60}$	$\frac{2}{60}$	$\frac{22}{60}$	$\frac{42}{60}$	$\frac{8}{60}$	$-\frac{28}{60}$	0	$\frac{46}{60}$	$\frac{34}{60}$	$\frac{60}{900}$
	b	—	$-\frac{46}{60}$	$+\frac{12}{60}$	$+\frac{40}{60}$	$-\frac{2}{60}$	$-\frac{24}{60}$	$+\frac{8}{60}$	$+\frac{14}{60}$	$-\frac{24}{60}$	$-\frac{20}{60}$	$+\frac{34}{60}$	$+\frac{36}{60}$	$-\frac{28}{60}$	$-\frac{46}{60}$	0
	c	$\frac{46}{60}$	$-\frac{12}{60}$	$\frac{6}{60}$	$\frac{36}{60}$	$\frac{18}{60}$	$-\frac{12}{60}$	$\frac{6}{60}$	$\frac{36}{60}$	$\frac{18}{60}$	$-\frac{12}{60}$	$\frac{6}{60}$	$\frac{36}{60}$	$\frac{18}{60}$	$-\frac{12}{60}$	$\frac{60}{900}$
	d	—	$-\frac{12}{60}$	$\frac{46}{60}$	$-\frac{12}{60}$	$\frac{6}{60}$	$\frac{36}{60}$	$\frac{18}{60}$	$-\frac{12}{60}$	$\frac{6}{60}$	$\frac{36}{60}$	$\frac{18}{60}$	$-\frac{12}{60}$	$\frac{6}{60}$	$\frac{36}{60}$	$\frac{60}{900}$
	e	$\frac{46}{60}$	$-\frac{12}{60}$	$\frac{52}{60}$	$\frac{24}{60}$	$\frac{24}{60}$	$\frac{24}{60}$	$\frac{24}{60}$	$\frac{24}{60}$	$\frac{24}{60}$	$\frac{24}{60}$	$\frac{24}{60}$	$\frac{24}{60}$	$\frac{24}{60}$	$\frac{24}{60}$	$\frac{120}{900}$

Table 5.5.2 (continued)

		1	2	3	4	5	6	7	8	9	10	11	12	13	14	average
g_{y_A}	a	$\frac{30}{60}$	$\frac{24}{60}$	$-\frac{0}{60}$	$\frac{6}{60}$	$\frac{24}{60}$	$\frac{12}{60}$	$-\frac{6}{60}$	$\frac{12}{60}$	$\frac{36}{60}$	$\frac{18}{60}$	$-\frac{12}{60}$	0	$\frac{30}{60}$	$\frac{24}{60}$	$\frac{1}{5}$
	b	—	$-\frac{30}{60}$	$+\frac{6}{60}$	$+\frac{24}{60}$	$-\frac{6}{60}$	$-\frac{18}{60}$	$+\frac{12}{60}$	$+\frac{18}{60}$	$-\frac{18}{60}$	$-\frac{24}{60}$	$+\frac{18}{60}$	$+\frac{30}{60}$	$-\frac{12}{60}$	$-\frac{30}{60}$	0
	c	$\frac{30}{60}$	$-\frac{6}{60}$	$\frac{6}{60}$	$\frac{30}{60}$	$\frac{18}{60}$	$-\frac{6}{60}$	$\frac{6}{60}$	$\frac{30}{60}$	$\frac{18}{60}$	$-\frac{6}{60}$	$\frac{6}{60}$	$\frac{30}{60}$	$\frac{18}{60}$	$-\frac{6}{60}$	$\frac{6.0}{900}$
	d	—	—	$\frac{30}{60}$	$-\frac{6}{60}$	$\frac{6}{60}$	$\frac{30}{60}$	$\frac{18}{60}$	$-\frac{6}{60}$	$\frac{6}{60}$	$\frac{30}{60}$	$\frac{18}{60}$	$-\frac{6}{60}$	$\frac{6}{60}$	$\frac{30}{60}$	$\frac{6.0}{900}$
	e	$\frac{30}{60}$	$-\frac{6}{60}$	$\frac{36}{60}$	$\frac{24}{60}$	$\frac{24}{60}$	$\frac{24}{60}$	$\frac{24}{60}$	$\frac{24}{60}$	$\frac{24}{60}$	$\frac{24}{60}$	$\frac{24}{60}$	$\frac{24}{60}$	$\frac{24}{60}$	$\frac{24}{60}$	$\frac{120}{900}$
$s_{u_A} = s_{u_B}$	a	$-\frac{10}{60}$	$-\frac{10}{60}$	0	$\frac{10}{60}$	$\frac{10}{60}$	0	$-\frac{10}{60}$	$-\frac{10}{60}$	0	$\frac{10}{60}$	$\frac{10}{60}$	0	$-\frac{10}{60}$	$-\frac{10}{60}$	0
	b	—	$\frac{10}{60}$	0	$-\frac{10}{60}$	$-\frac{10}{60}$	0	$\frac{10}{60}$	$\frac{10}{60}$	0	$-\frac{10}{60}$	$-\frac{10}{60}$	0	$\frac{10}{60}$	$\frac{10}{60}$	0
	c	$-\frac{10}{60}$	0	0	0	0	0	0	0	0	0	0	0	0	0	0
	d	—	—	$-\frac{10}{60}$	0	0	0	0	0	0	0	0	0	0	0	0
	e	$-\frac{10}{60}$	0	$-\frac{10}{60}$	0	0	0	0	0	0	0	0	0	0	0	0

structural or cyclical objectives. Nevertheless, we may now ask whether the cyclically careless behaviour of one region can be corrected by the partners. No absolute answer can be given to this, of course, since disturbances caused by the active region must be described exactly. If, therefore, region A tries to achieve its aim of an increase in the real wage rate by the simple application of a continued capacity-pull, without concern for the cyclical consequences, which measures can best be applied in region B to restore order at least within the region itself?

It is not difficult to understand that such a situation is only possible if region B resorts to continual measures – for example in the investment field – whose intensity would, moreover, have to be continually increased. In other words, A's careless cyclical behaviour could provoke an escalation of counter-measures in B, with all the associated structurally disrupting consequences.

It is indeed possible to deduce from table 5.4.1 that no (at least no simple) line of policy can be laid for region B which guarantees that passive region B will avoid the cyclical instability instigated by A.

Table 5.5.2 describes the matter in detail.

Appendices

1.1.1 *Introduction*

Up till now we have been considering regional economic structures which are similar in all respects, including size. We will now be abandoning the assumption of identical size and will be turning our attention to a system in which region A is twice as large as region B.

In reality, this situation is more interesting than one of complete symmetry.

We have already seen that in the symmetrical case, problems of economic strategy arise with regard to resistance to less desirable internal situations, or with regard to the resistance to the effect of measures taken by the partner. However, when the regions differ greatly in size, the strategic policy just referred to, acquires new dimensions. In particular, problems regarding the economic dominance of large regions over smaller regions then arise.

In this appendix it is simply our intention to show how the asymmetry in our theoretical models could be introduced. The reader will discover that even the problem of differences in size, will give rise to a casuistry which cannot be settled within a reasonable space. We felt obliged to confine ourselves to a brief résumé of a few, in our view important, results.

Of the autonomous impulses, we will again discuss spending-pull and wage-push only.

In the new situation, it would seem at first glance to be of importance if the autonomous impulses are introduced in the small or the large region.

The following system, based on the above, can be worked out for this appendix.
1. The effects of a one-time spending-pull in the large region.
2. The effects of a one-time spending-pull in the small region.

137

3. The effects of one-time wage-pushes.

All these impulses will be numerically illustrated, in the usual way. Before presenting the relevant tables, we will pause briefly to consider the construction of the new model.

1.1.2 *The new model and the solution: the data*

We assume – and that is somewhat more general than we announced in the introduction to this appendix – that the working population of region A is a factor ϕ times as large as that of region B. In the situation of equilibrium growth therefore, all variables in A are ϕ times as large, at least if there is otherwise symmetry.

Only one structural parameter assumes logically different values in the two regions i.e. the average import ratio. In an equilibrium growth situation this will be ϕ times as big in the small region B as in A. Of the relations, summarised in model 1.2.1, only equation (5) undergoes a change. In the new model, the import and export equation will read as follows:

$$\{e - m\} = -\mu'_A \begin{bmatrix} 1 & -\phi \\ -\phi & 1 \end{bmatrix} \{ y'_R \}_{-1} - e_E \eta \psi \begin{bmatrix} 1 & -1 \\ -1 & 1 \end{bmatrix} \{\underline{p_L}\}_{-1}$$

(A 1.1.1)

Here is:

$$\mu'_A = \frac{\mu_{0_A} \eta \psi \beta}{1 - \lambda_m}$$

If we take into account the relations dealt with previously, we obtain the following as final equation for the new model:

$$\{y'_R\} = \left(1 - \delta + \frac{\sigma_R}{\kappa_R}\right) \{y'_{R-1}\} - \zeta M \mu' \begin{bmatrix} 1 & -\phi \\ -1 & \phi \end{bmatrix} \{y'_{R-2}\}$$

$$- e_E \eta \psi \zeta M \begin{bmatrix} 1 & -1 \\ -1 & 1 \end{bmatrix} \{p_{L-1}\} + \zeta M x_{R-1} + \frac{1}{\kappa_R} i_{-1}$$

(A 1.1.2)

If we keep the earlier structural parameters (so that, among others, $\delta = \sigma_R/\kappa_R$), it can easily be shown that the characteristic equation of the system (A 1.1.2) reads:

$$\lambda'(1 - \lambda') \{\lambda'(1 - \lambda') - \zeta M \mu'_A(1 + \phi)\} = 0$$

(A 1.1.3)

138

In (A 1.1.3), λ' symbolises the eigenvalue of the system. A cyclical movement almost identical to an earlier one, arises if we take:

$$\zeta M \mu'_A (1 + \phi) = 1 \tag{A 1.1.4}$$

This last condition is satisfied if all details of the symmetrical structure are kept, with the exception of

$$\beta = \tfrac{1}{3} \qquad \mu_{0_A} = \tfrac{1}{4} \qquad \mu'_A = \tfrac{2}{3} \qquad \phi = 2 \qquad l_A = 200$$

This paragraph ends with a not uninteresting conclusion. The system stability increases as ϕ becomes smaller (see A 1.1.3). In other words: a system composed of regions (countries) of equal size, suffers from a greater instability than a system composed of a larger and a smaller region.

This deduction encourages further generalisation to systems larger than two regions. Unfortunately, this was not possible, within the scope of this study.

1.1.3 Description of the business cycle and some conclusions

Since we have given a detailed explanation of the symmetrical model, we feel we can be brief in describing the reaction of the new model to autonomous impulses. The details can be found in the following tables: A 1.1–A 1.3. A few interesting conclusions arising specifically from the differences in size can be described as follows.

1. In the case of a consumption-pull, only the *absolute size* of the impulse and the size of the region where the impulse is initiated are important for the structural interregional influence. The cyclical course differs according to whether the spending impulse originates from the small or the large region (see tables A 1.1 and A 1.2).

2. A similar conclusion can be drawn in the case of the wage-push. In that case not only the structural consequences but also the cyclical course of the real quantities does not depend on the region where the wage-push is given.

This is understandable, since one and the same initial wage and price mutation involves one and the same quantitative mutation in the balance on current account, irrespective of the source.

The conclusion made in paragraph 1.4.2 is still applicable, to an undiminished degree, i.e. the effects in the active region, except those regarding the nominal quantities are exactly opposite to those in the passive region.

Table A 1.1   One-time consumption-pull in the large country of 6 (15%)

(in absolute deviations from equilibrium values)	t	1	2	3	4	5	6	7	8	average
Land A ($l = 200$, $\bar{e}_E = 100$)										
$\underline{c_R}$	6	0	0	0	0	0	0	0	0	0
$y'_R \quad = l$	0	0	3	3	2	1	1	2	3	2
$y_R \quad = \underline{y'_R} + 5(e-m) + 5\underline{c_R}$	30	0	3	-7	-8	1	11	12	3	2
$i_B \quad = \frac{4}{5}y_R$	24	0	2.4	-5.6	-6.4	0.8	8.8	9.6	2.4	1.6
$c_R \quad = \frac{1}{5}\underline{y'_R} + \underline{c_R}$	6	0	0.6	0.6	0.4	0.2	0.2	0.4	0.6	0.4
$(e-m) \quad = -4(p_A - p_B)$	0	0	0	-2	-2	0	2	2	0	0
$(p_L-1) = p-1 = \beta \dfrac{L_{-1}}{l_a}$ (:100)	0	0	0	$\frac{1}{2}$	$\frac{1}{2}$	$\frac{1}{3}$	$\frac{1}{6}$	$\frac{1}{6}$	$\frac{1}{3}$	$\frac{1}{3}$
$d \quad = 0.8\,y'_R$	0	0	2.4	2.4	1.6	0.8	0.8	1.6	2.4	1.6
i_N	24	0	0	-8	-8	0	8	8	0	0

Table A 1.1 (continued)

(in absolute deviations from equilibrium values)	t	1	2	3	4	5	6	7	8	average
Land B ($\bar{l}=100$)										
y'_R		0	0	0	1	2	2	1	0	1
$y_R \quad = y'_R + 5(e-m) + 5\underline{c_R}$		0	0	10	11	2	-8	-9	0	1
$i_B \quad = 0.8\,y_R$		0	0	8	8.8	1.6	-6.4	-7.2	0	0.8
$c_R \quad = 0.2\,y'_R + \underline{c_R}$		0	0	0	0.2	0.4	0.4	0.2	0	0.2
$(e-m)$		0	0	2	2	0	-2	-2	0	0
$(p_L - 1) = p-1 = \beta\dfrac{l_{-1}}{\bar{l}}$ (: 100)		0	0	0	0	$\frac{1}{3}$	$\frac{2}{3}$	$\frac{2}{3}$	$\frac{1}{3}$	$\frac{1}{3}$
d		0	0	0	0.8	1.6	1.6	0.8	0	0.8
i_N		0	0	8	8	0	-8	-8	0	0
General										
$p_A - p_B$ (: 100)		0	0	$\frac{1}{2}$	$\frac{1}{2}$	0	$-\frac{1}{2}$	$-\frac{1}{2}$	0	0

141

Table A 1.2 One-time consumption-pull in the small country of 6 (30%)

(in absolute deviations from equilibrium values)	t	1	2	3	4	5	6	7	8	average
Land A ($l = 200$, $e_E = 100$)										
$y'_R = l$		0	0	0	2	4	4	2	0	2
$y_R = y'_R + 5(e-m)$		0	0	20	22	4	-16	-18	0	2
$i_B = 0.8y_R$		0	0	16	17.6	3.2	-12.8	-14.4	0	1.6
$c_R = 0.2y'_R$		0	0	0	0.4	0.8	0.8	0.4	0	0.4
$(e-m) = -4(p_A - p_B)$		0	0	4	4	0	-4	-4	0	0
$p_L - 1 = p - 1 = \beta \dfrac{l_{-1}}{l}$ (: 100)		0	0	0	0	$\frac{1}{3}$	$\frac{2}{3}$	$\frac{2}{3}$	$\frac{1}{3}$	$\frac{1}{3}$
$d = 0.8y'_R$		0	0	0	1.6	3.2	3.2	1.6	0	1.6
i_N		0	0	16	16	0	-16	-16	0	0

Table A 1.2 (continued)

(in absolute deviations from equilibrium values)	t	1	2	3	4	5	6	7	8	average
Land B ($l = 100$)										
$\underline{c_R}$		6	0	0	0	0	0	0	0	0
$y'_R \;\; = l$		0	3	3	1	-1	-1	1	3	1
$y_R \;\; = y'_R + 5(e-m) + 5\underline{c_R}$		30	3	-17	-19	-1	19	21	3	1
$i_B \;\; = 0.8 y_R$		24	2.4	-13.6	-15.2	-0.8	15.2	16.8	2.4	0.8
$c_R \;\; = 0.2 y'_R + \underline{c_R}$		6	0.6	0.6	0.2	-0.2	-0.2	0.2	0.6	0.2
$(e-m)$		0	0	-4	-4	0	4	4	0	0
$p_L - 1 = p - 1 = \beta \dfrac{L_{-1}}{l}$		0	0	1	1	$\frac{1}{3}$	$-\frac{1}{3}$	$-\frac{1}{3}$	$\frac{1}{3}$	$\frac{1}{3}$
$d \;\; = 0.8 y'_r$		0	2.4	2.4	0.8	-0.8	-0.8	0.8	2.4	0.8
i_N		24	0	-16	-16	0	16	16	0	0
General										
$p_A - p_B$		0	0	-1	-1	0	1	1	0	0

143

Table A 1.3 One-time wage-push in the small country B of $\frac{1}{2}\%$

Deviations from equilibrium values	t	1	2	3	4	5	6	7	8	average
Land B (the consequences for A are the opposite)										
p_L	(: 100)	$\frac{1}{2}$	$\frac{1}{2}$	$\frac{1}{2}$	$\frac{1}{2}$	$\frac{1}{2}$	$\frac{1}{2}$	$\frac{1}{2}$	$\frac{1}{2}$	$\frac{1}{2}$
$y'_R \quad = l$		0	-1	-2	-2	-1	0	0	-1	-1
$y_R \quad = y'_R + 5(e-m)$		-10	-11	-2	8	9	0	-10	-11	-1
$i_B \quad = 0.8 y_R$		-8	-8.8	-1.6	6.4	7.2	0	-8	-8.8	-0.8
$c_R \quad = 0.2 y'_R$		0	-0.2	-0.4	-0.4	-0.1	0	0	-0.2	-0.2
$(e-m) = 4(p_A - p_B)$		-2	-2	0	2	2	0	-2	-2	0
d		0	-0.8	-1.6	-1.8	-0.8	0	0	-0.8	-0.8
i_N		-8	-8	0	8	8	0	-8	-8	0
$p_{L_A} - 1 = (p_A - 1) = \beta \frac{l-1}{l}$	(: 100)	0	0	$\frac{1}{6}$	$\frac{1}{3}$	$\frac{1}{3}$	$\frac{1}{6}$	0	0	$\frac{1}{6}$
$p_{L_B} - 1 = (p_B - 1) = \beta \frac{l-1}{l} + p_L$	(: 100)	$\frac{1}{2}$	$\frac{1}{2}$	$\frac{1}{6}$	$-\frac{1}{6}$	$-\frac{1}{6}$	$\frac{1}{6}$	$\frac{1}{2}$	$\frac{1}{2}$	$\frac{1}{6}$
$p_A - p_B$	(: 100)	$-\frac{1}{2}$	$-\frac{1}{2}$	0	$\frac{1}{2}$	$\frac{1}{2}$	0	$-\frac{1}{2}$	$-\frac{1}{2}$	0

3. Nominal prices and wages should also be mentioned. Not only does their development deviate from all other variables but as we have seen there is also an important difference between a one-time wage-push, given in the small region on the one hand and a similar impulse given in the large region, on the other hand. This difference can be summarised as follows:

The results of a one-time wage-push given in the large region are completely analogous with those in the small region on the understanding that the general level is only half $(1/\phi)$ that of a wage-push in the large region.

Tables A 1.1–A 1.3 can be consulted for further details.

APPENDIX 1.2 SYSTEMS OF LINEAR DIFFERENCE EQUATIONS

1.2.1 The matrix presentation of a linear difference equation

Let us consider the following homogeneous linear difference equation of the nth degree.

$$x_t + a_1 x_{t-1} + a_2 x_{t-2} + \ldots + a_n x_{t-n} = 0 \tag{1}$$

$$x_{t-i} \in R \qquad i = 1, \ldots, n; \qquad t \in GH, (GH = \{\text{integers}\})$$

$$a_j \in R \qquad j = 1, \ldots, n; \qquad a_n \neq 0$$

The characteristic equation of (1) reads:

$$\lambda^n + a_1 \lambda^{n-1} + \ldots a_{n-1}\lambda + a_n = 0 \tag{2}$$

The root(s) of (2) are called the characteristic roots of difference equation (1).

(1) can also be written as follows:

$$\{x\}_t = [A] \{x\}_{t-1}, \tag{3}$$

in which:

$$\{x\}_t = \begin{Bmatrix} x_t \\ x_{t-1} \\ \vdots \\ x_{t-(n-1)} \end{Bmatrix}$$

145

and

$$[A] = \begin{bmatrix} -a_1 & -a_2 & -a_3 & \cdots & -a_n \\ 1 & 0 & 0 & \cdots & 0 \\ 0 & 1 & 0 & \cdots & 0 \\ \cdot & \cdot & \cdot & \cdots & \cdot \\ 0 & 0 & 0 & \cdots & 1 & 0 \end{bmatrix}$$

According to this matrix a difference equation in scale of the nth degree as in (1) can be given with a vector-difference equation of the first degree.

It can be proved that the roots of the characteristic equation (2) are the eigenvalues of A in (4).

The importance of this is that the investigation of the dynamic qualities of difference equation (1) amounts in fact to an investigation of the eigenvalues of A.

1.2.2 *Systems of difference equations*

Not only the description of the dynamic qualities of one single difference equation (such as (1)) but also that of many simultaneous difference equations can be presented similarly to the system of (1) by means of a system of the 1st degree.

We can define for this purpose a 'vector of vectors' $\{\underline{y}_t\}$ as follows:

$$\{y\}_t \begin{Bmatrix} y(t) \\ y(t-1) \\ \vdots \\ y(t-(n-1)) \end{Bmatrix} \tag{3}$$

with

$$y(t) = \begin{Bmatrix} y_1(t) \\ y_2(t) \\ \vdots \\ y_m(t) \end{Bmatrix} \quad y(t) \in R_m \tag{4}$$

A system of m soluble difference equations (in m variables) can then be set out as follows:

$$y(t) + [A_1]\, y(t-1) + \ldots + [A_n]\, y(t-n) = 0 \tag{5}$$

System (5) is analogous to (1) on the understanding that the variables are now vectors and the 'co-efficients' $[A]$ matrices.

146

System (5) can be presented by the following system of the 1st degree.

$$\{y\}_t = [\underline{A}] \{y\}_{t-1} \tag{6}$$

$$(\underline{A}: R_{nxm} \rightarrow R_{nxm})$$

The explanation of $[\underline{A}]$ is

$$\underline{A} = \begin{bmatrix} -[A_1] & -[A_2] & \cdots & -[A_n] \\ I & 0 & \cdots & 0 \\ \cdot & \cdot & \cdots & \cdot \\ 0 & 0 & \cdots I & 0 \end{bmatrix} \tag{7}$$

Once again we can prove that the dynamic characteristics can be described by the eigenvalues of the square matrix $\underline{A}$ in (7).

APPENDIX 2.1 YIELD DEFINITIONS AND INVESTMENT FUNCTION

In Chapters II–IV, the variable $\check{r}$ played an important role, both in the investment function and in the spending function. For this reason a more detailed explanation seems appropriate here.

2.1.1 *The closed economy*

The definition of the actual yield from invested capital reads:

$$r = \frac{y - lw}{k} \tag{1}$$

where:

r = actual yield
y = production volume
l = labour volume
w = real wage rate
k = capital goods volume

With an equilibrium wage ratio of λ_0 and a normal (equilibrium) average capital-coefficient of κ the formula of the capital yield accompanying equilibrium growth is:

$$r_E = \frac{1 - \lambda_0}{\kappa} \tag{2}$$

Deduction of (1) and (2) provides the difference between actual yield and equilibrium yield.

$$\check{r}_f \equiv r - r_E \tag{3}$$

Meanwhile, we have not used the yield in investment functions and spendings functions as defined in (3) but instead the actual yield deviation (from the equilibrium yield), overlooking cyclical over- (under-) utilisation or over- (under-) manning of the capital goods supply. The definition of what we have indicated by 'calculation yield', using (1) then becomes:

$$r_c \equiv \frac{y}{k}(E) - \frac{l}{k}(E)w = \frac{1}{\kappa} - \frac{\alpha}{\kappa}w \tag{4}$$

Since the following applies:

$$w = w_E(1 + \check{w}), \tag{5}$$

we can also write for (4):

$$r_c = \frac{1}{\kappa} - \frac{\alpha w_E}{\kappa}(1 + \check{w}) = \frac{1}{\kappa} - \frac{\lambda_0}{\kappa}(1 + \check{w}) \tag{6}$$

(since $\alpha w_E = \lambda_0$).

If we deduct the equilibrium yield from (6) we obtain the calculation yield as opposed to the equilibrium yield

$$\check{r} = r_c - r_E = - \frac{\lambda_0}{\kappa}\check{w} \tag{7}$$

The difference between $\check{r}$ and $\check{r}_f$ is obviously determined by the degree of utilisation, using the formula:

$$\check{r}_f - \check{r} = \frac{1 - \tilde{\alpha}_y \lambda_0}{\kappa}(g_y - g_k) = - \frac{1 - \tilde{\alpha}_y \lambda_0}{\kappa} s_b \tag{8}$$

2.1.2 *The open economy*

In this case, the terms of trade help to determine the capital yield. The following applies:

$$r \equiv \frac{y - lw - \left(l\dfrac{p_E}{p} - m\dfrac{p_m}{p}\right)}{k} \tag{9}$$

148

We have now defined the calculation yield on the basis of equilibrium internal production relationships thereby assuming that when determining profitability, the companies overlook any unbalanced relationships possibly existing between actual export volume (or import volume) on the one hand and production and production capacity on the other hand. Contrary to the equilibrium yield percentage, the definition of the calculation yield will then read:

$$\check{r} = -\frac{\lambda_0}{\kappa}\check{w} + \frac{\mu_0}{\kappa}(\check{p}_e - \check{p}_m) \tag{10}$$

(See formula (3.2.14).)

2.1.3 *The investment function*

In Chapters II–V, we have assumed that the calculation yield was decisive for investments. A simple delay of one period is thereby assumed. The investment function, in terms of relative deviations from the equilibrium growth is said to be:

$$g_i = g_k + \tilde{\sigma}_R \frac{\check{r}_{-1}}{r_E} \tag{11}$$

This could be interpreted in the following way. Investers aim firstly at a normal growth, considering the actual available capital goods supply but corrections are introduced through the behaviour parameters $\tilde{\sigma}_R$, according to whether the relative deviation of the calculation from equilibrium yield is higher or lower.

Furthermore it is possible, beginning with the accumulation of capital function (in absolute terms):

$$k_t = k_{t-1}(1 - \delta) + i_{-1} \tag{12}$$

(in which i represents gross investments), and keeping in mind the following definitions:

$$k \equiv k_E(1 + g_k) \quad \text{and} \quad i_E \equiv i_E(1 + g_i) \tag{13}$$

to formulate the following accumulation function in relative deviations.

$$g_k = g_{k-1} + \frac{g_n + \delta}{1 + g_n}(g_{i-1} - g_{k-1}) \tag{14}$$

Here, g_n: the natural (net) growth rate,
$\quad\;\;\delta$: the constant depreciation ratio.

A combination of (11) and (14) produces:

$$g_k = g_{k-1} + \sigma_R \check{r}_{-2},\tag{15}$$

in which σ_R is a rather complicated coefficient which, under the given premises is equal to:

$$\sigma_R = \tilde{\sigma}_R \frac{g_n + \delta}{1 + g_n} \frac{1}{r_E}.\tag{16}$$

APPENDIX 2.2 THE WAGE DETERMINATION FUNCTION

Up till now we have continually assumed that the nominal wage rate $(\check{p}_L)$, irrespective of the autonomous impulses, is dependent on the price level $(\check{p})$ on the one hand and on the *situation* on the labour market (g_l) on the other hand. This implies, in terms of changes in the wage rate that the *change* in the wage rate is related to the *change* in employment.

In the original specification of the Phillips curve, a sort of excess-demand theory was assumed: the wage rate *change* is dependent on the employment situation, thus:

$$\check{w} = \check{w}_{-1} + \beta g_L + \underline{\check{w}}\tag{1}$$

Since the labour demand function indicates no change, we can derive the following final equation in the case of a wage-push:

$$(1 - \beta M_l \tilde{\alpha}_y \lambda_0)\,\check{w} - (2 - 2\,\beta M_l \tilde{\alpha}_y \lambda_0)\,\check{w}_{-1} +$$

$$+ \left(1 + \beta \sigma_R \frac{\lambda_0}{\kappa} - \beta M_l \tilde{\alpha}_y \lambda_0\right)\check{w}_{-2} = \underline{\check{w}}\tag{2}$$

Two important conclusions can be drawn.
1. The new determination of wages function produces a more unstable cyclical situation, compared with that mentioned earlier. This can be easily checked by filling in the data of paragraph 2.4 in (2), after which a modulus of 3 arises.
2. Structurally, the new function is 'more stable' in that the full-employment tendencies are more pronounced. In the following explanation, this is easy to understand. In the new system, the wage rate adapts itself to the 'right' direction (and thereby the creation of labour positions), *as long as* there is no full-employment, while in the text of Chapter II no feed-back effects emanate from the employment situation itself. This is because, in that case, adjustment stops as soon as wages no longer change.

150

However, it does make rather a difference from a cyclical and structural point of view, which of the two mechanisms is in operation. It is therefore even more remarkable that the Central Planning Bureau has changed from one to the other without any further comment (compare for example the specification in the model 63D (Verdoorn and Post) with that of the CEP 1971).

In the meantime of course, the question of which mechanism dominates the real situation must be solved empirically. The best relation, obtained by estimating about 150 wage determination functions (for the Netherlands) was as follows:[1]

$$\frac{\dot{p}_L}{p_L} = \frac{0,98}{1-0,20\,E^{-1}}\,\frac{\dot{p}_c}{p_c} + 0,64\,\rho + 0,61\,g_L + 2,67\,\Delta g_L + 2,89 \quad (^2)$$

period of estimation: 1950–1968; $R^2 = 0.95$.

We can conclude that in actual fact, both of the mechanisms discussed here are operating. We may presume, however, that the 'old' mechanism is dominant, although the delay is longer than we have assumed. It would seem, therefore, that we are justified in placing most of the emphasis on the mechanism postulated by us beforehand. There are at least no empirical objections.

APPENDIX 3.1 THE $\tilde{\mu}$-MECHANISM

In table A 3.1 below, we present the results of one-time internal impulses in a model which is the same as that elaborated in the body of Chapter III, with the exception of the import function. For this we have taken:

$$g_m = \frac{\tilde{\mu}}{\mu_0}\,g_y \tag{1}$$

using the following data:

$$\tilde{\alpha}_k = \frac{3}{4} \qquad \tilde{\alpha}_y = \frac{3}{8} \qquad \beta = 2 \qquad \varepsilon = 1 \qquad \eta_w = \frac{4}{5}$$

$$\kappa = \frac{10}{9} \qquad \lambda_0 = \frac{2}{3} \qquad \mu_0 = \frac{1}{2} \qquad \tilde{\mu} = \frac{1}{2} \qquad \sigma_R = 1 \qquad \psi_w = \frac{2}{15}$$

1. We hope to publish the results of this investigation in more detail, in a future study.
2. p_L: nominal wage rate ρ : change in production of labour
    p_c: price level of consumption goods g_L: percentage of overemployment.

Table A 3.1   Consequences of a number of one-time internal impulses in period 1

a. wage-push;   b. spending-pull;   c. capacity-pull

Variable	Kind of impulse	t	1	2	3	4	5	6	average
	a	$\hat{\underline{w}}$	$\frac{3}{5}$	0	0	0	0	0	0
	b	$\hat{\underline{g}}_x$	1	0	0	0	0	0	0
	c	$\hat{\underline{g}}_k$	$\frac{3}{10}$	0	0	0	0	0	0
		a. $\hat{\underline{p}}_L$							
$\check{w}$	F.E.	$A_0\check{w} - A_1\check{w}_{-1} + A_2\check{w}_{-2} = \frac{3}{5}\check{w}_{-2} +$ b. $\beta M_1\tilde{\alpha}_y\,M_m\hat{\underline{g}}_x$	1	0	-1	0	1	0	0
		c. $\beta M_1\tilde{\alpha}'_k\hat{\underline{g}}_k$							
$\check{r}$	abc	$\check{r} = -\dfrac{\lambda_0}{\kappa}\check{w} = -\dfrac{3}{5}\check{w}$	$-\frac{3}{5}$	0	$\frac{3}{5}$	0	$-\frac{3}{5}$	0	0
g_k	ab	$g_k = g_{k-1} + \sigma_R\check{r}_{-2} = g_{k-1} + \check{r}_{-2}$	0	0	$-\frac{3}{5}$	$-\frac{3}{5}$	0	0	$-\frac{3}{10}$
	c	$g_k = \text{idem} + \hat{\underline{g}}_k$	$\frac{3}{10}$	$\frac{3}{10}$	$-\frac{3}{10}$	$-\frac{3}{10}$	$\frac{3}{10}$	$\frac{3}{10}$	0
g_L	a	$g_L = M_1[\tilde{\alpha}'_k g_k + \tilde{\alpha}_y\,M_m\{\lambda_0\check{w} - (\lambda' + \mu_0\eta_w)\check{w}_{-1}\}] =$ $= g_k + \frac{1}{5}\check{w} - \frac{3}{10}\check{w}$	$\frac{1}{5}$	$-\frac{3}{10}$	$-\frac{4}{5}$	$-\frac{3}{10}$	$\frac{1}{5}$	$-\frac{3}{10}$	$-\frac{3}{10}$
	b	$g_L = \text{idem} + M_1\tilde{\alpha}_y M_m\hat{\underline{g}}_x = \text{idem} + \frac{3}{10}\hat{\underline{g}}_x$	$\frac{1}{2}$	0	$-\frac{1}{2}$	0	$\frac{1}{2}$	0	0

152

Variable	Kind of impulse	t	1	2	3	4	5	6	average
$\mathring{w}$	a	$\mathring{w} = \beta_{g_L} + \breve{\mathring{w}} = 2g_L + \underline{\breve{\mathring{w}}}$	1	0	-1	0	1	0	0
	b	$\mathring{w} = \beta_{g_L} = 2g_L$							
	c	$\mathring{w} = \beta_{g_L} = 2g_L$							
g_x	a	$g_x = \lambda_0(g_L + \breve{\mathring{w}}) + (1-\lambda_0)g_k + \kappa\breve{r}_{-1} = $ $= \frac{2}{3}(g_L + \breve{\mathring{w}}) + \frac{1}{3}g_k + \breve{r}_{-1}$	$\frac{4}{5}$	$-\frac{4}{5}$	$-\frac{7}{5}$	$\frac{1}{5}$	$\frac{4}{5}$	$-\frac{4}{5}$	$-\frac{3}{10}$
	b	$g_x = \text{idem} + \underline{\breve{g}_x}$	2	$\frac{2}{5}$	$-\frac{1}{5}$	$\frac{7}{5}$	2	$\frac{2}{5}$	$\frac{9}{10}$
	c	$g_x = \text{idem as a}$	$\frac{11}{10}$	$-\frac{1}{2}$	$-\frac{11}{10}$	$\frac{1}{2}$	$\frac{11}{10}$	$-\frac{1}{2}$	0
g_y	a	$g_y = M_m(g_x + \mu_0 g_E) = \frac{2}{3}(g_x + \frac{1}{2}g_E)$	$\frac{8}{15}$	$-\frac{12}{15}$	$-\frac{14}{15}$	$\frac{6}{15}$	$\frac{8}{15}$	$-\frac{12}{15}$	$-\frac{1}{5}$
	b	$g_y = \text{idem}$	$\frac{20}{15}$	0	$-\frac{2}{15}$	$\frac{18}{15}$	$\frac{20}{15}$	0	$\frac{3}{5}$
	c	$g_y = \text{idem}$	$\frac{11}{15}$	$-\frac{9}{15}$	$-\frac{11}{15}$	$\frac{9}{15}$	$\frac{11}{15}$	$-\frac{9}{15}$	0
s_b	a	$s_b = g_k - g_y$	$-\frac{8}{15}$	$\frac{12}{15}$	$\frac{5}{15}$	$-\frac{15}{15}$	$-\frac{8}{15}$	$\frac{12}{15}$	$-\frac{1}{10}$
	b	$s_b = \text{idem}$	$-\frac{20}{15}$	0	$-\frac{7}{15}$	$-\frac{27}{15}$	$-\frac{20}{15}$	0	$-\frac{9}{10}$
	c	$s_b = \text{idem}$	$-\frac{13}{30}$	$\frac{27}{30}$	$\frac{13}{30}$	$-\frac{27}{30}$	$-\frac{13}{30}$	$\frac{27}{30}$	0

Table A 3.1 *(continued)*

Variable	Kind of impulse	t	1	2	3	4	5	6	*average*
$\mu_0 g_E$	abc	$\mu_0 g_E = -\mu_0 \eta_w \ddot{w}_{-1} = -\frac{2}{5}\ddot{w}_{-1}$	0	0	0	$\frac{2}{5}$	0	$-\frac{2}{5}$	0
$\mu_0 g_m$	a	$\mu_0 g_m = \tilde{\mu} g_y = \frac{1}{2} g_y$	$\frac{4}{15}$	$-\frac{6}{15}$	$-\frac{7}{15}$	$\frac{3}{15}$	$\frac{4}{15}$	$-\frac{6}{15}$	$-\frac{1}{10}$
	b	$\mu_0 g_m$ = idem	$\frac{10}{15}$	0	$-\frac{1}{15}$	$\frac{9}{15}$	$\frac{10}{15}$	0	$\frac{3}{15}$
	c	$\mu_0 g_m$ = idem	$\frac{11}{30}$	$-\frac{9}{30}$	$-\frac{11}{30}$	$\frac{9}{30}$	$\frac{11}{30}$	$-\frac{9}{30}$	0
s_u	a	$s_u = \mu_0(g_E - g_m)$	$-\frac{4}{15}$	0	$\frac{7}{15}$	$\frac{3}{15}$	$-\frac{4}{15}$	0	$\frac{1}{10}$
	b	s_u = idem	$-\frac{2}{3}$	$-\frac{2}{5}$	$\frac{1}{15}$	$-\frac{3}{15}$	$-\frac{2}{3}$	$-\frac{2}{5}$	$-\frac{3}{10}$
	c	s_u = idem	$-\frac{11}{30}$	$-\frac{1}{10}$	$\frac{11}{30}$	$\frac{1}{10}$	$-\frac{11}{30}$	$-\frac{1}{10}$	0
S_u	a	$S_u = s_u + \mu_0 \psi_w w$	$-\frac{1}{5}$	0	$\frac{2}{5}$	$\frac{1}{5}$	$-\frac{1}{5}$	0	$\frac{1}{10}$
	b	S_u = idem	$-\frac{3}{5}$	$-\frac{2}{5}$	0	$-\frac{1}{5}$	$-\frac{3}{5}$	$-\frac{2}{5}$	$-\frac{3}{10}$
	c	S_u = idem	$-\frac{3}{10}$	$-\frac{1}{10}$	$\frac{3}{10}$	$\frac{1}{10}$	$-\frac{3}{10}$	$-\frac{1}{10}$	0

Composite expressions:

$$\tilde{\alpha}'_k = \frac{5}{6} \qquad \lambda' = \frac{3}{5}$$

$$M_l = \frac{6}{5}$$

$$A_0 = \frac{1}{M_w} = \frac{3}{5}.$$

We may conclude that the effects differ only slightly from the effects of the ω-mechanism. An exception must be made for the effect of a positive wage-push on the balance on current account (structural). For this (in contrast to the ω-mechanism) we may draw the more usual conclusion that a positive wage-push causes a negative balance on current account (for both value and volume).

Summary

1. In the second half of the sixties, integrated business cycle-structure models (also called BCS models) were developed by a small number of people in which the short term economic process was said to be based on ideas of development found in the growth theory.

In the Netherlands, Schouten in particular, has conducted much work in this field, on a theoretical level; results of more empirically designed studies by the Central Planning Bureau were published by Van den Beld. Outside the Netherlands, authors such as Smithies, Phillips and Bergstrom also concerned themselves with the above-mentioned integration of business cycle and structure.

The few publications in our possession deal exclusively with macro-economics. In our study we have tried to extend this line by applying the BCS analysis to models of several countries, regions or (if one wishes) of several sectors. In formal terms, the substance of our study narrows down to the des-aggregation of more or less familiar macroeconomic BCS models. The division between the regions (countries or sectors) has been made by presuming an independently operating Phillips mechanism for the labour markets.

In more concrete terms the problem just outlined leads us to a theory of the inter-regional (international) coordination of economic policy: is coordination of economic policy necessary or desired, yes or no? In view of this last question, we also had to investigate how the consequences of the actions of large countries are transmitted internationally, to be confronted sooner or later with the consequences of their own actions. A theoretically interesting question here is, what the components of the dynamic characteristics of the system are; in any case these are not solely determined by the macroeconomic behaviour parameters of an isolated region or country, but are also determined by the behaviour parameters of the trade partners. A general conclusion, which arises from the above and which has been developed in detail in the body of our study is that recommendations made to open economies from a purely macroeconomic point of view (i.e. in which the external demand and price development is regarded as an exogenous factor) do not always lead to the desired result.

2. As early as in Chapter I, a model was developed which emphasises the integrated operation of two regions. The model is however still very simple. One of the characteristic assumptions is that businesses rely on a constant profitability of the available production capacity, irrespective of the actual development of costs. This assumed rigidity of the profit margins reveals in fact an extremely high degree of monopoly within the business world. A second important simplification concerns the demand for labour function, in which it is assumed that the demand for labour is wholly dependent on the production capacity, because the businesses man the available production capacity with the normal strength irrespective of the actual effective demand. It was also assumed that inter-regional trade is determined solely by the inter-regional price relationships via the traditional import and export elasticities.

In the two-region model built on these rigid foundations, a cyclical movement arises which propagates itself through both regions, after autonomous impulses have been given in *one* of the two. The inter-regional cyclical movement is reflected in the current account of the balance of payments (actually, of the balance of trade, since we have ignored the inter-regional mobility of production factors).

We have discussed in detail, two kinds of impulses, i.e. the unilateral (given in *one* region) consumption or spending-pull and the (also unilateral) wage-push. The effects of both these impulses differ greatly. Although the unilateral spending-pull is characterised by an effect in both regions which is structurally the same (the diffusion effect of the spending-pull), a unilateral wage-push has an effect on all real variables which is exactly the opposite in the two regions.[1]

With regard to economic policy, we have limited ourselves to employment policy and the stabilisation policy associated with it. We could conclude that in the given model, both the instrument of the spending-pull and that of the wage-push are in theory possible means of attaining objectives connected with employment. If a region wishes to change its employment situation permanently, without causing any inter-regional side effects, it can only do this by applying a proper combination of negative wage-push and a positive spending-pull (if an *increase* in employment is desired).

1. Both the structural effect and cyclical effect of a unilateral spending-pull are similar in the two regions, although the passive region lags half a business cycle-phase behind.

The correct stabilisation policy arises directly from the similarity in character in both regions of the effects of a spending-pull contrasted with the opposite effect of a wage-push. This implies that, if the initial disturbance is, for example, a positive wage-push in region A, then it can be neutralised by a similarly positive wage-push in region B ('keeping in step'). The originally passive region B can also avoid the cyclical and structural effects of A's positive wage-push by applying a negative spending-pull (after some delay, however).

3. It will be clear that the assumptions we have just repeated, place too many limitations on the actuality of the obtained results. It can, after all, be concluded that in actual fact the profitability, in any case in the short run, is indeed influenced by the costs and that the demand for labour is also (in some models even solely) determined by the effective demand and that finally in the field of inter-regional trade more mechanisms are in operation, than the traditional price mechanism.

It would have undoubtedly been possible to use the method of diminishing abstraction by building a large model, in which all the aspects we have mentioned (plus any others), would have been intensely observed. We have, however, chosen the gradual approach and have, in Chapter II, discussed a macromodel of the closed economy in which the two abstractions first mentioned (constant profit margins and the independence of the labour demand from actual production) have been dropped. An important simplification in comparison with Chapter I is of course that the nature of the macrotheory is such that inter-regional problems are disregarded. The Chapter II model must however be seen as the aggregate of the multi-region models which follow. As such, it supplies the indispensable background for subsequent explanations.

But, apart from that, a number of conclusions can be drawn from the Chapter II model, which retain their validity in the multi-region model also, because an autonomous impulse, initiated in one of the regions also has implications for the closed system of the community of the regions.

Chapter II deals not only with the wage-push and the spending-pull but also with an autonomous change in the growth of the capital goods supply (the capacity-pull). Of these three instruments, the last mentioned has structurally the most neutral effect, but does strongly resemble the wage-push. The spending-pull appears to cause the largest structural disturbances.

It can be said of employment policy that the wage policy instrument

158

is the most effective to be used for structural objectives. A positive capacity-pull can best be employed to stabilise, for example, a negative wage-push aimed at enlarging employment.

In addition to employment policy and its stabilisation, we have in Chapter II investigated the possibilities for a lasting change in the real wage rate. We could conclude that the continual capacity-pull is the appropriate measure to use. For the complete readjustment of the cyclical side effects, wage-push (one-time) and spending-pull (opposite, one-time) are necessary components.

The above remarks apply of course only in the case of a certain speed of reaction on the part of the economic authorities. When there is a different speed of reaction, different recommendations may have to be made; general remarks are not possible. We have devoted a paragraph to this problem also.

4. In Chapter III the macroanalysis was continued, now for the open economy. Firstly, we included in this chapter a discussion of the mechanisms which regulate the inter-regional (international) flow of goods, hereby taking into account a number of empirical results which among others have been published by the Central Planning Bureau. It has become evident that although the price mechanism of Chapter I is active in the real situation, there are other factors as well which play just as important a part. On the export side, these are the autonomous development of the world demand and the so-called 'home pressure of demand'. On the import side they are the internal actual production, because of the complementary connection between import volume and production and again the 'home pressure' mentioned above.

Then we studied the operation of the model complete with the new mechanisms, after another autonomous wage-push, spending-pull and capacity-pull had been administered.

The results of the employment and distribution of income policy did not appear to be fundamentally different from those in the closed economy. In the new chapter therefore the emphasis in our economic-political analyses was on the balance of payments policy. In this context, the spending instrument and the exchange rate instrument were discussed.

Our analysis did not produce any spectacular facts with regard to the first point. An autonomous decrease in internal spendings leads to a surplus on current account, measured both in value and volume. The cyclical effects could be absorbed by means of a positive capacity-pull. A structural under-utilisation of capital goods must of course be reckoned with since the capital goods supply increases and the actual production decreases because of the negative spending-pull (i.e. a positive saving-pull).

Not only the spending instrument but also an alteration of the exchange rate can be used in order to attain objectives related to the balance of payments. It is however difficult to fully estimate the consequences of a change in the exchange rate.

The complexity is caused by the fact that a change in the exchange rate affects important structural relations in three places, i.e. in the export and the import functions (because of the changed competition position) and also in the capital yield (because of the changed terms of trade). An extra difficulty is the compensating effect on the balance of payments of the competition effect on the one hand and the terms of trade effect on the other hand. In accordance with current ideas, we have emphasised the competition effect of an alteration of the exchange rate, which is, in fact, virtually the same (as far as internal effects are concerned) as an autonomous change in the volume of world trade. In turn, the terms of trade effect in our model can be transformed into an autonomous yield-push.

Summed up, the conclusion was as follows: the competition effect of a revaluation leads to a structural shortage on the current account. This shortage diminishes as a result of the improved terms of trade. As well, the improved terms of trade induce a positive yield-push, the effect of which can be compared on the one hand with a spending-pull and on the other hand with a (continual) capacity-pull. Here we have the obvious stabilising measures for a post revaluation period: both competition effect and terms of trade effect require a spending-pull, while the latter also necessitates a continual negative capacity-pull.

Partly in connection with the problem of the exchange rate, we concluded Chapter III with an examination of autonomous changes in the development of world demand. It was found that world trade itself exhibits cyclical fluctuations in prices and volume. We have shown that the periodicity of these fluctuations compared to the endogenous periodicity, is very important for the instability of the open macromodel. This instability can increase considerably if the frequency of the exogenous fluctuation is about the same as the dominant endogenous vibration number (resonance effect).

In our opinion, if this resonance effect does appear, then a policy aimed at stabilising the business cycle can in theory still be designed. However, when put into practice, the policy will be faced with an accumulation of difficulties.

160

5. Apart from its significance within the macroeconomic context, the resonance effect provides a good introduction to Chapters IV and V, in which we resumed the discussion of the regional des-aggregated models begun in Chapter I. In the regional models, it may be recalled, each region is individually faced with a cyclical course of the prices and the demand of the trade partner. It differs from macroeconomics of course in that the cycles in question are no longer of exogenous origin but can be explained endogenously.

The connecting link between the regions is in Chapter IV the inter-regional price mechanism. In the changed model, the impulses already mentioned several times are once more investigated.

With regard to the wage-push we could conclude that whereas in Chapter I it had an effect in the active region opposite to that in the passive, this opposition only partly remains. It applies only to the real wage rate and the degree of utilisation (structural), while effects of several other variables (accumulation of capital and employment) are now similar, in both regions.

We repeat that most of the variables connected with the unilateral consumption-pull (employment, production and accumulation of capital) display a similar development (the diffusion effect of the consumption-pull thus remains intact). The real wage rate is an exception since it reaches values which are opposite to each other in the active and the passive regions.

The opposed effect in active and passive regions is however most pronounced in the case of a unilateral capacity-pull. An important distinction from the macroeconomy is now revealed to us.

In the macroeconomy, the effects of wage-push and capacity-pull are virtually the same, except with regard to the accumulation of capital and employment. In the regions model based on the price mechanism, however, this is no longer the case.

With regard to economic policy, we have confined ourselves to employment policy and its stabilisation measures. A distinction was made between two possible situations:
A. The region that pursues the employment policy, also takes care of cyclical stabilisation.
B. The region that is active regarding employment, leaves the cyclical stabilisation in the hands of the trade partner.

ref. A. In this case it is advisable, with a view to increasing employment, to apply a powerful combination of a negative wage-push and a positive capacity-pull. Both measures compensate each other to a large extent, with regard to the cyclical effects. Supplemented by a negative consumption-pull even complete stabilisation can be acquired, while no disturbance arises in the partner region from either a cyclical or a structural point of view.

ref. B. Assuming that region *A* wishes to realise an increase in employment by applying a negative wage-push, it is possible for the trade partner to avoid the cyclical and structural effects of *A*'s action. The most important of the possible measures likely to be taken by region *B* is a lagged but also negative capacity-pull.

6. Chapter v differs from Chapter iv in that it is no longer the price mechanism but instead the 'home pressure of demand' which now regulates the relations. A striking result is that the cyclical fluctuations following a unilateral wage-push and a unilateral capacity-pull do not go in opposite directions in the active and passive region but instead follow almost the same course.

The effects of the unilateral spending-pull are, with the odd exception, identical in both regions.

With regard to economic policy, we can note that the heart of employment policy is once again the wage-push. The region active in this regard can take care of the cyclical stabilisation by means of a capacity-pull in the opposite direction. In this way, neither cyclical nor structural repercussions for the partner region need appear.

The question again arises whether the partner has means at its disposal to avoid the consequences of *A*'s intervention.

This question can be answered in the affirmative: a negative capacity-pull in region *B* brings most of the cyclical results of a negative wage-push in region *A* to zero.

We concluded Chapter v with a few words about an equilibrium income policy. As in the macroeconomy, the core of this is a continued increase in the investment tendency by a continual operation of the capacity-pull.

Our final general conclusion is that a region or a country can by pursuing an independent policy, realise objectives concerning employment and distribution of income without causing cyclical instability. If, however, a region fails to redress the inter-regional cyclical side effects of its structural policy then this can usually be done by the partner region, again without otherwise interfering with the efforts of the active region to achieve structural change.

162

References

Allen, R. G. D., *Mathematical economics*, Macmillan, London, 1956.
Allen, R. G. D., *Macro-economic theory*, Macmillan, London, 1967.

Ball, R. J., *Inflation and the theory of money*, George Allen & Unwin, London, 1964.
Baumol, W. J., *Economic dynamics*, Macmillan, London, 1959.
Beld, C. A. van den, *Dynamiek der ontwikkeling op middellange termijn*, Wolters, Groningen (Neth.), 1967.
Bergstrom, A. R., A model of technical progress, the production function and cyclical growth, in: *Economica*, 1962.
Bhatia, R. J., Unemployment and the rate of change in money earnings in the United States, 1900–'58, in: *Economica*, 1961.
Bhatia, R. J., Profits and the rate of change in money earnings in the United States, 1935–'59, in: *Economica*, 1962.
Bowen, W. G., and Berry, R. A., Unemployment conditions and movements of the money-wage level, in: *Review of Economics and Statistics*, 1963.

Central Planning Bureau, Central Economic Plans, 1960–1972.

Dicks-Mireaux, L. A., The interrelationship between cost and price changes, 1946–'59: a study of inflation in postwar Britain, *Oxford Economic Papers*, 1961.
Domar, E. D., Capital expansion, rate of growth and employment, in: *Econometrica*, 1946.
Driehuis, W., *Fluctuations and growth in a near full employment economy*, Rotterdam University Press, Rotterdam, 1972.
Duesenberry, J. S., *Business cycles and economic growth*, McGraw-Hill, New York, 1958.

Eckstein, O., Money wage determination revisited, in: *American Economic Review*, 1968.
Eyk, C. J. van, Conjunctuur-structuurmodellen, in: *Orbis Economicus*, 1969.

Goldberg, S., *Introduction to difference equations*, John Wiley & Sons Inc., London, 1958.

Harrod, R. F., An essay in dynamic theory, in: *Economic Journal*, 1939.

Kaldor, N., Alternative theories of distribution, in: *Review of Economic Studies*, 1955.
Kalecki, Michal, *Selected essays on the dynamics of the capitalist economy, 1933–1970*, Cambridge University Press, Cambridge, 1971.

163

Karlin, S., *Mathematical methods and theory in games, programming, and economics* (volume 1), Addison-Wesley, London, 1959.

Kolnaar, A.H.J.J., *Werktijdverkorting en dynamiek*, Stenfert Kroese, Leyden, 1969.

Kolnaar, A.H.J.J., Inkomenspolitiek en afwenteling, I-II, in: *Maandschrift Economie*, 1970.

Kolnaar, A.H.J.J., *Planning en prijsmechanisme*, Stenfert Kroese, Leyden, 1971.

Kuh, E., A productive theory of wage levels – an alternative to the Phillips curve, in: *Review of Economic Studies*, 1967.

Kurz, M., The general instability of a class of competitive growth models, in: *Review of Economic Studies*, 1968.

Lancaster, K., *Mathematical economics*, Macmillan, New York, 1968.

Lipsey, R.G., The relation between unemployment and the rate of change of money wage rates in the United Kingdom, 1862–1957: a further analysis, in: *Economica*, 1961.

Lundberg, E., *Instability and economic growth*, Yale University Press, New Haven and London, 1968.

Pease, Marshall C., *Methods of matrix algebra*, Academic Press, New York/London, 1965.

Pen, J., Waaraan is de Nederlandse loonpolitiek bezweken? in: *Hollands Maandblad*, 1970.

Phellps Brown, E.H., The long-term movement of real wages, in: Dunlop, *The theory of wage determination*.

Phellps Brown, E.H., Wage drift, in: *Economica*, 1962.

Phillips, A.W., A simple model of employment, money and prices in a growing economy, in: *Economica*, 1961.

Phillips, A.W., The relation between unemployment and the rate of change of money wage rates in the United Kingdom, 1862–1957, in: *Economica*, 1958.

Sargan, J.D., Wages and prices in the United Kingdom: a study in econometric methodology, in: Hart, Mills and Whitaker, *Econometric analysis for national economic planning*, London, 1964.

Schilderinck, J.H.F., *Een econometrisch model van de Nederlandse economie*, Tilburg, 1970.

Schouten, D.B.J., *Exacte economie*, Stenfert Kroese, Leyden, 1957.

Schouten, D.B.J., *Dynamische macro-economie*, I-II, Stenfert Kroese, Leyden, 1967.

Schouten, D.B.J., Conjunctuurpolitiek versus structuurpolitiek, een macro-economische beschouwing over het investeringsloon, in: *Maandschrift Economie*, 1968.

Schouten, D.B.J., Konjunktuur, lonen en bestedingen op basis van een konjunktureel twee-landenmodel, in: *Maandschrift Economie*, 1971.

SER (Social and Economic Council), Report of the Commission of economic specialists, 1971.

Smithies, A., Economic fluctuations and growth, in: *Econometrica*, 1957.

Smulders, A.A.J., Het rendement als macro-economisch kerngegeven, in: *Maandschrift Economie*, 1972.

Solow, R.M., Note on Uzawa's two sector model of economic growth, in: *Review of Economic Studies*, 1961.

164

Uzawa, H., On a two-sector model of economic growth, in: *Review of Economic Studies*, 1961.

Uzawa, H., On a two-sector model of economic growth, II, in: *Review of Economic Studies*, 1963.

Verdoorn, P.J., and Post, J.J., Comparison of the prewar and postwar business cycles in the Netherlands: an experiment in econometrics, in: Bronfenbrenner, Martin (ed.), *Is the business cycle obsolete?*, Wiley, New York, 1969.

Williams, C.G., *Labor economics*, John Wiley & Sons, New York, 1970.

List of symbols and some abbreviations

The most important symbols and abbreviations have been included in this list. The meaning of those that are not included is indicated in the context. The classification is as follows:

I. ABBREVIATIONS
II. SYMBOLS

1. *Variables* (divided into volumina, prices and money values),
2. *Autonomous impulses,*
3. *Coefficients and constant parameters,*
4. *Subindices,*
5. *Operators et al.*

I. ABBREVIATIONS

A   Appendix.
CEP   Central Economic Plan.
CPB   Central Planning Bureau.
CPM   Central Planning Bureau Model.
F.E.   Final equation.

II. SYMBOLS

1. *Variables*

1.1 *Volumina – absolute levels*
c_L consumption by wage earners
c_R consumption by non wage earners

d	depreciation
e	export
$i \equiv i_B$	gross investments
i_{net}	net investments
k	available capital goods
l	employment
l_v	demand for labour
$\check{l}$	supply of labour
m	import
y	gross national income
y'	production capacity, expressed in goods
y_L	real wage incomes
y_R	real profit sum
$y'_R \equiv (1 - \lambda_m) y'$	the part of production capacity (in goods) included in capital goods

1.2 Volumina – (relative) deviations from equilibrium growth values

g_e	export
g_i	investments
g_k	available capital goods
$\bar{g}_k$	id. as g_k but average trend value
$g_l \equiv g_L$	demand for labour
$\bar{g}_l$	id. as g_l but average trend value
g_m	import
g_x	internal spendings
g_y	actual production
$\bar{g}_y$	id. as g_y but average trend value
$s \equiv g_k - g_x$	difference between production capacity and internal spendings
s_b	under-utilisation percentage of the available capital goods
s_u	balance on current account

1.3 Prices – absolute levels

p	internal general price level
$p_l \equiv p_L$	nominal wage rate
r	actual yield (see A 2.1)
$r_0 \equiv r_E$	id. as r but in the case of equilibrium growth
$w \equiv \dfrac{p_L}{p}$	real wage rate

1.4 *Prices – (relative) deviations from equilibrium growth*

$\check{p} \equiv \check{p}_x$ internal general price level

$\check{p}_e$ export price level

$\check{p}_l \equiv \check{p}_L$ nominal wage rate

$\check{r}$ calculation yield (is a differentiation, see A 2.1, page 148)

$\check{r}_f$ actual yield

$\check{w}$ real wage rate

1.5 *Prices – money values*

S_u balance in money on current account (deviation from equilibrium growth)

2. *Autonomous impulses*

2.1 *Absolute levels*

$\underline{c}_R$ consumption-pull

$\underline{i}$ capacity-pull

$\underline{p}_l = \underline{p}_L$ nominal wage-push

$\underline{x}$ spending-pull

2.2 *Deviations from equilibrium growth values*

$\hat{\underline{g}}_e \equiv g_e - g_{e_E}$ growth rate of world trade

$\hat{\underline{g}}_k \equiv g_k - g_n$ growth rate of the volume of capital

$\check{\underline{g}}_x$ autonomous increase of internal spendings

$\hat{\underline{g}}_x \equiv g_x - g_n$ growth rate of internal spendings

$\check{\underline{p}}$ nominal price-push

$\check{\underline{p}}_b$ foreign price level

$\check{\underline{p}}_l \equiv \underline{p}_L$ nominal wage-push

$\hat{\underline{p}}_L \equiv \check{\underline{p}}_L - \check{\underline{p}}_{L-1}$ nominal wage rate increase

$\check{\underline{p}}_m$ import price level

$\check{\underline{r}}'$ induced yield-push

$\check{\underline{w}}$ real wage-push

$\hat{\underline{w}} \equiv \check{\underline{w}} - \check{\underline{w}}_{-1}$ real wage costs increase

3. *Coefficients and constant parameters*

α average labour ratio

$\tilde{\alpha}_k$ elasticity of the demand for labour with regard to production capacity

$\tilde{\alpha}_y$ idem as $\tilde{\alpha}_k$ but with regard to the actual production

β	elasticity of the nominal wage rate with regard to the employment situation
$\tilde{\gamma}_L$	marginal consumption ratio of wage earners
$\tilde{\gamma}_R$	idem as $\tilde{\gamma}_L$ but of non wage earners
g_n	(net) natural growth rate
δ	depreciation rate (perunage)
ε	elasticity of the nominal wage rate with regard to the general price level
ζ	acceleration coefficient
η	sum of import and export elasticities with regard to the nominal import and export prices
η_e	export elasticity with regard to the nominal export price
η_m	import elasticity with regard to the nominal import price
η_{PL}	export elasticity with regard to the difference in wage rate and foreign price level
κ	average capital coefficient
λ_0	wage costs ratio (equilibrium growth)
$(1-\lambda_m)$	constant monopolistic profit margin
$\tilde{\mu}$	marginal import ratio of the actual production
μ_0	average import and export ratio (equilibrium growth)
π	growth rate of the professional population
ρ	autonomous increase in productivity of labour
$\sigma_R \equiv \sigma_r$	investment parameter (see A 2.1, page 150)
$\tilde{\sigma}_R$	investment parameter
ϕ	size ratios of the regions
ψ, ψ_1, ψ_2	transmission coefficients of the nominal wage costs in the general price level
$\psi_B, \psi_E, \psi_{ME}$	transmission coefficients in the export price function
ψ_{MX}, ψ_X	transmission coefficients in the internal price determination functions
$(1-\omega_e)$	part of s that leads to extra exports
$(1-\omega_m)$	idem as $(1-\omega_e)$ but in relation to imports
$(1-\omega)$	part of s that leads to a volume balance on current account

3.1 *Composite expressions*

$\tilde{\alpha}'_k$	corrected elasticity of the demand for labour with regard to available capital goods (labour positions)
A_0, A_1, A_2	coefficients in the final equation

η_w composite elasticity coefficient of the export volume compared with the real wage rate

$\kappa_R \equiv \dfrac{\kappa}{1-\lambda_m}$ capital coefficient, related to the real profit income

λ' wage costs ratio corrected for the terms of trade

μ' proportion coefficient between the real export balance and the inter-regional difference in tension

$M \equiv 1/(1-\zeta\kappa_R)$ spending multiplier

M_l employment multiplier

M_m import multiplier

$M_w \equiv \dfrac{1}{A_0}$ wage rate multiplier

ψ_w transmission coefficient of the real wage rate in the export price level

4. Subindices

A, B region A respectively region B

$E \equiv 0$ equilibrium growth

t time (period)

$-1, -2$, etc. period $-1, -2$, etc.

5. Operators et al.

Δ linear differentiator

E increase operator (definition: $Ex_t \equiv x_{t+1}$)

I_0 identity operator

λ value(s) of the characteristic equation (eigenvalues)

Σ summation symbol

(B 1547) Printed in Belgium by Ceuterick s.a.
Brusselse straat 153   B 3000-Louvain
A. Struyf   Oude Baan 353   B 3040-Korbeek-Lo